D1060098

ODYSSEY OF A DESERT PROSPECTOR

ODYSSEY OF A DESERT PROSPECTOR

BY HERMAN W. ALBERT

NORMAN

UNIVERSITY OF OKLAHOMA PRESS

RARE
F
595
.A 5

LIBRARY OF CONGRESS CATALOG CARD NUMBER: 67–15590

Copyright 1967 by the University of Oklahoma Press, Publishing Division of the University. Composed and printed at Norman, Oklahoma, U.S.A., by the University of Oklahoma Press. First edition.
GRAND VALLEY LIBRARY

*To you, kind reader, who have
volunteered to string along
with me via these pages as I
revisit the scenes and characters
of my unforgettable odyssey.*

PREFACE

THE LITERATURE OF MINING of the American West contains few personal accounts by men who took up prospecting—the real and lonely but richly rewarding kind, with burros as pack animals and a skillet over an open fire for food preparation. This was my life soon after the twentieth century opened. It is of this life that I write.

I have tried to recreate as faithfully as possible what I experienced, the conversations I heard, and the rainbows my contemporaries and I pursued. The narrative reflects perhaps typically for prospecting as a craft this quality of pursuit. Only a reading will reveal the treasures found—and they may vary from reader to reader.

Dialogue long remembered is the special dispensation of the autobiographer. The historian will have none of it, unless it can be documented. But, as anyone who knows me well can perhaps attest, I have a good and accurate memory, not simply for such details but for facts and figures of a rather intricate character, encountered in my banking and accounting experiences subsequent to my prospecting career. I have tried to put down precisely what I heard in conversation, and I did not keep notes.

The men and women who figure in this account are the persons of my prospecting days. To my deep sorrow the Maud referred to herein, who became my adored wife, died several years ago.

HERMAN W. ALBERT

Los Angeles, California
August 1, 1967

ODYSSEY OF A DESERT PROSPECTOR

IT WAS AN EVENTFUL DAY when on that balmy May morning I struck out alone from the Headlight Corral in Tonopah, Nevada, with four burros and headed for parts totally unknown to me. I was all aglow and sure that I was on the royal road to romance and riches; I was even giving serious thought to how the sudden acquisition of wealth might affect the future course of my life. My exuberance and optimism then and there knew no bounds. Nighttime brought that unforgettable day to its close, out there on the desert some twenty miles north of Tonopah, when I, an unmitigated tenderfoot twenty-four years old, found myself called upon to do something about making camp, preparing a supper of sorts, unpacking, and hobbling the meekly submissive burros before turning them loose to rustle their sustenance as best they could on the little tufts of bunch grass among the sheltering twigs of sagebrush. I wondered how I'd ever manage to reassemble things and secure them to the little beasts' backs in the morning without the help of my friend Still Wandell, who had started me off with such first-rate packs.

All, however, worked out smoothly, and early on the following morning I was off again and on my way.

Now for the how, when, and why of it all—my decision to enroll in that ancient and honorable craft whose members in those days were referred to as "Desert Rats." Frankly, it was all pure and simple chance, and as it turned out I wouldn't have missed it for all the wealth of Croesus.

It began on a fine Saturday evening in the year 1907, in the month of May, when the days were growing longer and the sunsets over Paradise Peak far off to the north became more and more dazzling and spectacular. I had dined at my boardinghouse in the upper end of Tonopah and was sauntering along the main street in the heart of town till I saw a crowd gathered in front of the Tonopah Club, a busy gambling and saloon rendezvous. The center of attraction was an outfit of four expertly packed burros just in from the hills, apparently, standing unperturbed at the curb in the street. One of them, a big intelligent-looking brown, had on a McClellan army saddle to which was attached a cardboard sign reading "For Sale—$150." Everyone seemed keenly interested and exchanged admiring comments concerning the sturdy-looking quartet. I overheard a pair of Cornish miners say the outfit was a great bargain and if they weren't tied down with their wives they'd snap it up in a jiffy and make for the hills to go prospecting. One woman remarked to her companion, "I suppose the poor darlings were left standing there while their owner went inside to fill himself with liquor." It developed that the owner had indeed gone inside, but definitely not for the purpose the woman had hinted. He let it be known that he needed the money to get to San Francisco to have his eyes operated on for cataracts. I entered the club to see what was going on, and there I spotted a well-known miner and prospector named Still Wandell—whom I have already mentioned—just up from Greenwater, where a terrific boom was under way. Still was at the bar with another man, a skinny little fellow who looked as if he belonged with a circus or carnival outfit. He was togged out in brand-new khaki pants, white silk shirt, bright yellow necktie, patent leather shoes, and a fifty-dollar Stetson hat.

Still motioned me over and said he wanted me to meet his friend, the Greenwater Kid. So that was who the grinning, baby-faced, pint-sized chappie was—the Greenwater Kid!

Everyone knew all about him and his luck. He had been washing dishes in a mine boardinghouse in Rhyolite when he talked a waitress into staking him to go to Greenwater, not too far away, where he promptly located a number of inside claims and sold them for a mint of money—the waitress taking her half of the proceeds and returning back East with it as fast as she could pack her grip. The Kid proceeded to poop away all of his half on the roulette wheel and the crap table. It all came back to me as I looked at him. I asked Still and the Kid if they had noticed the burro outfit outside.

"Yes," said Still, "we were just talking about it, weren't we, Kid?"

"That's right," the Kid replied, "an' I was sayin' how I wisht I had them *bureaus* 'cause I know where they's a great big gold mine, an' she's open to location." I looked at Still and he nodded approvingly.

"Yes, sir," the Kid went on, fixing me with his innocent blue eyes, "it's up on the Black Rock Desert. I know a Injun, a good Injun, an' he told me all about it. It's a whole hill o'good millin' ore—millions o'tons of it!"

"Those are the kind that make the best mines," Still Wandell added, "those big, low-grade propositions."

"What about that Indian?" I asked. "How do you know he's any good?"

"Oh, One-Eyed Tom's all right, ain't he, Still?" the Kid replied.

"Yes, he's reliable as long as he don't get hold of any booze," Still said. "You see," he said to me, "Old Tom was run out of his tribe up there for killing an Indian. If it weren't for that, he'd a'never mentioned that hill of gold ore. Indians never tell us white men about those things. Seems to be part of their religion or something."

"Would Tom go up there with you?" I asked.

5

up that much in cash right then, but that he'd stake half of his interest in the club against the Kid's pile—a fair enough offer. The Kid, smiling and with a wink at the crowd, took him up on it. A rack of dice was brought forward and the Kid was given his choice. He reached nonchalantly for a pair. It was his roll first. Picking up the dice, he breathed on them in his closed hand to warm them up, and addressed them endearingly, beseechingly, in the voodoo jargon of the street urchin. With a snap of his fingers he tossed them out. It was a good throw—a five and a trey—hard indeed to beat. He was all smiles. Now Goodrich, his face blankly expressionless, took a pair at random from the scrambled rack of dice and tossed it the length of the crap table. They came to rest with two fives up. The onlookers gasped, and all eyes were fixed on the Kid, who merely stood there with a vacant grin on his face, according to the swamper, who added, "He sure was a good sport" and told how drink after drink was showered on the Kid.

Outside I consulted with Still Wandell. He said he felt guilty and ashamed for getting me into such a mess. In a way, he couldn't have helped it. He said he liked the Kid and didn't have the heart to turn him down. He just took a chance on his making good, and that's what he got for trying to be a good Samaritan. Yes, that's exactly as good old Still put it.

"What about the burros?" I asked. "Do you suppose they're all right?"

"Oh sure," he said. "There's plenty of hay and water down there in the corral."

"What am I going to do with them now?"

"Well, you can sell 'em, I suppose, that is, if you're calling it off with the Kid," Still replied.

"I've got to call it off, haven't I?" I said.

Still shrugged his shoulders. I sensed that he did not want to say anything against the Kid. Finally, after a protracted moment of silence between us, I had an inspiration.

"Gosh," I said, "if I knew the least thing about prospecting, I'd take that outfit myself and head for the hills in a hurry!"

"Maybe that's just what you ought to do," Still said. "There's not a whole lot to know. You just kinda pick it up as you go, from day to day. I can show you in a few minutes how to get the packs on and off the burros."

"When?" I asked, excitedly.

"Right away," Still said, "but, first, I've got to get the Kid out of there and put him to bed."

I helped him. Then he and I headed down the street for the Headlight Corral, on below the red-light district.

There stood the four disconsolate-looking beasties, no doubt trying to figure what next. They could have passed for statues but for their overworked tails flailing away at pesky flies. Their packs were in an adjoining shed where the Kid and I had stored them.

"Now the question is which is which and who's who," Still said as he surveyed the pile of dunnage. Still and I gathered up the whole works and laid it on the ground. Still loudly called out, "Dan!" The big brown jack instantly alerted his long, plushy ears, pointing them straight at Still, while his beautiful big eyes beamed in sure-fire recognition of his moniker.

"How'd you know his name?" I asked.

"Scratched right here," Still replied, indicating the cantle of the riding saddle. Soon, Mr. Dan stood there all saddled and bridled, ready to be off. Still followed through with the rest of the packs, using the same technique. On each of the crosstrees he found the name of the respective animal. There was no guesswork about it. Rickey, Old Gal, and Jennie B were the only ones to whom the packsaddles thus marked could possibly belong.

"The bell goes on Jennie B," Still said. "Her neck shows she's been wearing it." He picked it up by the black leather strap to which it was riveted and gave it a shake. "You only put it on when you turn 'em loose," he added. "A burro only rings a bell four times in a forenoon," he warned with a chuckle.

"How's that?" I asked.

"Oh, it's just an old saying," he replied. "There's a lot of truth in it though. You see, they feed all night long after their day's travel. Then come sunup, they sneak up some draw or behind some rocks or junipers to keep out of sight while they take a snooze for themselves. You'll learn in time."

"Don't they eat in the daytime?" I asked.

"All I know," Still replied, "is they try their best to stay hid. A man down on the Amargosa told me he caught his burros packing feed to the one that had a bell on, so's to keep her from ringing it and giving the hideout away. They're plenty cute; you'll find out soon enough!"

Still reeled off a barrage of instructions, warnings, advice, hints, suggestions, and especially taboos, in the course of our loading the packs on the uncomplaining jacks and two jennies. His do's and don't's were about equally divided. Sample: Never mix packsaddles and blankets—always put the same pack on the same animal—don't pack canned foods (too heavy)—stick to dried fruits, beans, flour, baking powder—go light on sugar—don't get sore at the burros when you have to hunt them a long ways (that's how you find mines)—jack rabbits are good eating unless there's grubs under their hides—don't pass up hawks either (they're good parboiled and fried in bacon grease). These are just a few of Still's injunctions which covered the sum total of that most alluring of all professions—prospecting—on which I was now embarked.

2

Now FOR A BRIEF SKETCH of my background, which I regard as being germane to my story.

I was born in the Garden State of New Jersey, where the buzz of the mosquito is heard of a hot summer's night. The year was 1882, the year before Richard Wagner died. I have always been grateful that I had the privilege of sharing even such a short community of time on this earth with that great artist. My revered father was a cleric on the staff of Old Trinity Church on lower Broadway, New York, and it had been his expressed desire, most understandably, that I dedicate my life, as he had done, to the service of God and my fellow man. Naturally, I wound up in New York's Union Theological Seminary, where I tackled in earnest all the ingredients that comprise a priest's indoctrination. I soon learned it was not for me, especially after I had heard a venerable bishop declare one day in chapel that any of us candidates for holy orders who could picture himself happier and more contented in any other sphere of life than that of a humble servant of God should forthwith abandon all thought of becoming a priest, for in that case he was utterly devoid of a true calling. That settled it for me. I quizzed myself and was forced to confess that I could be at least as happy, if not more so, in any number of roles, ranging from taxi driver, heading a bank like J. P. Morgan and Company, even being president of the New York Central Railroad, with a private car equipped with all the comforts of home in which to travel whenever so disposed.

I had some good friends in East Orange who had been sending me snapshots of their cousin, Tasker Oddie, who had stumbled across a huge fortune at a desolate spot on the desert of central Nevada, which had been christened Tonopah, an Indian word denoting a species of sagebrush indicating the nearness of moisture under the surface. The photos showed the jubilant Oddie standing beside a great pile of high-grade silver-and-gold ore extracted from a shallow shaft on a cone-shaped butte, which his confreres had named Mount Oddie in his honor.

I left the seminary and worked for the Lehigh Valley Railroad Company on the docks of Black Tom's Island in New York Harbor, trundling freight in and out of boxcars and storage buildings via hand truck and baling hook at the wage of a dollar and seventy-five cents for a ten-hour shift. It was hardly a way to amass a fortune, but the ministry hadn't offered much more. I had seen my father's struggles to provide the bare necessities of life for his family. It wasn't easy.

Oddie, with his great showing of pay ore, excited me. I hate to admit it, but I envied him, shipping that rich rock to the smelters in a steady stream of freight wagons, pending through rail service which was already in the offing. The Tonopah and Goldfield Railroad was being rushed to completion from Mina, on the Southern Pacific. It was too much to resist. I said as much to Oddie's charming cousins, who retorted with Horace Greeley's famous advice, fortifying it with a letter of introduction to the fortunate young mining mogul. As fast as I could close out my business interests in the effete East, which actually amounted to less than a hill of beans, I was off for the West with that precious letter and my life's savings of some two hundred and fifty dollars in my pocket.

I set out via the Erie Railroad, which offered the cheapest fare I could find by shopping around. I was glad to give my business to the poor old Erie, which even at that time was just about gasping for breath. By dint of something or other it got me to Chicago with my Gladstone bag and fiddle. From there on, after changing trains to the Southern Pacific, Omaha, Laramie, and a host of fabulous Wild West names breezed by my tourist-car window as one state after another was crossed.

On a memorable night the conductor gave me a poke in the ribs and said the next station was Hazen, Nevada, where I'd have to lay over till nine in the morning when a train of sorts would pull out for points south connecting at Mina with the prosperous new Tonopah and Goldfield Railroad.

It was at Hazen that the business of fitting myself into the game of life as it is played, where a mining boom is under way, really began. With bag and fiddle, I headed through the darkness for a brightly-lighted, false-fronted, wooden, jerry-built affair, which the conductor had pointed out to me as being the hotel, a few yards back of the tracks. In spite of the hour, there was no lack of activity inside the wide-opened front entrance. There were two or three card games going on and considerable animated conversation was buzzing. The proprietor left the bar briefly to have me sign the register and be assigned to a room upstairs, for which I paid fifty cents in advance for the night's lodging. He told me to take the room on the left because the one on the right was full. When I asked for the key, he looked surprised and said there wasn't any. Well, I surely wasn't going to argue with him, because it could only have ended in his favor, and I certainly did not relish the idea of sleeping in the sagebrush. I entered the room on the left as he had directed. He must have made a mistake, I figured. There were two beds in it, both occupied. One had two men sleeping in it. I tiptoed across to the room on the right, which he had said was full—an understatement if ever I had heard one. This room also contained two beds and both beds had a couple of men in them. They were blissfully asleep. I returned to the room on the left intending to pick up my luggage and go downstairs to ask for further instructions, when the man alone in the one bed spoke up and said, "Crawl right in here, feller, alongside me. Call yourself lucky, 'cause it's all there's left in this hotel."

I thanked him, removed my outer garments and shoes, and gingerly took my place beside him. To my amazement he reached for something at the foot of the bed, and the next thing I knew he had settled back and was lighting a cigar. Billows of smoke enveloped both of us.

"This nightcap smoke is the one I enjoy most of all," he informed me, puffing away.

If this is a hotel, I said to myself, then an Eskimo igloo cannot be too bad, but I made up my mind not to let it get me down.

I slept not only soundly but too well. When I awoke I found that my bedmate had quietly departed. I dressed as fast as I could and went down to the restaurant. A washstand stood beside the doorway with a big pitcher of water resting on it. A man who had just finished washing his face and hands was combing his wet hair before the cheap mirror on the wall. Its uneven glass gave some very distorted reflections, as I found out when I used it. The roller towel had been rolled and rerolled time and again. Filthy was the word for it, and I had to grit my teeth to use it.

I went inside and found an empty seat at one of the tables. Three rough-clad men, who were eating there, responded with friendly nods to my morning greeting. Before I knew it, a buxom waitress stood beside me with a toothpick in her mouth. She looked me straight in the eye and snapped, "Mush?"

I had no idea what she was driving at and she must have sensed my discomfort.

"Listen 'ere," she said, "I just ast' you a civil question, an' I can't stand 'ere waitin' for you to make up ya' mind."

"I'm very sorry, lady," I said, "but I didn't quite understand what you meant."

"Oh, English, ain't ya'?" she replied. Well, at's what I am too—Cornish—but don't ya' start callin' me a Cousin Jenny. I suppose if I'd a'said porridge you'd a'understood."

"Ah," I said, "if 'mush' means porridge I'd certainly like some."

"Now we're goin' to town," she replied. "Ham an' eggs straight up or face down, spuds hash-brown or shoestring, an' o'course ya' want java, white or black?"

After I told her what I wanted, she swished off to the kitchen. My three tablemates broke into a hearty laugh. I joined them, and the four of us were soon having a jolly time of it. The three men were important members of the mining fraternity. One of them was the well-known Don Gillis, who, as I later learned, was a particular friend of Tasker Oddie's, the man to whom I had a letter of introduction. The others took turns reciting doggerels. One was neatly inscribed on the wall of the privy which was out back in the sagebrush:

> *She was slingin' hash in Hazen.*
> *Was she cute—and was she brazen!*

"Sounds like Will Irwin," Gillis said. "Wasn't he the one that wrote about a lady named Nell? All I can recall of it are the last two lines which have a way of sticking in my mind:

> *She had her boots on when she fell,*
> *So what the hell, Bill, what the hell!*

On that note and with the arrival of my excellent breakfast, my genial companions, much to my regret, got up and went about their business.

My bill? Four bits! Can you believe it?

3

I'D LIKE TO GO BACK to Tonopah for a moment to pick up a few loose ends of our journey, before we carry on from where we left off that morning on the San Antonio Flat where I performed the miracle of repacking my long-eared worthies and in high spirits shooed them northward riding that noble jack, Dan. I'll be brief about my sojourn in Tonopah, from the spring of 1906 to that of 1907, but far be it from me to brush off with a ho-hum that "Queen of Desert Mining Camps" to which we'll be returning in due season.

First, about my letter of introduction, which was received with characteristic graciousness by Tonopah's leading citizen, Tasker Lowndes Oddie, who was then at the pinnacle of his financial success. He was a fellow New Jerseyite, from Montclair, an Essex Trooper, and naturally a fine horseman. Through him I was placed on the engineering staff of the now-flourishing Tonopah Mining Company, as a surveyor's helper, which gave me the privilege of putting up at the company's fine clubhouse—a lucky break, for I was down to less than ten dollars after a session with the crap table.

The motto of the gambling place was framed on the wall. It read:

NOTHING VENTURED, NOTHING GAINED

It had truly fascinated me. These must be literate people, I mused, and the first man I spoke to really looked the part.

He was handsome and venerable, seated in an armchair on a platform where he watched the moves made below him by a seriously engrossed group of men who were placing chips and keeping score with a kind of abacus on the layout as the cards issued from the metal case manipulated by the dealer. A Chinaman beside me said it was faro bank. Taking advantage of a lull, while the dealer was reshuffling his deck of cards, I said to the gray-haired man sitting up there in the chair—he was known as the lookout—"I wish I understood that game."

He looked down at me benignly and replied, "Take an old fool's advice and don't learn."

My job at the Tonopah Mining Company would have been 100 per cent as far as I was concerned. I got so I could run a transit and set off latitude and departure in plotting the map of the underground workings. In fact, it was a good course in draftsmanship, and it stood me in good stead later on, as will be seen. However, I detested the little squirt of an engineer under whom I worked. When I had had my fill of him I told him so, which brought to a conclusion my otherwise pleasant association with the Tonopah Mining Company and its sumptuous clubhouse.

Now came break number two, and a mighty good one it was. As I was leaving the hill with my duds, I passed the big Mizpah shaft where miners were coming up from the day shift, while others were going down on the afternoon shift. A well-dressed, pleasant-faced man, unquestionably a gentleman, stood there taking it all in, and as I drew near he nodded and I could see he wanted to speak to me.

"I've just been wondering," he began, "why all those men have scissors in their hands. What do they use them for in the mine?"

I laughed, and immediately regretted it, for there was no doubt he was serious and asked in good faith.

"Oh," I said, "I thought you were joking. They do look

like scissors, now that you mention it, but as a matter of fact they're candlesticks, very handy for sticking in the wall while they work by candlelight—just can't get along without them."

He laughed and said, "My name is Lyon."

I told him mine, and we shook hands.

"Of course," he said, "I don't have to tell you now that I'm a tenderfoot right out of the East."

"The same here," I said. "Only been west about six months."

"Do you like it out here?" he asked.

"I do, very much," I replied. "Here's where I want to spend the rest of my days. No more stuffy, crowded East for me."

"That's encouraging," he said. Then he amplified that remark by informing me he had been appointed auditor for the Tonopah and Goldfield Railroad and was to assume his duties right away. He said he badly needed a bookkeeper, and he wondered if I knew where he might find one.

"Unfortunately I don't," I said, "and I'm only sorry that I'm not a bookkeeper myself. All I know about railroading is moving freight on a hand truck."

"Where did you learn that?" he asked.

"On Black Tom's Island," I replied.

"What! In Jersey City?"

"Exactly," I said.

"Well, then you were working for the Lehigh Valley Railroad."

"That's a fact," I said.

"Great heavens, this beats anything I ever heard of!" he exclaimed.

"How so?" I asked.

"Because I was with the Lehigh Valley before I came out here. It was at Mr. M. B. Cutter's request that I took this appointment. Mr. Cutter, as you probably know, has been made president of the Tonopah and Goldfield."

"Well, well," I said. "I used to see him when he came down to the docks to find out how things were going."

"Well, well, indeed," he replied. "Maybe I've found my bookkeeper right here. Would you consider taking the job?"

"Surely you're not serious," I replied. "Why, I don't know the first thing about bookkeeping."

"You don't have to," he said. "It's so simple I could break you in while I'm getting organized. I can see by the tag on your grip that you write a good hand, and that's all that's necessary."

That's the long and short of it, principally the latter. When spring came, fate, or whatever it was, entangled me with that burro outfit and with genuine regret I arranged with Mr. Lyon to be relieved of my bookkeeping job and was assured by that magnanimous gentleman that he not only didn't blame me but envied me and wished me good luck.

Now I'd like to push on from my first night's campsite into the second day of my emancipation from the routine and restrictions of community existence.

That first night, snug under my tarpaulin during drizzling rain, I felt I was a guest in God's own hotel, and that thought abided with me from night to night as I lay in my bed under the open sky gazing at the sight of sights—the stars I could almost touch. There I was, drinking it all in, flattering my-self that I was an essential part of it, essential, else how could I see it? How was it that my eyes could light instantly on the farthest star, more than one hundred light-years from the earth? Was not that fact sufficient to dispel the illusions of time and space? I had to give up. It was truly a luxurious hotel without electric lights for reading, one in which there was no stale air, no noise of revelry, no bellboys, but just the distant tinkle of Jennie B's bell, the plaintive tweet of a night bird, and often the shrilllllllllll yap-yap-yap of the lovesick coyote.

My second camp was on the rim of a big wash which drained the cloudbursts off the north end of the San Antonio Mountains. I really felt lonesome, and it bothered me, till I figured out the probable cause was the fact that for the first time in my life I had spent a whole day without seeing a human being, man, woman, or child. I reflected that lonesomeness was a blessing in that it brings about a closer unity with Nature, which I submit is another way of saying God.

The next afternoon the spell, whatever it was, lost its rule over me and was broken. I saw lots of fellow men, not only the entire L. H. Sly outfit of honest-to-God cowboys, buckaroos, cowpunchers, *vaqueros*, or however one wishes to designate the breed, but the almost legendary, well-nigh notorious Bar Francis. That daredevil had captured a whole band of mustang horses high up in the Shoshone Mountains and was driving the wild lot, aided by a pair of his cronies, one of them a half-blood Indian, down to Goldfield, where he was sure to find a ready market for them to be broken for riding. They were in the big round corral on Sly's headquarters ranch at the mouth of Cloverdale Canyon, where I, too, found an ideal spot to camp in the willows at the lower end.

I stayed up late that night listening to the boys as they talked shop in the roomy ranch house. Two of them struck me as being real men of action in the raw, without frills or stand-ins. One was Bar Francis, a free-lance prankster and horse trainer, whose utter fearlessness stood out in the cool, good-natured blue of his keen eyes. The other, a California Mexican named Juan Nava, was boss of the cow outfit. He was cheerful, though inherently of a dignified demeanor. I observed that these two outstanding men held each other in genuine respect. I saw a lot of them as time went on.

There was considerable talk of a new gold strike up Cloverdale Canyon in a side gulch that had been christened Golden. The discoverer was Jack Weeks, a half-blood Indian, marvelous roper and bronco buster. He had, so the boys said, sold his claims for twenty-five thousand dollars. Lots of prospecting was going on there. I thought maybe I was still in time to do myself some good thereabouts. In the morning I told my big Dan, he of the long plushy ears and knowing eyes, that he and his colleagues would have to relinquish their lush feed down there along the creek, for we were moving on to Golden.

Three miles or so up the canyon I came to a side dirt road and a makeshift sign with the word "Golden" daubed on it and an arrow pointing toward the foothills. But what caught my eyes was some scribbling on a scrap of paper tacked to the post. Of course nosey old Dan was just dying to read what it said, and, reading between his big cocked ears, this is what I saw:

HALT PEDESTRIAN! KNOWEST THOU NOT THAT THOU APPROACHEST THE LAND OF MISERY?

"Now who the hell wrote that?" I could literally feel Dan saying to himself even before he gave out with the goldurndest bray to which those hills had ever resounded. The perpetrator, whoever he was, was guilty of an act of the most abject depravity—knocking a mining camp. Compared with him a horse thief was—oh, well, what's the use?

Golden was in a setting of scattered pine nut and juniper trees. Jack Weeks never showed up at all while I was there, which was about ten days. I wanted to meet him, and did later on—a remarkable personality.

One great enthusiast whom I did meet was Judge Copper-noll whose bailiwick was the famous old bonanza silver camp of Austin, a hundred miles to the north, county seat of Lander County, Nevada. "Cop," as he was called, showed me a fine assortment of jewelry rock which had come off his ground. The Williamson boys had more of the same dazzling stuff.

I finally gave up looking for some promising ground that was not already staked out. It was suggested that I take a lease and do some prospecting work on it, but it seemed too soon for me to think of settling down to a grind like that. In that frame of mind I bade adieu to Golden. I do believe there's a real gold mine up there which some fine day will reward the right outfit, that is, one that is adequately financed.

After a one-night stand at Black Springs, I shoved on to the spot in Ione Valley where it was my good fortune to meet Hot Steam Boyd.

4

SOMEWHERE ALONG THE LINE he had come to be known and referred to as Hot Steam Boyd, and I was soon to learn why that moniker had been bestowed on him.

He was not only an able prospector but a real philosopher and gentleman of the hills. He had made several small fortunes along the Mother Lode of California as a "pocket-hunter."

What is a pocket- hunter, exactly? Well, he's—or she's—an individual that digs and pans around the grassroots in "them thar hills" looking for those deposits of jewelry rock close to the surface. It's a game of skill, perseverance, dreams, and optimism which has rewarded many of its practitioners with sudden, often fabulous, wealth.

"There's lots more pockets to be found in California," Hot Steam averred when I first met him out there in the shadow of Paradise Peak in northern Nye County, Nevada. He added that the Mother Lode had become so jammed with folk bent on the search for poor-man's gold that they were getting in one another's way, and for that reason he had decided to try his luck in Nevada.

One balmy evening, only a couple of weeks after I had taken to the hills, I made dry camp in the volcanic foothills across Ione Valley from Paradise Peak. My four burros were starting on their nocturnal nibbling, wherever they could find a bite amongst the sagebrush, hobbled, as usual. A batch of "yeast-powder" biscuits was coming along in my dutch-oven, a pot of tea was steeping on a hot rock, and slices of bacon were beginning to sizzle fragrantly in the pan. The whole works was in reach of my arm as I sat on my roll of bedding. A few minutes more and I'd be eating. My appetite was equal to the occasion, needless to say.

What a sunset over the opposite hills! The bell on Jennie B's neck was all that intruded on the silence of that veritable paradise of silence. Paradise Peak! A real poet must have named it as he watched a brilliant, flaming sunset outline its summit, suggesting that heaven itself was just beyond. Jennie B's bell tolled a sudden volley. I looked to see what was up. She was standing a hundred yards off, head erect. Smart little critter! Her equine radar had picked up a lone rider down on that lifeless flat, at least two miles away, headed up my way. I hadn't seen a soul in over a week. I wondered who it could be. He must have seen my smoke. Better hold up supper a bit, I thought.

"Evening, partner!" his voice rang with a cordial assurance.

Pulling up close to my fire the gray-bearded, stooped-shouldered, khaki-clad rider appeared several sizes too big for the stocky little white gelding between his long, gangling legs. His high-laced buckskin boots had hobnailed soles and heels. In the afterglow of that lingering twilight his appearance was somewhat quixotic.

"My name's Boyd," he announced as he dismounted stiffly. Our mutual introductions were accompanied with handshakes. I caught him casting an approving eye over my layout.

"Fine to have you eat supper with me," I said. "Soon's you're ready we'll fall to." My invitation was accepted with thanks and obvious eagerness.

"I'll just loosen Shorty's cinch," he said, "and drop the reins on the ground. He'll stand right there while we eat."

In spite of his stoop, my guest stood a good six feet tall. He was spare-built and rangy.

"Over there's a basin and water if you care to wash a bit," I said.

He hesitated an instant. "How much water is left in your cans?" he asked.

"A good ten gallons," I replied. "Just help yourself. I'm moving on in the morning anyway."

"Then I'll just take a cup or two for a wash," he said, "and if you say the word I'll give Shorty about a quart."

I told him to go right ahead. I hoped he'd be quick about it, for my appetite was demanding action and refused to be put off much longer.

At last he came and sat beside me on my bedroll. He forked himself a couple of strips of bacon and reached into the Dutch oven for a biscuit. Tea was poured in big tin cups, sugar stirred in, and supper was under way to the tune of my guest's unstinted compliments.

"Know what?" he asked, after he had washed down a big mouthful. "You're the first person I've seen in over a month. What day is it, anyway? I've lost track."

"Eighteenth of June," I replied.

"Ha, then it's my birthday!" he exclaimed. "What luck! You're giving me a real party!"

I offered my congratulations mingled with regret that there wasn't a cake with candles on it for him.

"Nothing could beat all this," he assured me.

I was anxious to get him started talking about himself. Who was he? What was he doing, riding around on Shorty and not seeing anybody for a month at a crack?

"Wonderful spot here to spend the night," he said, as he gazed over the spooky valley from which he had so recently appeared and on which the shadows were fast closing in. From the distance came the feeble, hollow tonk of Jennie B's bell.

"That's music to a prospector," he said. "Real music that tells him God's in his heaven and all's well with the world!"

"A wonderful thought," I said, "just suits the occasion."

"Yes," he said, "I often use it as prayer. I learned it in Sunday school as a boy. It braces a fellow up when he's down-hearted."

We continued to eat in silence a while. Finally he began to talk again.

"I see you tended your burros before you sat down to eat," he said.

"Yes," I replied, "I always do that, but I didn't give them a drink this time. I understand that burros can get along without water for several days at a time."

"That's true," he said, "but they like to have it just the same. Fine animals you've got there. I noticed them as I rode up. Where'd you come from today?"

"Black Springs," I replied. "How far would you call that from here?"

"A good twenty miles and more—almost as far as where I came from, over there across the valley—Ellsworth. Ever hear of it?" he asked.

I admitted I hadn't, and he went on to say it looked promising, gold, but the big thing there was iron ore, which he described as being just about inexhaustible in his opinion. He came pretty near being right. Millions of tons of it were shipped to Japan from Ellsworth after World War I, at a great profit to the owner, Anson Phelps Stokes, of New York. It could have been mine, had I but known! It was open to location as Hot Steam and I sat there that fine summer's evening.

"Well, sir, you've had quite a trip," I remarked, casually.

"Yes," he replied, "and I've still got about eight more miles ahead of me to reach my camp. Guess I'd better be on my way. It'll be getting dark before long, but Shorty could make it blindfolded."

"How about staying here tonight?" I suggested. "This bed's big enough for two." I could revel in solitude up to a certain point, but right then it struck me that to watch him riding off into the dusk would be pouring it on a bit too thick.

"If you're dead sure I wouldn't be inconveniencing you," he temporized, "I'd enjoy staying here."

It was settled. I had taken on a house guest for the night—a very welcome one at that. I told him we'd light out together in the morning.

"Headed anywhere in particular?" he asked.

"Just anywhere and everywhere," I replied. "Where is there a good place to prospect? Tell me, and I'll go there."

"Sunnyside—none better," he declared without hesitation. "There's where I'm camped, in those big hills yonder." He swung his arm around toward the north. "What's more, your burros'll find lots of good feed around there."

26

What a break! Sure, I'd go to Sunnyside. Maybe I could learn a few things. God knows I needed to.

"I'll go break the news to Shorty," he said, and that's exactly what he did. I rose to watch the proceedings. All the while he was unsaddling the pony he kept talking to him as if he had more than horse sense. Shorty stood there stark naked, even the rope removed from around his neck. No human actor could have registered disbelief more convincingly than Shorty did just then. It took a sharp slap on his rump and a hearty "Run along, Shorty," to snap him out of it. With a startled snort, head high and tail arched, he struck out at a prancing trot, looking back at us over his shoulder with a mixture of incredulity and a bid to "come and catch me" in his challenging eyes. It was all too much for me. I had never seen anything like it.

"Don't you have to hobble him?" I asked.

"Oh, yes, that is, if I want him to stay around."

"Well, what'll he do now? Where'll he go?"

"Oh, he'll just mosey along, feeding on the way most of the night. He'll be home by sunup, waiting for us when we get there."

I had a notion to add, "and have lunch ready for us to sit down to?"

"Now you just take it easy a few minutes while I clean up around here," I advised. When the dishes and pans were put away I sat down beside him on the bed.

"Mind if I smoke?" he asked. He had his pipe out and a yellow package of tobacco.

"Of course not," I said. "Please go right ahead. Matter of fact I have a pipe too, brand new, never been smoked." There's where I made my mistake—imagine, a new unbroken pipe, which he invited me to pack tight with his diabolical tobacco—"Imperial," as the wrapper read!

"How is it?" I asked.

"I like it," he replied. "Got lots of body to it." That's what it had indeed, and lots more than I could stomach, as I found after just three puffs of it. My head began swimming around contrariwise to the direction of the earth's rotation. Everything was not only upside down but inside out as well. Unsteadily I managed to lay the pipe down on the ground beside me.

"How do you like it?" he asked.

"Wish I had a fan," I replied, all a-sweat. "I'll be all right—no fault of the tobacco—just that I'm out of practice I guess."

"Now that's too bad," he said, getting up and knocking the burning contents out of his own pipe. It was well that he did; I am sure that just one more whiff of the sickening smoke would have laid me out for keeps. Fortunately, a gentle breeze sprang up about that time and dried the cold sweat on my forehead. Gradually the vile dizziness, which had threatened to ruin the whole evening for us both, left. I at last felt equal to prodding my guest into telling me about Sunnyside—all about it, his claims, if any, and if he had struck gold on them.

"Oh, yes, I've got a group of six claims up there," he said. "I haven't struck the ore body yet, but there's a stringer that's going to lead me to it, I hope."

I had no idea what a "stringer" was but refrained from asking him because I did not want to interrupt him just then.

"You see," he went on, "it's a case of picking up some bits of high-grade float. It just had to come from my ground. It was rich—assayed over a hundred dollars to the ton. You wouldn't need a very big vein of that grade ore. Any round of shots might bring it in, and then again it might fool me. Those blind veins are not so easy to pick up, especially in a formation that's been broken up and faulted. There you are again—it's along the faults that the ore occurs."

"How do you account for that?" I asked, thoroughly confused.

"Well, I don't claim to be a graduate geologist," he said, "but I've got my own theories on the subject. Like to hear them?"

"Very much," I replied.

"Good," he said. "Now, a fault's a slide in the earth's crust that makes a crack or a fissure. You follow me?"

I nodded ignorantly, yet hopefully.

"Now, the hot steam that carries the gold and silver in solution," he continued, "shoots up from the bowels of the earth and escapes through the fissure, and when it gets near the surface the hot steam gradually cools off and the gold and silver precipitate and stay behind in the country rock while the rest of the steam escapes into the atmosphere."

I had a sudden inspiration. "Are you by any chance the well-known Hot Steam Boyd?" I asked.

"Yes, that's what the boys call me around here," he acknowledged.

I'd heard of Hot Steam Boyd many a time, and each time I had wondered what other kind of steam there could possibly be than the hot variety.

The fire was down to a little bed of coals, glowing with that resinous pungency remindful of fine Turkish tobacco—true desert incense. The brilliant hues of the western sky had given way to a lusterless gray against which Paradise Peak and the range trailing northward therefrom loomed black and gloomy. One by one the stars with seeming reluctance took their places on the night shift.

"Tell me," Hot Steam asked, "are you out on your own?

I know I have no business asking you, but what I'd like to know is where did you get hold of those fine burros?"

"Glad you approve of them," I said. "I think they're fine too. Yes, I'm on my own. This whole outfit belongs to me. I bought it in Tonopah for a hundred and fifty dollars."

"You don't say," he exclaimed. "Well, you surely got a bargain. I never saw a finer jack than that big brown."

"Oh, that's Dan," I replied. "Yes, he's a wonder. He's the one I ride. I talk to him just as you do to Shorty, and he loves it. I'm sure he knows what I'm saying. Sometimes he acts like a teacher's pet polishing apples, comes and pokes his head under my arm and wants to be rubbed behind the ears. He's a powerful animal, but I don't always ride him when we travel. I walk a good part of the time."

"That stocky muddy gray one—tell me about him."

"Ah, Rickey! He's strictly business," I said. "He's no pet like Dan, but they're great pals, those two. Rickey takes the lead when we're on the go and keeps up a fine steady pace. I believe he's even stronger than Dan, though he's quite a bit smaller. I admire the little cuss even though he's not much on personality. He makes it up with his mighty stout heart. Did you happen to notice the way his left ear's all chewed up? Must have been in a fight one time or another."

"Yes sir, I noticed that," he replied. "Did you know that a tough little jack like him can lick the stuffing out of a big stud horse?"

"No, you don't tell me," I said.

"It's a fact," he insisted. "A jack fights with both his teeth and his hoofs. Once he clamps his jaws on a horse's neck he hangs on like a bulldog."

"Imagine Rickey doing that!" I said. "Why, he's so gentle and patient, actually retiring."

"Ah, that's what fools people," said Hot Steam. "Some men are like that, mild-mannered, soft-spoken, baby-blue eyed, but don't let that fool you. They're wonderful to get along with, but don't try to play any tricks on them! Same way with these jacks. They're an entirely different animal once they get riled up. Let's see now, what about your other burros, those two jennies? That white one with the bell looks to me as if she's coming in."

"Coming in?" I asked. "How do you mean?"

"Why, don't you know?" he said. "She's about ready to foal."

"Honest?" I asked, dumbfounded. It had never occurred to me that Jennie B might be anything other than just plain pot-bellied.

"Yes," he assured me, "you can look for a colt any time now."

"Gosh," I said ruefully, "I suppose I should have been more tolerant of the poor thing. She's the only one that ever makes trouble—keeps breaking out of line for no reason at all when she's supposed to follow right behind Rickey. Besides, she's the one that leads the others 'way off at night, in spite of her hobbles. Best thing about her is her white hide—shows up a long ways off. Well, well, so Jennie B's going to be a mother!"

"That other one is a pretty animal—the mouse-colored one," Hot Steam went on talking.

"Isn't she?" I said. "She's as good as gold. Her name's Old Gal. Puts me in mind of some prim old maid—nice disposition, perfect lady, and minds her own business."

In response to his futher prodding I told him about the circumstances leading up to my acquiring the outfit, with special emphasis on the part Still Wandell had played in it.

"Oh, you know Still, do you?" Hot Steam asked.

"Very well," I replied. "He was just up from Greenwater."

"How did he say it was looking down there?" Hot Steam asked.

"Still seemed a little worried," I replied.

"That so? Then the ore bodies didn't turn out so good, I guess."

"No, not that," I corrected. "He's afraid they're so big and rich that copper'll be a glut on the market once Greenwater starts shipping."

"H'm! The boys must still be busy selling stock down there," Hot Steam remarked dryly.

"Yes, they can't print certificates fast enough. Charles M. Schwab of United States Steel is sinking a shaft a thousand feet deep. Anything with the word Greenwater on it sells like hotcakes."

"Is Charlie Schwab worried too?" Hot Steam asked with a chuckle.

"Now, you don't seriously believe Mr. Charles M. Schwab would encourage that line of talk, do you?" I asked.

"Well, he wouldn't order it stopped," Hot Steam declared. "Remember what he did at Rhyolite—bought in for a song. No sir, Charlie's nobody's sucker."

Hot Steam assured me he knew about the Greenwater Kid and said the last he had heard about him he was flat broke.

"I can vouch for that," I said. "If it hadn't been for the Greenwater Kid, I wouldn't be sitting out here with you like this tonight."

"Well, I'm grateful to him for that," Hot Steam was kind enough to say.

5

I WAS SORRY to see it come bedtime. The old boy was good. His observations on any given subject were unique and nothing is farther from my intentions than to hold any of them up to ridicule. One doesn't ridicule sincerity. Take, for instance, his nickname—Hot Steam. Of course, all steam is hot, but when he used the term in advancing his geological ideas it connoted more than immediately struck the ear. The steam he was talking about, steam under millions of pounds of pressure in the bowels of the earth, steam so hot that there's vaporized gold and silver in it—that really could be fairly hot steam—hotter, at least, than the common or teakettle variety. He was brimful of ideas—some of which could well have been years ahead of his time. One of them had to do with the proper position for lying in bed. He insisted on lying in line with the earth's magnetic currents so that they would pass through his body in a straight line from head to toe, or vice versa, and never should one sleep "crosswise of the magnet," as he put it.

When the bed was unrolled, I asked him which side he liked to sleep on.

"Either one," he said, "just so my head's a mite higher than my feet. That drains the blood out of the brain and gives it a chance to relax."

As we worked ourselves under the blankets I observed that he was wearing heavy woolen underwear, which by the light of the Milky Way showed up a blood red.

"Don't you find those flannels pretty warm this season of the year?" I asked.

"Oh my, no," he said. "I wear it the year 'round. It's cool in summer in this dry climate, and it keeps a fellow clean, much cleaner than if he took a bath every day. The wool draws everything out of the pores and then you wash the wool instead of the body. It's the same with wool stockings. They keep your feet in good condition."

I feared morning would never come. The night seemed

like an eternity of praying that the earth's magnetic currents would blow a fuse or something and become disconnected with Hot Steam's snoring. One man's bliss can truly be another man's misery. Along about dawn the power went off, and I did manage to sneak in a few winks of short-lived sleep before the sun came up and I saw my energetic bed-fellow sitting up and lacing his boots.

"Good morning" I called out as I began fishing for my clothes at the foot of the bed.

"Good morning, good morning," Hot Steam sang out gaily. "Did you have a good sleep?"

"Did I?" I replied. "Why, I just woke up this minute. How about you?"

"Never slept better," he replied. "I was dead to the world."

I let it go at that. He got up, stretched, and took some deep breaths.

"Ah," he said, "I see your burros down there on the flat, all bunched up together." He walked off a few yards.

In a minute I was up and joined him where he kept looking at the unusual sight. Suddenly he grabbed my arm.

"It's a colt!"

"Where?" I asked.

"Don't you see that black bundle under Jennie B's nose, down on the ground?" He pointed.

"Is that a colt, that little black spot?"

"You bet it is," he said. "It's kind of half sitting up. See the big ears?"

I still couldn't believe it. How in the world could my snow-white Jennie B have a coal-black colt? Surely Hot Steam was wrong.

"Often happens," he said when I put the question to him. "Chances are that little feller'll turn white like his mother, by and by."

34

This unexpected development floored me. "What do I do now?" I asked.

"They're all right where they are for now," he said. "We'll go fetch 'em after we've had breakfast."

"Can that little thing walk?" I asked.

"Hardly," he replied. "We'll have to take turns carrying it."

I felt a mounting impatience to get down there and have a look at the brand-new baby burro. Hot Steam was one of those exasperating slow eaters. At last he was finished. His second big cup of tea was downed, and he wiped his beard on his big blue bandanna. I could tell he didn't approve of our leaving the dishes unwashed, but he was too polite to mention it. We hurried down the slope.

The little chap was all velvety fuzz—a baby jack. There we stood, burros and men, gazing at the young hero, one and all simply crazy about him. Even the unromantic Rickey edged up as close to Jennie B as she would let him and frankly admired her offspring. Hot Steam leaned forward, patted the fluffy baby's head, and addressed him in gentle terms of affection. Jennie B looked none too pleased about it.

"Now let's see if she'll let me pick him up," he said.

"Here, let me," I protested; I wanted to be the first to handle him.

But Hot Steam already had his long arms around the little body, just back of the forelegs, and set it up on its uncertain, spraddling underpinning. He steadied the body a moment. Then he knelt to poke his head between its fore and aft extremities, rose from his knees, and there he stood with a throw of genuine desert sable draped across his shoulders.

"He's had a grand bath," he said, "same as cats give their kittens."

We headed back for camp. I soon insisted on relieving Hot

Steam of his burden, and with the warm, silky feel of the throbbing little body on the back of my neck, what else could I do but forgive Jennie B her past cussedness? The shedding of some thirty-odd pounds had transformed her figure. There was only one possible name for that little son of a desert— Blackie! Then a thought came to me.

"What if he turns white?" I asked.

"So'll his name," Hot Steam assured me.

No driving, no urging had been needed. The burros docilely trailed after their lode star, Blackie, back to camp as they would have into hell itself, so completely were they spellbound by the dramatic nativity they had beheld. I soon realized that my well-versed guest had not been talking through his hat when he told me that all I needed to do from then on was to tether his little nibs and the grown-ups would remain close by, even without hobbles. In particular would that be true of Jennie B, the miscreant who had been leading them so far astray.

The next order of business was to break camp and prepare for our trip to Sunnyside. Hot Steam was an able packer, as was to be expected. He seemed to be adept at anything whatsoever. He didn't go in for the diamond hitch, that much-touted "sparkler" which he said was "all for fancy— cowboys and such, with their silver conchas and orange chaps." He said he'd be glad to teach me how to throw it if I should decide to stay at Sunnyside.

We took turns riding that wise old boy Dan and holding Blackie on our laps. Each time we changed places we gave the tiny mascot a chance to try out his wobbly legs as well as to refresh himself at the delicious fount which was maintained for his exclusive benefit by Jennie B.

We headed for the mouth of a canyon separating twin

high ridges which sloped down from the crest of the range and broke off sharply, suggesting the bastions of a giant fortress. Floods racing through that rugged portal had written their own history in the deep draw extending down to the floor of the valley, six or seven miles below. A well-worn trail led us to its bed and continued on up the canyon.

A short ways on, the canyon widened out into a grassy meadow rent through its middle by the deep wash of the ages. On the anomalous little plateau we came upon an old, rusty cast-iron cookstove set on a pier of slab rock. As I was in the lead, and afoot, I stopped to ponder the strange sight and, of course, it was a foregone conclusion that I must step closer and open the oven door, which was slightly ajar. Instantly I jumped backwards and all but landed in the deep ditch.

"What's the matter?" Hot Steam called out. "What is it? I can't see from here." I relieved him of Blackie so he could dismount. He stepped over to the stove and stooped to peer into the oven.

"Snakes!" he exclaimed. "Well, well, cozy and snug!"

"Rattlers?" I asked. He had edged closer and squatted on his haunches to study the reptiles.

"No," he said at last, straightening, "they're a beautiful pair of bull snakes. Come take a look at them. They're gentle and harmless." I took him at his word but moved cautiously anyway.

"The way to tell is by their heads."

"And their slender, tapering tails?" I added.

"No," he corrected, "you can't altogether trust their tails. There's a dangerous snake on these deserts that's supposed to be a cross between a bull snake and a rattler. It has a slim tapering tail and the same color and markings as a bull snake, but its head is flat and triangular like a rattler's only a little smaller. I've only run across one of 'em, but I've heard others say they'd seen them. I never believed them till I saw that one with my own eyes.

"Did you kill it?" I asked.

"You bet I did," Hot Steam declared. "I opened its mouth and sure enough it had a rattler's pair of fangs in the upper jaw."

"Don't the scientists know about it?"

"I heard the professors at the state university laughed it off," Hot Steam replied. "They said snakes like that only come in bottles."

"You should have sent them your specimen," I said.

"You're right," he agreed, "and if I ever find another one that's just what I'll do. Take a look at those two in there. They're as friendly as kittens—make fine pets around a camp—wonderful mousers, and best of all they keep rattlers away."

I asked what in the world that stove was doing there. It seemed funny to me.

"Cowboys brought it in last winter," he told me. "They camped up here while the cattle were feeding on the white sage down on the alkali flat." I had never heard of white sage, but he described it as a dwarf species only a few inches tall with silvery leaves. It thrives on 'dobe ground and the first frost adds something or other to its edibility for cattle and sheep. They love it and go all out for it.

Continuing on up the canyon, I couldn't get that hybrid snake out of my mind. Finally, I came right out with it.

"I thought bull snakes and rattlers were deadly enemies," I said. "How do you account for their ever mating?"

"All you can do is guess at that," he replied. "One fellow had it figured out that if you kill a male bull snake, his mate'll take up with an unattached rattler, if she happens to meet up with one. This man said it only happens once in a great while, and the reason the half-rattler is so scarce is because hybrids can't reproduce. You can take that or leave it. I just don't know."

"Wait till we reach the top of this blowout," Hot Steam said. "You'll see a campsite that's hard to beat. Just look at the feed around here!"

Soon we emerged on a level patch surfaced with finely chipped pink-and-white chalky rock that squeaked musically under foot. Hot Steam called it volcanic tufa.

"Ah, there's your pony," I said. Across the gulch stood Shorty, lazily switching his tail. He was hugging the base of a bluff which shut off the sun's supercharged rays in the heat of the day.

No one could ask for a more ideal, more commanding hideout than Hot Steam's camp at Sunnyside. No brigand, no moonshiner, no prospector, nor, in fact, any man that wanted to get away from it all could ever find a spot more to his heart's content—a nature-lover's sanctuary I truly believed.

I should have known that Hot Steam's hangout would be just like that—a model establishment, every detail well thought out, pin-neat. First to greet the eye was the tent-shack up against the face of a cliff-like rock which hovered protectingly over it. The lumber of the walls and doorway had quite evidently been salvaged from some wrecking job. A legend, done in some kind of black pigment, appeared over the door:

WELCOME. PLEASE CLOSE DOOR WHEN LEAVING. BOYD.

I followed Hot Steam inside. "No one's been here," he observed.

This was "batching" in luxury—stove, table, bench, cupboards, washstand, with mirror of sorts, skillets, dishes, supplies, and at the far end as inviting a bunk as ever a man tucked himself into on a chilly night.

Deferring to the "animals first" tradition, we unburdened the burros and left them to their own devices, unhobbled, which was not the magnanimous gesture it might sound like. The guileless creatures were more effectively shackled by their infatuation for Blackie, who meant to make a night of it right there where he was. The next chore was to fetch a bucket of water. A few dozen steps across the musical tufa led me to a stockaded water hole in which a whisky barrel was sunk. The hole was full to the brim, though at first glance it appeared empty because the water was so clear and transparent. Outside the inclosure was an iron trough which could at one time have been part of a milling plant but now was catching the overflow from the spring—a boon to straying animals. Soon enough my burros would be up there helping themselves to that godsend which had been developed by the cattlemen of Reese River.

Reese River! That name was beginning to do things to me. Hot Steam had spoken of it so many times that I thought it had him hypnotized, and I told him so.

"There are many places that folks call God's Country," he said, "but to me Reese River is the capital of them all."

Just what was the source of those vague memories the mention of Reese River evoked in me? It bothered me all during the splendid lunch of fried potatoes, bacon, and tea, which my good host had prepared. Just where was this fabulous stream anyway and was it a real river with water, or just another Amargosa?

"It's right over the range from where we're sitting," Hot Steam said, "and you bet it's a real river with water all the way from Arc Dome to the Humboldt River, over two hundred miles north."

Cattle, thousands and thousands of 'em, high up in the headwaters of Reese River and its tributary canyons in the snowcapped Toiyabes ranged in that summer paradise, enjoyed alike by the sportsman, the fisherman, and the prospector. It was the habitat of deer, bighorn mountain sheep, grouse, sage hen, trout, and—yes, that predatory balancer of nature, the mountain lion. That's how Hot Steam painted Reese River for me, adding that its mineral potentialities, gold, silver, and other metals, were unlimited. Rugged country, that, with Arc Dome twelve thousand feet in elevation and the whole Toiyabe Range averaging better than ten thousand feet all the way north to Austin and beyond.

At last it all came back to me! Several years before I had read about the Reese River boom of the 1860's in a book by an early-day engineer named Ross Brown. At that time it was claimed that Austin, on the Pony Express trail, would surpass the Comstock itself—Austin, the scene of the lusty Reese River excitement. Come what may, my mind was made up then and there. That's where I'd go eventually—to Reese River!

I was jarred out of my reverie when I saw my host feeding potato peels to Jennie B. It would never have occurred to me to do that.

"Why," he chuckled, "that's candy to her. It'll make sweet milk for Blackie too. You know, there's hardly anything a burro won't eat. They're like goats in that respect. I saw one eat a piece of oilcloth once that was a label on a pair of overalls. There was a trick to it, though. One fellow bet another that his jack would eat it. When the other fellow took him up on it, he spread some bacon grease on the label and offered it to the jack. You should have seen him eat it and hang around for more!" Hot Steam laughed heartily.

Sloppiness in any form was strictly out, as far as Hot

Steam's camp was concerned. I was to find the same true of prospectors as a class, generally speaking, also of cowboys, whose code called for washing the hands and face and combing the hair before starting to cook. As for table manners, that was something else again. Their code granted considerable latitude. Conveying food, even peas, on a knife to the mouth was a matter of personal discretion. That and bolting one's food and resounding belches, provided there was no evidence of malice involved, were the principal points of departure from generally accepted standards of prandial procedure that drew my attention as I moved from camp to camp. Alas, I am unable to report so favorably on the sheepherders. Those hardy souls are bottled up in the rocks 'way above timberline all summer long with neither the opportunity nor the inclination to wash themselves, much less bathe. Their whole outfit is packed on one lone burro, and often I have seen them turn their dishes over to their hungry dogs for washing.

Now came the big moment to have a look at Hot Steam's diggings. It was a stiff hike to get up there, the elevation being some five hundred feet greater than at the camp. He was running a tunnel into the hillside, following a seam that looked to me like nothing but a crack. It was in over a hundred feet, all of it having been hand-drilled and mucked out by wheelbarrow.

"It's a tight formation, hard on drill bits," he said. All the way in to the face he held his candle up so I'd see the seam in the roof. It was impossible for me to share his enthusiasm over the showing. I was a greenie, and it didn't mean much to me.

"A true fissure," he said, as we stood looking at it. "Every inch of it pans like a house afire. Any day it could bulge out into a bonanza ore body." He started nicking away with his poll pick at the seam while I held the candle for him. He would catch the pay dirt in his hand and carefully place it on his handkerchief spread open at his feet. Outside I watched with interest as he pulverized the dry dirt in a mortar, dumped it into an old rusty frying pan, and washed it out in the slack tub alongside the blower where he did his blacksmithing. He panned as expertly as he packed, swishing and swirling the pulp in the half-submerged pan, coaxing it over the rim till only a minute quantity of concentrate remained.

Now for the showdown. Would there be colors—or just a skunking? Pouring away all but a thimbleful of the water, he raised the pan, jolted it lightly a few times with his free hand, and then with a grin held it out for me to inspect. There in the pan I saw a miniature Halley's Comet, gleaming gold at the head or core and shading off for an inch or more into a tail of lustrous yellow particles. A hundred-dollar panning, Hot Steam pronounced it, meaning that the dirt he had panned would assay in the neighborhood of one hundred dollars to the ton. But it takes a good many handfuls to make a ton, alas.

It had been Hot Steam's Mother-Lode pocket-hunting experience that enabled him to pick up his narrow but rich seam. How on earth he had done it, I couldn't begin to figure out. I was anxious to learn.

"It's as simple as ABC," he explained. "All it takes is a lot of time and patience."

Before he got through explaining, I was ready to throw up my hands. He must have dug a thousand postholes in the course of panning his way up the hillside to find the source of the gold he had encountered in the dirt down below. Lord, was that what I had let myself in for when I took up prospecting? It seemed like a grim future. I had thought that mines always stuck their noses out boldly on the surface, like the

Mizpah at Tonopah, when Jim Butler accidentally stubbed his toe on it while hunting his burros in 1901. I didn't think brains ever entered into it. This blind gophering didn't appeal to me one bit. I thought it was all a matter of luck.

Hot Steam just smiled and told me to cheer up.

"They're still finding those surface showings," he said, "and they always will, because cloudbursts and earthquakes keep changing the face of the country and exposing new sections of the earth's crust. Many times outcrops that people have passed up for years and years turn out to be rich in precious metals. This is the kind of work for me. There's excitement in it, like detective work. The good Lord didn't intend for all the mines to be discovered at once. He kept a lot of them under cover so as to make us work to find them."

6

RICH FLOAT! Wherever you go when you're out prospecting you hear about it. Ranchers, sheepmen, buckaroos, and especially fellow prospectors, all come up with the same old story. "They's been some powerful rich float picked up in that thar gulch," they say, knowingly. Sometimes it's "down that a'wash," or "around them blowouts." In one respect, however, the story never varies—it's always "rich" float. I have yet to have someone tell me "there's been some awful hungry-looking rock picked up," etc., etc.

I told Hot Steam I couldn't see that it would be to the advantage of either one of us for me to stay on at Sunnyside. Of course, I could locate some claims adjoining his ground, do the required amount of location work on them, namely two hundred and forty cubic feet of excavation for each claim, put up monuments on the corners and sides, have the claims recorded with the county clerk, and then just sit tight waiting for Hot Steam to prove up my ground by opening up a bonanza on his. He had admitted that it might be several months before he'd strike it in his tunnel, if ever.

"Always a gamble," he had said. Hence, it just had to be Reese River for me.

"Why not stick here a while," the hospitable gentleman asked, "and give Old Baldy a rub? There's been some *rich float* picked up around there." He was referring to Bald Mountain, the highest peak in the range we were in—the Shoshones. He added that he'd look into it himself if he weren't tied down where he was.

Rich float! Sounded mighty good—must have sloughed off some vein—maybe sticking right out of the ground—sure might be worth looking into. I told Hot Steam I'd sleep on that.

Next morning I announced I had decided to tackle Old Baldy. I'd just make a reconnaissance trip, size things up, and be back early in the afternoon.

"That's a pretty big job," he warned. "It's a good big ten miles up there, steep, rough going." It hadn't looked like even three miles to my untutored eye. Anyway, I was going. That's one of the beauties of being a prospector. One did as one bally well pleased.

After breakfast I took my hand pick, a sample sack, a quart canteen of water, and struck out for the high places. One thing I had found out about myself—I could manage without water much longer than the average person could. Why, I don't know. Hot Steam handed me a "dough god" to take along for lunch—a thick, slow-baked hotcake made of whatever batter was left over from breakfast.

Leisurely, I went about the task of conquering Old Baldy, stopping every so often to knock off a chunk from this or that cropping or to crack open an interesting bit of rock, wet it with my tongue as I had observed Hot Steam do, and then

45

intently train my magnifying glass on what might, with beginner's luck, turn out to be rich float. Eventually it occurred to me that even if I were to find a piece of the real McCoy I probably wouldn't know it from green cheese. Besides, although geologizing was an undeniably fascinating way to pass the time of day, even to one not knowing a thing about it, still two hours or more had slipped away from me without bringing the top of Old Baldy any nearer to speak of. I had reached the top of the crest, yes, but the noble peak now looked higher than ever, still miles off to the north.

But what a wonderland it was up there! I was in a park, no less, surfaced with finely chipped pink tufa through which the backbone of the range jutted in a jumble of shattered segments. The air was rife with delicate fragrance, which I soon traced to the diminutive white blossoms of a scraggly shrub which appeared to exist by sufferance of the friendly rocks around which it sprouted. Well-defined trails, that I mistakenly ascribed to cattle, threaded the general course of the range. Here one was really up in the sky, intensely blue and cloudless, not only overhead but all around one. The silence was not a mere negative state; it was a tangible entity existing by itself, independent of all else. Its intensity magnified whatever it was that buzzed in one's ears—either the cosmic roar from without or the throb of my own power-plant from within.

These speculations, however, were destined to be short-lived and came to an abrupt halt. Out of the blue there came a sudden, unearthly, ferocious snort which set my heart to thumping in double time. I had visions of all the fierce, blood-thirsty wild beasts of India and Africa at once. Nothing I had ever heard in circus or zoo was invested with the diabolical menace of that piercing snort. I was scared, and I don't mean maybe. Yes, sir, I was certain I was being stalked. I frenziedly racked my brains for some means of defense against that unseen monster, when there it was again off in the direction of Old Baldy! This time it was followed by a thundering rumble lasting seconds only then stopping cold. Now came the briefest silence, then once again the same sequence of sounds, only this time from farther off—and with it came its own explanation when I dared look for it.

On a bluff, scarcely two hundred yards away, like a pedestalled statue, stood a magnificently poised horse, motionless as a West Point cadet at attention, looking at me with the fire of defiance and distrust in his blazing eyes. Beyond him, nonchalantly grazing, were some fifty-odd head of sleek mustangs—mares with streaming tails and luxurious manes to match—grays, buckskins, browns, pintos, and colts, newborn and older. Only their czar, the solid midnight black with head aloft and tail arched like a plume, paid the least attention to me. The rest of the band evidenced by their utter indifference that they had implicit faith in his ability to cope with any situation that might arise affecting their well-being. Here, indeed, was an equine totalitarian state, complete with its dictator who brooked no rival. It was time enough for the band to think of taking to their heels when Comrade Black gave the command.

There we stood, exchanging fixed stares, each watching for the other's next move. I was reluctant to break the spell, to bring down the curtain on that enthralling tableau. In the stallion's noble eyes I was a hated intruder up there in that last refuge, that horse-heaven of untamed cayuses who only asked to be left alone.

I was not unfamiliar with the black stallion's story. I had read about the precariousness of his status as overlord of his harem of mares, how he had risen to power, and what his eventual end would be. Perhaps at that very moment he was standing guard over his own doom. The male colt suckling one of his mares there in the distance might one day stand forth and challenge him to a battle that must end in death or banishment for one or the other of them. Or it could be that some outside stallion would be the one to lift his crown and take over his harem, adding it to his own if he already had one. In either event, his ultimate, inevitable downfall would evoke not so much as a neigh of regret from his mares. All they loved, and that but briefly, was their colts. So the vanquished stallion, provided his conqueror had let him off with his life, would pass the rest of his days as an exile in some rocky canyon until his teeth and hoofs grew long and useless and, unable to walk or chew any more, he would lie down never to get up again, fully aware that he was the cynosure of eager-eyed coyotes and buzzards.

Well, aside from all that—what if that powerful brute should take after me—what chance should I have of defending myself or of escaping? I was unarmed, completely at his mercy it struck me. At about that time there actually existed a horse in captivity, named Cruiser, a vicious, dangerous man-killer who was kept for exhibition purposes only. I thanked heaven that wasn't Cruiser eyeing me from off yonder. Then again, this fellow might be just as tough a customer, if not worse.

Putting my fingers to my lips, I blew a sharp whistle. In response, I drew an especially enraged snort, and away tore the band on a dead run with the stallion bringing up the rear, turning to face me from time to time with parting snorts, until all were out of sight beyond where the trail skirted a bold, rocky bluff.

So, exit mustangs. Old Baldy? There it was—and still is, for all of me. Alas, though, when and if someone strikes it rich along the slopes of that sharp peak, it will serve me right for not having heeded Hot Steam's endorsement of it.

From where I stood, two contrasting views presented themselves. To the west, Ione Valley, asleep, lifeless, saddening, and to the right it was, yes, Reese River!

I sought out a position where I could rest while feasting on the heavenliness of that picture, Reese River, far and away the most beautiful valley on earth, right in the center of that matchless state, Nevada! Across there were the towering snowcapped Toiyabes, with massive Arc Dome like a bookend at their southern extremity. But how can I, how can anyone, do justice to such a scene in mere words? From my vantage point I could take in a sweep of say sixty miles of the valley with the ribbon of green winding down its middle where the river flowed between its willow-fringed banks—the sharply outlined green meadows, the clusters of cottonwoods on ranch after ranch, buildings, corrals, haystacks, all so distant as to appear like mere specks on the landscape.

Despite that alluring prospect, I felt myself growing drowsy in the warmth of the sun, and I stretched myself out full length on the gently yielding tufa for a brief nap. Pleased with myself for having taken up prospecting, which now more than ever appealed to me as being the most carefree, independent, and altogether delightful existence attainable in this life, if not in the next, I soon dozed off into blissful oblivion.

What had meant to be just a forty-winker had elongated itself into a snooze of major proportions during which the sun had taken unfair advantage of me by stealthily sinking into its late afternoon declivity. Coming to, I realized there was little time to spare if I meant to join Hot Steam at six o'clock supper.

I reached camp just as my methodical host had finished washing himself preparatory to cooking the meal I could scarcely wait to sit down to. He was wiping himself—which is to say his face, neck, beard, scalp, hands, and forearms up to the elbows—dry on his tawny towel. He looked as fresh and clean as a daisy. I told him I had never seen anyone with clearer, bluer eyes than his, and in return I was treated to a brief discourse on eye hygiene.

"I always use cold water to wash," he said, "the colder the better. The first thing I do is hold my face down in it with my eyes wide open. That stimulates them and washes out all the grit."

I was glad to learn that, but what I wanted was for him to talk about Reese River. I asked so many questions that the poor man hardly had a chance to eat, what with giving his all to answering them.

What sort of people were the ranchers over there? What was the best way to get into that country with burros? Was any prospecting going on in those deep, rugged canyons? My questions flowed on and on.

"They're big-hearted folks over there on the river," he said. It seemed he knew them all, clear down to Battle Mountain. Reese River flows north, which tended to confuse me when he spoke of Austin's being "down" the river. All the ranches along the entire stream could about be counted on one's fingers and toes. There was a marked preponderance of Irish names—Keough, Bowler, Walsh, Ryan, O'Toole, with here and there an Italian like Gandolfo, a Scot like Watt or Litster, a German like Dieringer or Gooding or Schmaling. However, Thomas Jefferson Bell cut a commanding figure as owner of an outfit on the upper river second only to that of his friend Patrick Walsh, forty miles below, one of whose barbed-wire fences ran twenty-two miles in a straight line.

The magnificent Bell ranch adjoined the equally splendid Keough ranch at the latter's upper end. Bell had six stalwart sons, one of whom, Elmer, later lost his life in World War I. The Keoughs and Bells were on the friendliest of terms, both running large herds of cattle on the mountain range. T. J. Bell was a member of the state senate and was well regarded and respected by all his colleagues.

Patrick Michael Bowler had a miniature empire about midway between the Bell and Walsh ranches. According to Hot Steam, Bowler was well along in his eighties but still given to spending hours a day in the saddle, trusting no one but himself to see that all was kept in shipshape running order. Behind his back, he was generally referred to as Grandpa Bowler. It had been said that he once ran a hired man off the ranch at the business end of a pitchfork for having indulged in that unseemly familiarity. As a young cocksure immigrant from Cahirisaveen, County Kerry, Ireland, he had landed at New Orleans, where he lost no time pulling the strings to get on the police force. One hot day, as Hot Steam related it, he had the misfortune to fall asleep on his beat and awoke to find that, as he expressed it, "some dirty Dutchman" had made off with his helmet. Unable to offer a satisfactory explanation of his bareheadedness on reporting at headquarters, he was fined a month's pay, which so riled him that he threw up the job. Somewhere along the line he had gotten wind of Reese River, Nevada, and there he went with his meager savings, his loyal Irish wife, and a non-magnificent obsession, namely, "those Dutch so-and-sos!"

In Reese River Valley he prospered, as did his progeny.

Hot Steam knew them all. Soon my thoughts began to wander, all interlaced with that alluring view of the valley with the green streak where the river flowed. It was all settled. In the morning, I'd light out. Already I was beginning to miss Hot Steam. There was no end to what I could learn from him by staying at Sunnyside, but he had his work all mapped out, and I was probably only in his way. So it was good-by, Hot Steam. I heard of him indirectly from time to time but never saw him again. His stingy seam refused to open up for him and finally disappeared altogether in a fault. I'm sure he's in that heavenly abode where the streets are paved with gold.

7

REESE RIVER could be reached by any number of routes. Hot Steam had advised me to go by way of Ione, a famous gold camp of yesteryear with a rich legend of shootings and diversified perfidy.

Early in the afternoon I dropped into the mouth of Ione Canyon and made camp alongside an old neglected graveyard. Blackie had walked a good part of the way, sticking close to his mother's protecting and nourishing flanks. We had gone about eight miles at snail's pace, on Blackie's account, even though I had given him frequent lifts on my lap aboard the incomparable Dan.

I unpacked, tied Blackie to a black sage bush, and with a laugh at the expense of all four adult burros for letting little Mr. Big Shot make such boobs of them as to render hobbles superfluous—a laugh that was to boomerang, however—I was off for "uptown" to take in the sights.

Strolling up along the narrow wagon road, I saw on both sides of the canyon the foundations and stumps of mine and mill buildings, their superstructures having long since gone the way of dismantling and fire. At about midtown, if such it might be called, I saw a man bent double at the tail end of a horse he was shoeing. In a corral nearby stood a few scrawny-looking nags. As I approached, he let down the critter's hind foot and greeted me, hammer in hand. He was red-headed, freckled, and wore blue denim overalls with the manufacturer's warranty still attached.

"My name's Phillips—Harry Phillips," he said, offering me his hand. I was happy to shake the big, rough, friendly paw. He was about my own age, say twenty-two, and of course I wanted to hear his life's story. It was such a long one that I began to worry about getting back to my camp in time to cook supper before dark. That fear, however, was allayed by Harry's insistence on my staying for supper with him and his mother. They lived in an oversized, one-story wooden building, the converted quarters of a store of bygone days. The rear had been rigged up as a combined kitchen, dining room, and lounge, as snug a setup as one could want. In one corner was the wood-burning range, which no doubt had come around the Horn, polished like new, with bright nickel trimmings. There stood Mrs. Phillips bringing things to a head thereon as Harry and I entered. Like him she had red hair, and what an abundance of it! She wore it in a turban of thick braids. She was trim of figure and agile appearing. All was spotless in there. The aroma of the food in the steaming and sizzling skillets hit the bull's-eye of my eager appetite. The gracious lady could spare me little more than a glance, a pleasant and smiling one, as Harry introduced me. Harry and I, all freshly washed up, sat at the places set for us, the good lady clearly preferring to serve us first and defer her own meal till we had finished. They called it a supper, this marvelous feast built around man-sized T-bone steaks, juicy and tender, which I was told had come from the George Keough ranch on Reese River.

I learned that these fine people were all connected with the far-flung Bowler clan, which even had its ramifications in the Pat Walsh family and other families on the river I was headed for. That warned me I had better watch my tongue upon reaching Reese River. An idle word dropped here or there could well upset the apple cart of one's pleasant and harmonious sojourn in that beautiful valley.

I was trying to figure out how Harry and his mother happened to be living in that isolated ghost camp instead of on a prosperous cattle ranch like their relatives on Reese River. The answer, it appeared, was that Harry's late father had chosen to be a mining man—'nuf said—and had been alternately rich and broke any number of times. Alas for his wife and young son, he was caught with his luck down when the bewhiskered Father Time came along and scythed him into eternity.

At least Harry enjoyed the distinction of being Ione's *de facto* mayor. He had plenty to keep him occupied—a string of shabby cayuses, which he was forever shoeing, and a few dozen head of variegated cattle, which he was continually rounding up, and an astronomical number of mining claims on which he was ceaselessly doing assessment work as required by law.

Soon it came time for me to think of getting back to my camp. I took my leave, having done my best to convey to those extraordinarily kind and friendly people my sincere appreciation of their generous hospitality toward me.

With a feeling of great inner well-being, I ambled down the canyon, facing the splendor of another desert sunset.

At camp I found others who apparently were not unappreciative of the color effects off there in the west. I couldn't imagine what possessed my burros. They were all standing still, gazing as if transfixed. Were they homesick for Sunnyside or something?

No, that wasn't it, bless their gentle hearts! My camp was a shambles! Everything was strewn around à la hurricane. Only my roll of bedding was intact. Burglars! Yes, and four-footed ones! The larder was cleaned out—sugar, flour, beans, prunes, tea, precious remnant of bacon, even salt and pepper—all had gone down the hatch. I couldn't help laughing. Noble Dan, covered with flour all down his front, looked like a fellow-Shriner in full regalia, apron and all. Which of these innocents had eaten my prunes—over five pounds of 'em? Could be an explosion around there any minute if the greedy one had followed up with a drink at the nearby trough!

Punishment, even the mildest reproof, was out of the question. Gentle scamps, they wouldn't have the slightest idea what it was for. They had only done what I myself should have done under the circumstances if I had been born a burro. Indeed, I owed them a vote of thanks. They had taught me a valuable lesson about safeguarding my larder in the future.

Five o'clock the following morning found me once more uptown in what once was the county seat of Nye County, that ghost-ridden sepulcher of departed hustle and bustle—Ione. I thought I'd take a look around the old ruins while waiting for the place to come to some semblance of life.

I had expected to have to kill a couple of hours before I could buy the ingredients of a makeshift breakfast at the store run there by a Mr. Fred Schmaling. I had reckoned without the demoniacal energy of that human dynamo Harry Phillips, who was at that unearthly hour bustling around his blacksmith shop and corral. One of his horses, he explained, had developed a quarter-crack in an aft hoof, and he was going to flange up a special shoe for it. I told him about the debacle at my camp and asked him when Mr. Schmaling opened for business.

"Then you haven't had breakfast," he said. "Come on—this

can wait," and he all but hauled me across to his mother's kitchen where that amazing lady was clearing away the breakfast things.

"Here 'tis after five," Harry said, "and this poor fellow hasn't had his breakfast yet."

"Tchk, tchk!" Mrs. Phillips tchk'd sympathetically, nor would she listen to my protests as she hastened to "rustle up," as Harry expressed it, a few odds and ends consisting of mush with cream, hotcakes, ham and eggs, fried potatoes, and steaming hot coffee!

"What coffee!" I exclaimed, as she poured me a second big cup.

"Nothing extra," she replied, "just Schmaling's best. The old robber charges me twenty cents a pound for the stuff."

"Coffee's all in the making," Harry added. Mrs. Phillips surely had it down to a science, and I told her so.

Fred Schmaling, right there in dead old Ione, carried a stock of goods that would do credit to the best of stores in the big, going mining camps. It was all hauled in from Fallon, one hundred miles west, by his own teams. He was rated the richest man in the county. In his sixties, a virtual recluse, honest, but as tight as Hetty Green and as warmhearted as Bluebeard, he yet enjoyed the liberal patronage of the Reese River ranchers, miners, and Indians strictly as a matter of convenience and fair prices. I found him distinctly unpleasant to be around. He resembled George Bernard Shaw, physically, that is, tall, lean, gray, and tidy. His premises, a done-over old mine building, were copious and in faultless order. Not an item was out of place. As I looked at him standing back of his counter, I felt sure he carried in his head a perpetual inventory of his cans and packages and would instantly miss the least item that was AWOL. His teamster, Castro Ynchausti, was all hooked up and ready to pull out for Fallon with his high-wheeled wagon and trailer and fine team of eight horses. Castro had been with him for fourteen years and had made the two-hundred-mile round trip between Ione and Fallon an average of three times a month, loaded both ways as a rule, taking out ore, hides, sheep, and lambs, and bringing back kegs of horseshoes, groceries, tobacco, work clothes, and ladies' finery for Indian as well as white belles. All that time Castro had stuck to his high seat and jerk line while more imaginative spirits were roaming the desolate hills along his route and striking it rich at places like Wonder, Fairview, and sundry others.

My exuberant salutation drew a thoroughly civil acknowledgment from Mr. Fred Schmaling like something right off the ice. I felt his eyes all over me. I couldn't altogether blame him for his indifferent attitude toward my patronage. How could he know for sure that I wasn't the slicker the sheriff was looking for? All in all, I just didn't like the man. I felt that he had no use for sunsets, that songbirds annoyed him, and that when he was alone he spent his time toting up his receipts and smacking his lips over the deposits entered in his bank book.

My purchases amounted to some forty pounds. I shouldered them and made for Harry Phillips' blacksmith shop where I deposited them for safekeeping while he and I set out on a tour of his mineral rights which reached in all directions as far as one could see and then some. It looked to me as though the old-timers had ripped up the landscape with shafts and tunnels, as evidenced by the great waste-dumps, until there was hardly an acre that hadn't been literally turned inside out in their frantic search for treasure. Still, Harry insisted that the surface had "barely been scratched."

Harry figured that he was worth anywhere from a million dollars up, just as surely as if the money were actually to his credit in the Bank of Austin, and right here I want to back him up with the prediction that time will prove him to have been conservative in his estimate. Among his locations was an enormous bluff of solid quartzite which is known to carry uniform gold values which, though not high, will some day be extracted when someone with vision and capital installs a mill there. That bluff was too low grade for the old-timers to work, but since history proves that the price of gold knows but one direction—up, up, and up—it would be a mistake to discount Harry's conclusions.

In a couple of hours I had seen enough to convince me that there was nothing to hold me longer in Ione. Harry had the situation completely tied up, and more power to him! Reese River was calling more and more insistently. Acknowledging my deep indebtedness to Mrs. Phillips and her most likable and big-hearted son, Harry, I bade them good-by and tramped back to my camp with my recent purchases.

There a strange sight awaited me. A man was stretched out on the ground beside my packs. Standing with drooped head over him was a saddled horse. I kept drawing closer, but the man made no move. He was sound asleep, dead to the world. He was garbed in blue overalls and jumper, high-laced, brown boots with hobnailed soles, and his wide-brimmed gray felt hat lay loosely over his forehead so that all I could see of his head was his bushy, carrot-red beard.

"Hello, there!" I called out to him. Finally he raised himself to a semireclining position, leaning on one elbow, looking much younger than I had expected. He seemed to be trying to recollect where he was.

"Oh, howdy, howdy!" he said, smiling, displaying a healthy set of even white teeth.

"Sorry to disturb you," I said.

"Not at all," he replied. "The sun gets pretty warm around

noontime and first thing you know you doze off." He now stood up, flexed his arms in a mighty stretch, drew a sack of Bull Durham from his vest pocket, and soon was drawing at a freshly rolled cigarette. All in all, he was quite a figure of a man, well proportioned, a six-footer.

"I just dropped by to say howdy," he said. I told him that was mighty good of him.

"Which way you're headed, if it's okay for me to ask?" he said.

"Reese River," I told him, warily, as we shook hands and introduced ourselves.

He gave his name as Bob Hanchett. I said I hoped he'd excuse me for going ahead with my packing while we talked, and just to keep the ball rolling I asked him what he knew about Reese River. From what I subsequently learned about this bird, it's a wonder he didn't tell me he had swum the length of it. However, he did claim that what he didn't know about that great valley, its inhabitants, white as well as Injun, you could put in your eye.

"Like it?" I asked.

"Sure do," he allowed. "Prettiest country y'ever saw, but if'n I was you I wouldn't go over there right now."

"Why not?" I demanded. "Why shouldn't I go right now, as you say, or any other time?"

"On account er'Grantsville," he replied. "That's where you'd oughter head for."

"Grantsville? Where's that?" I asked.

"Oh, about ten miles south o'here," he said. "Gettin' all set for the biggest boom since the Comstock! Place is fillin' up with prospectors an' promoters. Quite a few big engineers is pokin' around there too. Better get yerse'f a claim or two afore it's too late. That's my advice."

"Have you any ground there?" I asked.

"You just bet I have," he replied. "Just so happens the big strike all the excitement's about is right on my ground. I'm on my way back there now. Thinks I to myself, we might travel together. What say—any objections?"

"The whole place is surely all located by this time," I said, "isn't it?"

"What if it is?" he replied. "Maybe if'n you act fast you can get yerse'f an option or two—tie up some ground for thirty, sixty, ninety days—won't cost you much—then turn it over for big money. That's how it's did in this business. Take a chance like Columbus done. You can't lose, I'm tellin'ya'."

So, I fell for this big windbag Hanchett and his line of simon-pure, unadulterated bull. Instead of crossing the Shoshone Range, via the Ione summit en route to Reese River, I wound up in the old mining camp of Civil War days, Grantsville, which had indeed been named after the great Yankee general himself. Let it now be said that this revival of the old worked-out camp was conceived in Hanchett's own brain. Fate, perverse or fortuitous, had lured me there, a likely prospect in the eyes of that artful promoter. Later, I gleaned some interesting data pertaining to the scamp from sources I deemed reliable, such as that he had been run out of the Okanogan country up in Washington State and that his so-called strike at Grantsville was salted to his taste with some high-grade gold ore from the Berlin mine a couple of miles to the north.

In spite of it all, I am forced to admit that my trip to Grantsville was well worth the effort. My interest in the place was aroused the minute we struck the canyon whose steep walls were stained a blood red by mill tailings that had been swept by many a summer flood along its deeply rutted course. We passed a big milling plant which appeared to be in a good shape of preservation in spite of its having been shut down and idle for something like a quarter of a century. Farther up were the mine buildings—hoist house with gallows frame, boardinghouse, bunkhouses, shops, assay office, and superintendent's residence. The last was occupied and looked very cozy and homelike with flowers growing in the front yard. Just ahead the canyon widened into a fairly broad basin which presented a kind of carnival effect with numerous tents, wagons, mules, burros, and paraphernalia scattered among the tall sagebrush.

Facing this scene of general disarray was a fairly commodious building of frontier design with a high false front from which the word "SALOON" still beckoned as best it could through its dim, faded paint. It struck me as strange that business should be booming inside that place at such an early afternoon hour. A clamor of men's voices issued from the open door, mingled with an assortment of clinking and clattering noises.

Hanchett said he was camped farther up where his "strike" was. He suggested that I pick a suitable site for my camp right there among the other outfits.

"But first," he suggested, "what say we go in and hoist a little snort and see how the boys are making it?" I confessed that a cold bottle of beer would hit the spot, since we hadn't stopped on the way to eat lunch.

Inside the saloon, I counted over twenty men, prospectors presumably, sitting around circular tables that were covered with faded, torn green baize, playing with soiled old decks of cards. Others just stood around watching. Some leaned idly against the bar, talking, smoking, and chewing, most of them looking decidedly the worse for wear. Behind the bar was an alert little fellow with black hair plastered down on his flattish head. His face, too, was flat and broad with black snake eyes that fairly glittered when they met one's gaze. Yellow suspenders over a blue-and-white-striped shirt, open at the neck, black elastic arm bands at the elbows—that much of his garb one could see as he stood there polishing whisky glasses, chomping on an unlit cigar, and scrutinizing the house.

Hanchett, after breezing around and greeting everyone with exaggerated cordiality, he, the big wheel of the hour no less, eventually steered me up to the bar and introduced me to the factotum there presiding, Mr. Ed Kiefer, who honored me with a sidewise nod, or rather jerk, of the head, and hastened to ask, "What'll it be, gents?"

He took our orders, mine being that nice cold bottle of beer, and Hanchett's a mint julep, which came near deciding me to switch to the same. Up came Kiefer with two whisky glasses, two chaser glasses, and a bottle of clear, colorless fluid, announcing, "There you are, gents."

Hanchett stole a glance at me and then burst out laughing as he poured himself his "julep" to the very brim of his whisky glass. Then he shoved the bottle my way saying, "There's your beer." I helped myself to a mere taste of the vile stuff which I managed to down only by grace of a hasty swallow of water. The alleged joke was that while you had the privilege of ordering whatever you pleased, Mr. Kiefer reserved the right to serve you his one-and-only bar liquor, a villainous rotgut gin, of which he had hauled in a bountiful stock before he opened for business.

Now it came my treat. I took a cigar which I put in my pocket, and excused myself, explaining that I wanted to watch one of the solo games a while. I was fascinated by a little gray-bearded old fellow who shuffled and dealt the cards with professional deftness despite the fact that he was thumbless, born that way, with four fingers only on each hand. I learned that he was prospecting on a grubstake and was stone deaf. The boys referred to him as "Deef Bob."

Hanchett lingered on at the bar. I sensed that Kiefer was loath to extend him further credit. I got out. Danged if I'd buy him any more mint juleps!

8

"WHERE DO WE GO FROM HERE?" That's what my pack outfit out there in front of Kiefer's saloon seemed to be yelling at me when I rejoined it. "Let's get going!" my burros' expressions clearly indicated, "or else get us out from under these confounded packs so we can roll our itchy backs on the ground!"

It was pretty late in the day to strike out afresh for nowhere in particular. I decided I might as well stick around a bit, not that I thought for an instant that there was anything but Grade A bull to Hanchett's "strike." Still, as long as I was on the ground, I might as well see what it was all about. Right now this Grantsville thing looked to me more like a saloon boom than anything that had to do with mining. These boys were carrying on their prospecting, sinking their shafts, running their drifts, crosscuts, and tunnels, all at the expense of their respective grubstakers, right there inside Kiefer's saloon. Their claims were all staked out, and now all they had to do was wait for the fireworks to start. All hinged on Hanchett. He could be telling the truth, who knew?

I set up my little patented tent on a smooth plot of ground near the old house once occupied by the mine superintendent. On account of neighbors I deemed it best to sleep "indoors." A short way up a side draw I found a fine spring of water oozing up through the lava bedrock. It was fenced in, the water being piped to a small iron trough. It struck me that here was my chance for that long-promised bath. I was on the point of going back after a towel, soap, and clean clothes, when along came a man on horseback who pulled up for a chat. He was lean and lanky. I judged him to be in his late sixties but agile and alert. His name was John McComb. He had lived there in Grantsville ever since Civil War days. I told him I had just arrived—come to get in on that so-called boom.

"Boom!" he exploded. "It's all that loafer Hanchett's doing! He's been lying about a strike he says he's made up there in the canyon. The word's got around and now there's thirty or forty prospectors flocked in here, mostly grub-staked by old ladies and gamblers in Tonopah, Goldfield, and Manhattan, and more coming all the time."

"What about his strike?" I asked.

"Why, it's the biggest lot of bunk you ever listened to," he replied. "He went up there and jumped some of my claims and freshened up some old work I did on 'em years ago. I never could raise a color on that ground, but now it pans like all get-out, to hear him tell it. I know, because I went there myself. He's got it salted a-plenty, and that's what I keep telling everybody that'll listen to me, but there won't any of 'em believe me. Hanchett tells 'em I'm just sore on account of him jumping my ground and running into the high grade in a couple of shots. I tell you there's no sign of a vein up there and that's the truth. If it's as rich as he hollers, why don't he dig it out and ship it? No siree, not him. He's got somebody on his hook right now—nice young fellow by the name of Brandenburg that's got a rich uncle in the East. Hanchett got him to fork over one hundred dollars for a thirty-day option. The youngster was so excited that he dashed off to Tonopah to burn up the telegraph wires."

"Hanchett can't get by with that," I said. "The first engineer that comes out to examine the property'll turn it down."

"Sure," McComb agreed, "but that all takes time an' meanwhile Hanchett spreads the word around that he's optioned his ground for fifty thousand dollars and says he's looking for a big rush for options on his other claims. He's located God knows how many more claims up around there. Once he gets his hands on a few hundred dollars, he'll skip out and leave 'em all holding the sack."

McComb, with his bushy, faded eyebrows and his turkey-gobbler neck filled the bill for all that the term "old-timer" implies as he leaned over the horn of his saddle while his rough-coated brown nag relaxed drowsily under his weight. It was no trick to keep the man talking, especially when it came to airing his views concerning Hanchett.

I was curious about the alleged salting job, and I asked him if he knew how Hanchett had accomplished it.

"Sure I do," he said. "He shotgunned it. There's no trick to that."

"What do you mean—shotgunned?" I asked.

"Why, all he had to do was load his shells with a few specks of gold dust and then blaze away all around the shaft into the stuff he calls his shipping ore. That," McComb explained, "makes the gold specks stick tight, and you'd swear it grew there. You don't need a whole lot of high grade to do the job."

McComb also hinted that Hanchett had roped in Fred Schmaling for quite a bill, and I mentioned my hunch that he also owed Kiefer for drinks.

"Well now," he said, "if there's one fellow I've got no sympathy for it's that Kiefer. He's just plumb no good! He was hauling his low-grade gin to Phonolite to open a saloon there when this Hanchett got hold of him and steered him in here. Now he's got himself set up in that old saloon that's been closed tight for over thirty years. What a fine gang that is, hangin' around in there all day long when they're supposed to be out in the hills prospecting! They're just a lot of road runners knockin' around the country and living off the folks that's keeping them in beans and bacon. There's a few honest ones here though that're really hunting for something worth while. They'll all be on hand tonight. That old saloon'll be packed tight."

I told McComb I was figuring on taking a bath there at the trough.

"Good Lord, man," he exclaimed, "don't bathe in that!"

"Why not?" I asked. "Isn't it fit for a bath?"

"Fit?" he repeated vehemently. "Man alive, don't you know that's the only water there is around here?" Then he expatiated at length about the precious fount. A pipeline drew off the water from the spring inside the fence for domestic use, while the overflow was caught into the iron trough which he personally had set up there for his horse.

It all ended by my giving McComb my word that I wouldn't make actual bodily entry into the trough but would stand off at least three feet away while I dipped the water and poured it over me shower-fashion, being careful not to get any soap into the trough. His horse, he said, might not object to drinking after me if no soap was mixed in. Otherwise he'd balk for sure.

It was getting around time to be thinking about supper. I decided to have fried potatoes with bacon and a pot of cocoa. I peeled two big spuds, sliced them thin, and when the bacon was done I dumped them into the hot grease. I had the cocoa coming along nicely, just about ready to boil over, when I became aware of someone approaching me from behind. I turned around and there, smiling, stood a slight old lady, all tidy and pert, wearing a fresh-looking kitchen apron over her light figured dress. She was saucy eyed. Her white hair was smoothly parted in the middle with a small knot of it showing over the back of her head.

"Young man," she addressed me rather sternly, "what do you think you're doing?"

"Well," I said, straightening up, "this is certainly nice. You're just in time for supper. Do please be my guest." She let my audacity pass and came a step closer to peer into my pot.

"What's that you're boiling there?" she asked, pointing a finger at the pot.

"Cocoa," I replied. "Won't you have some?" Again she chose to ignore me.

"Is that all you're having—potatoes and cocoa?" she asked.

"No," I replied, "there's some delicious bacon on the rock over there. That's plenty for me. In fact, I don't often have the cocoa."

"Why not?" she asked. "It's not so expensive."

"That's not the idea," I said. "It takes a can of milk every time you make it."

"And what of that?" she persisted.

"You don't load your burros down with a lot of heavy canned goods," I said. "It happens I just stocked up at Ione, and I threw in a few little extras. Generally all you pack is flour, bacon, beans, dried fruits, and things like that."

"You don't have to tell me," she said, tartly. "I knew all those things long before you were born," and she stood up erect.

"Listen, young man," she said, suddenly turning all sweetness and light, "you haven't any bread, have you? That cocoa looks mighty good to me. I have an idea. Let's take all your stuff to my house. I've got a pan of biscuits baking in the

67

oven and plenty of butter and jelly. Come on, you bring the cocoa. I'll carry the rest."

So we went to the house that had domiciled the mine superintendent when Grantsville was in its heyday. Nobody, yes, nobody, ever enjoyed a supper more than I did, and I believe this grand lady did too, on that uniquely happy occasion.

Mrs. Post, my impromptu hostess, was a widow. Here was a woman who could talk and at the same time say something. It was by no means all personal history nor about her dear departed husband. The latter had been a metallurgist with the Grantsville company, sober, and competent, and that was that, Selah! Mrs. Post was eighty years old, holding down a man's job—watchwoman over all that idle plant. There was a lot of valuable machinery in the big mill, and every single day she made the full rounds of the plant from top to bottom. Her home was a museum filled with relics, specimens, and pictures that brought back days that had rolled down the gulch of time along with those red mill tailings I had seen on my way up the canyon. She had a young nephew who was making his home there with her. His name was Noble Getchel. He had gone to Austin to have some rock samples assayed and was expected back any day. It was in order that I might meet him, and also because of the way things in general were shaping up there, that I decided to stay a while at Grantsville.

No telephone, no mail except when someone happened to bring it over from Ione, and of course no radio in those days, and yet Mrs. Post scoffed at the notion of getting lonesome. Her only permanent neighbors were McComb and his wife, who lived at the upper end of the otherwise deserted camp. It had been so long since she had been on speaking terms with them that she had completely forgotten why they had fallen out. However, old friends, often traveling long distances over mountains and deserts in horse-drawn vehicles, called on her from time to time.

The outstanding character of the camp's active days seems to have been the man who then occupied the house in which Mrs. Post now lived, namely, Mitchell, the big boss of both mine and mill. His photographs, of which Mrs. Post showed me several, all of them full-length, made him out a tall, hefty individual with whiskers that reached from his chin to the floor when he stood erect. Even then they were not fully extended, and the overplus was arranged in a neat pile in front of his boots. I was wondering how he got around in the mine with all that hirsute adornment and if he wasn't afraid of getting it caught in a flywheel in the mill. Mrs. Post assured me that on the job he always wore it tucked inside his vest and only unfurled it on dress occasions.

Getchel finally arrived, after I had put in two full days prowling among the old waste dumps and exploring the adjacent terrain on all sides, often stopping to converse with claim owners whom I ran across out there engaged in excavating their required cubic footage for each claim.

Getchel had the mining bug in its most virulent form. It was in his blood, born in him, though there was a period in his life when he wasn't conscious of it. His father had mined successfully and had brought in a substantial silver producer near Battle Mountain, known as the Betty O'Neil mine. Young Getchel, though, had some talents that couldn't be kept down. Irresistibly they had led him to the theater, and it wasn't long before he found himself a headliner on the old Orpheum circuit. However, the excitement at Tonopah and Goldfield, with mining on the boom generally throughout Nevada, was a call of the wild to him. He left the footlights for good and was back now among the beloved hills of his old home state, scratching around on the trail that was destined to lead him in a few years to fame and immense fortune via the rich Getchel mine and his association with Barney Baruch, George Wingfield, *et al*.

Noble, as he asked me to call him, had Hanchett's number. He knew that his "strike" was a come-on, but he reasoned that with so many men scouring those hills for miles in all directions there was a chance that someone would stumble across something worth while. He suggested there was no valid reason why I couldn't be that lucky one. His enthusiasm was infectious. I decided to give it a try. Noble had to get at some location work of his own where time for doing so was running out. I wondered if I ought to be a good fellow and help him. No, that isn't done—might cloud his title. True, I could obviate that by giving him a quitclaim deed to any interest I might acquire in his claims. Again, if they should turn out to be bonanzas I might go around claiming my deed had been obtained by him through fraud, deceit, or what not. So, after all, there are some things a man prefers to do without anyone else's assistance—much safer.

Who stole my tent! It was gone, sure as shooting! Not a sign of it did I see as I approached the spot where it had stood out so prominently those past few days. I couldn't believe that any of those old desert rats that hung around Kiefer's all day would stoop to making off with a fellow craftsman's home on the range. I dashed to the spot. What did I find there? A heap of ashes—tent, bed, all burned to the ground. Holy smoke! The only means of identification were the blackened metal rods, that had held up the canvas which was now lying collapsed and useless, and one unburned corner of a particularly prized possession—my red wool double blanket which my mother had brought back from India. All the rest of my things—grub, utensils, tools, saddles—had escaped the holocaust, being stored in Mrs. Post's woodshed by her kind permission.

Strangely, no one around there apparently had seen the fire. It probably was all over in a jiffy, except that the bed must have smoldered through most of the day like rubbish burning itself out. It was all news to Noble, who had been down the canyon all day. He came out of the house to look the ruins over. With him was a tall young man—six feet of rangy, red-headed cowboy. Unless all my reading of westerns had been wasted, there it all was: telltale gait, overalls, boots, Bull Durham tab dangling from the vest pocket of his denim blouse, and about a week's growth of yellowish stubble sprouting around his cheeks and chin—yes, cowboy.

So this was Charlie Keough!

"Must've a spark blew on your tent," Charlie said when introductions were out of the way. He squatted down to roll himself a smoke. Now, Charlie could spout as good a brand of English as the next fellow. He was a graduate of the State University, but he chose to remain loyal to the range dialect as spoken by the boys among whom he had grown up. It was pure Reese River, guaranteed to be understood by white man and Injun alike. How right he was about the spark! I hadn't thoroughly extinguished my breakfast fire. I was surely learning the hard way.

"Come on over to the ranch," Charlie said. "We'll rustle you another bed." He meant it, and he insisted on it.

"We might be in for a boom over there," he added. "The Ward boys are takin' out specimen rock in Becker Canyon, not far from the ranch."

That did it! It meant Reese River for me in the morning, at last! Among the ashes of my tent I had found a piece of rock I had broken off a big dike the day before. It had a reddish stain running through it. I tossed it away in the sagebrush. Right there went an incalculable fortune that could have been mine. Had I only shown it to Noble or to Charlie Keough! Either of them would have informed me that my specimen was high-grade cinnabar—quicksilver ore! Hardly a year later someone came along and tapped that same dike and sold his discovery to a big mining outfit, the Bradleys. Afterwards, I had the painful experience of seeing the huge retorts that were set up there and the tramways by which the ore was fed into them to have the "quick" volatilized out of it, recondensed, and finally drawn off into flasks. I surely had missed the boat.

Charlie had come out of the house and was saying good-by to Mrs. Post and Noble. His splendid bay horse with the white snip curving downward from his forehead was pawing the dirt at the gate and noisily rolling the cricket in his Mexican bit. Charlie took down the black angora chaps from the horn of his saddle, stepped into them, and with one quick tug hooked the belt buckle at his waist. Barely had he put his left foot into the stirrup when the spirited animal swung toward home and was off at a triphammer gait leaving it strictly up to Charlie to finish mounting en route, a challenge to which his master was more than equal, settling his buttocks as lightly as a feather in the seat of the saddle.

"So long," he called to me. "See you on the river. Remember, first ranch north when you're out of the canyon."

Suddenly I had a bright idea. How would some gingerbread go for supper? There'd be loads of time to make some. I had the makings—that little can of blackstrap I had picked up at Fred Schmaling's and the ground Jamaica ginger I had fallen heir to when buying the outfit in Tonopah, one of the few things my burros had passed up during their recent raid. I decided to make a good-sized loaf while I was at it. I'd take along a piece of it for lunch the next day on my way to the river. I had no idea whatever how to go about making it, but what of that? This was an ideal time to experiment, while no one was around looking.

Now for my recipe: flour, salt, baking powder, all mixed in my general-purpose pan, add water to consistency of flapjack batter, then empty in the can of blackstrap and the package of ginger, mix together till the color is uniform, about the same shade as Dan, beat till it bubbles and rises.

But it did nothing of the kind. For ten solid minutes I stirred and beat the sludgy-looking concoction. I didn't raise a single bubble other than sweat on my brow. The stillness of death settled over it.

Playing possum on me, eh? Well, I'll fix that! Maybe this'll bring you to life, and with that I poured a gob of the viscid mix into my reliable old frying pan, covered it with a tin plate, and set it to bake on a bed of sagebrush coals. Of course, the heat would make it rise. No doubt about that.

My burros, always interested in scraps during cooking time, had been taking this all in. Master Blackie was tied to a stake. That was the only way to make mother stay home o' nights, especially this night, as I wanted to get an early start in the morning. That Jennie B! I was about fed up with the jade. She was just impossible. Numerous plans for getting by without her had been running through my mind. The sooner I was rid of her the better.

I don't rightly know what went wrong, but my batter simply squatted down and hugged the bottom of the pan in a state of complete exhaustion. It looked like anything but gingerbread—more like some kind of taffy. I had a job prying it loose with a screwdriver. It was tough and rubbery and smelled like hot asphalt. It looked a lot like the imitation leather used to half-sole boots. I offered Dan a bite of it, and

73

he was obviously delighted. Old Gal took hers in her usual ladylike way, so pleased that it wouldn't have surprised me to have her ask for the recipe. Rickey, never demonstrative, used his piece for chewing tobacco and, tough old customer that he was, he kept swallowing the juice.

Jennie B, as I would have bet a new hat, turned up her nose at the piece I offered her. When I tried rubbing her muzzle with it she swung around and got set to kick me.

There was enough batter for a few more discs, but I wasn't going to ruin my frying pan with it. Moreover, it was about time to be getting my supper started. What to do with that batter?

Ah yes, of course! Since the haughty Jennie B had disdained taking it internally why not see how she'd like it externally? I had the mixing dish in my hand and made as if to pass her, but instead I took her off guard and plastered her back all over with the sticky goo. She stood there the picture of unconcern, as if she meant to ignore the incident. She wasn't fooling me, though. I knew she was literally boiling inside. But whatever plans she was fostering to get even with me were upset by Dan. He was right at my heels, and before I realized what he was up to he brushed by me. His big brown ears went bobbing up and down as he greedily lapped up the enticing confection which was beginning to spread down Jennie B's flanks. The old boy's brash familiarity instantly roused her resentment and she let fly at him with everything she had in her lightning heels. Dan, however, merely crowded in closer, smothering her kicks, while his tongue never missed a single lap. Old Gal's feminine curiosity got the better of her. She must get her finger, rather her tongue, in the pie too. She took up a position on the opposite side, and now Jennie B was caught between two tongues and to imagine that she was liking it would have smacked of complete asininity, judging by her humped-up back and flattened ears. Pivot and swing as she might, she couldn't kick herself out of this indignity, much less so when Rickey horned in to see what was cooking and discovered that he had been missing a mighty good thing. He tore in for fair, to make up for lost time.

With three unbridled tongues massaging her spine and ribs Jennie B clearly was on the verge of hysteria. She let out an abortive bray and started to run, more intent on watching her pursuers than where she was going. I was afraid she would smash through Mrs. Post's fence and wreck her garden, to say nothing of damaging the house itself. How could I ever explain? I'd be ashamed to tell the good lady, or Noble either, that a gingerbread failure was at the bottom of the wild melee. I could, of course, say that the four animals had simply gone loco or that they had been nipped by a rabid coyote and were in the final throes of hydrophobia with their tongues hanging out. Sweeping like a great dust devil, they luckily just missed the fence as they headed in the general direction of Kiefer's saloon. Woe betide anyone that might be in their path!

Roughly they were describing a big circle. Dan and Rickey, getting in their licks on the same side, kept forcing the frantic Jennie B inwards toward the vortex against the pressure coming from the other side by the outnumbered Old Gal. Round and round they tore over the rough sage-grown area, one kicking, three licking, and I praying.

Then that which I prayed for happened. Jennie B went down in a heap. She would have been up again in a jiffy, for she was as nimble as a cat, but each time she got her front feet out from under her she was pushed back off balance by the unrestrained impetuosity of her erstwhile pals to whom she now was nothing more than an all-day sucker. I ran to fetch some ropes, hoping they'd keep her down meanwhile. And, hallelujah, that's exactly what they did. I speedily hitched ropes around the necks of the three aggressors making them fast to the trunks of stout black sage bushes, and then yanked Dan away from the prostrate form. With one less bearing down on her, she shortly managed to get up. Away she dashed with a series of parting kicks into empty space and she made a bee line for Blackie who was awaiting her with outstretched tongue. She recognized his claims as legitimate, appearing to find them soothing to her nerves.

I figured that my outfit of burros was now completely demoralized. Jennie B would be more flighty than ever. She always had been a misfit at best. I was going to banish her, turn her loose, bid her begone, and good riddance to her. It would mean saying good-by to Blackie too, and that thought hurt. I hated to think he might fall into unkind hands after the way I had petted him and the many sweet kisses I had stolen behind his silky, fuzzy ears. For fear I might weaken, I commenced untying him at once. All I had to do was turn him loose. Jennie B would lead him off, out of my life for good. I hoped they'd go over to Lodi Valley and join the band of wild burros that roam there. This time the other three wouldn't follow Jennie B. I was keeping them tied up for the night.

I sat down on the ground and pulled Blackie over on my lap for a last hug. I ran my hand back and forth over his soft, black muzzle while my cheek rested against his. Whispering, I bestowed my last blessing on him. "No one'll hold you like this again," I said softly. "You'll be running around in that big deserted valley with a harem of your own, pouring out your doleful desert-canary lament where it'll echo back and forth in the rocky canyons. Your baby days'll soon be over. Good-by, little feller!" Sure, I was crying.

I was about to get up when I heard my name called. It was Noble Getchel coming toward me.

"Don't you go to cooking any supper," he warned. "You're eating with us tonight."

I felt silly, not to say embarrassed, sitting there with Blackie in my arms like a baby. Still, I accepted his invitation without any show of feigned reluctance. At the same time I informed him that I was setting Jennie B and Blackie free, turning them loose to go wherever they liked. I brushed a couple of tears off my face.

"You really mean it?" he asked.

I made it clear to him that I meant every word of it. I was going to manage with three burros from then on. I was through with Jennie B.

Noble asked if I'd have any objections to his taking them over as he'd been planning to get a pack animal for moving stuff up to some of his ground.

"They're both yours," I said, delighted, handing over Blackie's rope and setting the little fellow up on his feet as I rose.

"What luck!" Noble said. "I was just in the nick of time, wasn't I?"

It was understood that I was only giving up the naked animals. From now on Jennie B's pack would adorn Dan's back while I traveled on foot. Once in a while I'd ride Dan on side trips. That's why I was hanging on to the McClellan saddle.

At supper I learned what it was that had brought Charlie Keough to Grantsville that afternoon. He had ridden over from his dad's ranch on Reese River to confer with Noble on the local beef situation. A real boom would call for plenty of beef, and that would mean keeping feeder steers coming in off the range for finishing on hay and grain.

If Charlie had consulted the boys over at Kiefer's saloon instead of seeking Noble's views and had taken their prognostications seriously, he would have hurried right back to the ranch and ordered the immediate rounding up of a couple of thousand head of steers. As it was, he steered shy of the gang he saw was running the show. If and when the time was opportune, he'd step into the picture. Like any smart advance agent, he had brought along a slight token of esteem in the form of a dozen choice T-bone steaks. That night Mrs. Post, Noble, and I each had one of them, done to a T, for dinner.

We relaxed in the cozy old parlor till around nine o'clock, when Mrs. Post announced it was her bedtime and bade us good night. It was all settled that I, being bedless and roof-less, was to crawl in with Noble. He suggested that first we stroll over to Kiefer's to see the boys and get a line on how the boom was coming along. Of course, Hanchett was there holding forth to a small group whose expressions ranged from rapt credulity to ill-concealed dubiosity. We exchanged the briefest of greetings with that mogul from where we were watching a solo game, entranced by the deftness of Deef Bob—Deefie for short—shuffling and dealing the cards with-out benefit of thumbs, and definitely holding his own in the game despite his deefness.

Kiefer seemed to be doing a flourishing business with his gin bottle at two bits a slug for the vile stuff.

After a while I got to talking with a fellow I had noticed a time or two. There was something about him that set him apart from the general run of desert rats. He was quite blond, blue-eyed and rosy-cheeked, looking clean and fresh as could be in his khakis and pink silk shirt. For a man of his age, about thirty I thought, there was a kind of boyish immaturity about him, a well-massaged, beauty-parlor suppleness, a wistful, vacuous stare, a miscast actor in a play. This exotic-looking chap was Deef Bob's partner! I read in his eyes that in his soul he had a hunger for sympathy, and he wanted me to listen to his troubles because no one else around there could possibly understand what was eating him. We drifted away to a corner apart from the crowd. He told me he had been a bareback rider with a circus that had gone "kerflooie." His act had consisted of doing somersaults and handstands and juggling Indian clubs while bouncing around on the capacious backs of fat, loping, snow-white mares as they lumbered around in a tanbark ring. Stranded, he had fallen in with Deef Bob at a railroad watertank on the Humboldt River a few weeks previously, but of late they hadn't been hitting it off too well. The outfit—a buckboard powered by a span of cute little jennets, the bedding, equipment, and all the rest—belonged to Deef Bob, except for this acrobat's few personal belongings, which included an exquisite little sorrel mare with a white tail and mane. She was born in the circus, he said, and he had bought her and raised her from a colt. Now she was crazy about the jennets and followed them wherever they went. He felt sure she'd feel the same way about my burros. But—and now he was getting to the point—he wanted to quit this "Godforsaken country" and go down to California and get a job around the race tracks—anything at all so long as it had to do with horses. That's all he knew, he said. Would I be interested in buying the little mare?

"Is she broke to ride?" I asked, trying to conceal the excitement the idea roused in me.

"Of course," he replied. "She's just like a rocking chair."

"What are you asking for her?" I asked.

"Look, sir," he said, "the only reason I'd sell her is because

I'm broke. Only for that I wouldn't take anything for her. She ought to bring $150 easy, but I'll let you have her for $75."

I was afraid he might change his mind. I had been admiring the lovely creature for days, and now—well, I simply must have her. I accepted his offer. Next morning he brought her up to Mrs. Post's gate, riding her bareback.

"Her name's Daisy," he said, handing me the halter rope.

As arranged the night before in Kiefer's saloon, he accepted my check for seventy-five dollars, drawn on the Tonopah Banking Corporation, in full payment for the mare. I took no bill of sale from him. What if he couldn't deliver a good merchantable title? What, on the other hand, if my check was no good? Each of us had to take a chance on the other.

9

I DREW UP at the George Keough ranch in mid-afternoon, halting in front of the low, rambling, unpretentious dwelling set in a garden of roses, pink, yellow, and white, plus a variety of smaller flowering plants and shrubs, through all of which a miniature irrigation ditch of water ran. The house stood on the edge of a bench left by ages of erosion. Less than a stone's throw below flowed the murmuring river between banks of overhanging willows and wild rosebushes in bloom. It was easy to imagine there were deep, shadowy pools where wary, gamey trout lurked.

Not a soul was in sight, and except for five or six work horses sleepily switching their tails under a mud-and-willows shed over by the barn and corrals the place seemed deserted.

I tied my Daisy mare to the hitching rail, opened the gate, and entered the yard. A wide roofed porch, with an inviting hammock, several chairs with rawhide woven seats, a long table covered with gaily flowered oilcloth, ran the full length of that side of the house. There, I thought, one could sit and dream hour after hour, facing the great Toiyabe Range with its deep, wooded canyons, gleaming snowbanks, and serrated crest. The house was wide open, so that I could peer in. I even heard the wall clock tick in the cheery dining room.

I tapped lightly with my heel on the floor of the porch. After a short pause a woman appeared in the far doorway. She was of ample proportions, middle-aged, and had flaming red hair. I was sure I had interrupted her afternoon siesta, but she came out smiling pleasantly. I greeted her, hat in hand.

"Quite an outfit you have there," she remarked.

"Thank you," I said. "I'm proud of it myself." Then I told her who I was and that I had had the pleasure of meeting Charlie Keough in Grantsville. "Aren't you Mrs. Keough?" I asked.

"Yes, I am," she replied.

"I thought so," I said, "because I had the pleasure of meeting your sister, Mrs. Phillips, in Ione, and she told me you were her sister, and I see you resemble each other."

"Yes, Kate's my sister," she said. "You can tell us Bowlers a mile off by our red hair. It runs through the family."

"I've heard that your father, Mr. Bowler, has a fine ranch somewhere in this valley," I said. "I hope to meet him some day."

"If you happen to strike him just right, you'll enjoy meeting him," she said with a smile.

An adorable little miss of ten or eleven now joined us. Without any preliminaries, she asked if it was my bed that had burned up.

So, her big brother had told them about me! My identification was clinched. Mrs. Keough invited me to have a cup of tea. She withdrew into the kitchen, and Miss Inez, her companionable young daughter, busied herself setting cups, plates, forks, and spoons for three on the table.

Lucky Charlie Keough! I thought. What a setting! What a life! His little sister said he had gone on horseback to Becker Canyon, about ten miles off to the northwest across the sage to look at the new gold strike. A man from Tonopah had gone with him, a Mr. Goodrich.

"Ed Goodrich?" I asked, wondering.

"Yes, that's his name", Miss Inez said. "He's a gambler. We like him anyway. He's very nice."

"And his word's as good as gold," Mrs. Keough added, setting down a chocolate cake on the table beside the teapot.

"Yes," I said, "his reputation is very good. He's one of the owners of the Tonopah Club."

And so might I have been, I thought to myself, ruefully, but for a roll of the dice!

Across the river the waving meadows of sweet wild hay stretched about as far as one could see up and down the valley. Some hundreds of yards away a man on horseback appeared from a willow-fringed slough. Over his shoulder he held a shovel. His coal-black horse came along at a leisurely gait.

"That's my husband, George, now," said Mrs. Keough. "He's been irrigating."

"All by himself?" I asked. "How does he do it?"

"Oh, yes," she replied, "he loves it. There's not much to it once the ditches are in—just a few pokes with the shovel here and there. That, and looking after the fences, is about all there's to do on these hay ranches."

George Keough rode the black horse, Nig, up to the gate, dismounted, and left him standing there with the reins on the ground, alongside my heterogeneous retinue. He leaned his shovel against the fence and, as he came through the gate, I saw he was carrying something in a wet gunny sack.

"How many?" his wife casually asked.

"Just eight," he said, and he emptied the sack on the grass so we could see his catch for ourselves—eight speckled rainbows, every one of them at least ten inches long, fresh out of Reese River.

What a tough life! I thought, especially for such a kindly man as George Keough. His hair showed silver white around the brim of his slouch felt hat, the band of which was stuck full of fishhooks. He gave me a cordial nod and a spontaneous "How do?" His frank blue eyes conveyed the best part of his greeting. Here was a man one couldn't help admiring at sight. I surmised he was in his mid-sixties. He was cowboy lean and stood very erect with shoulders thrown well back. Evidently he preferred a smoke to chocolate cake and tea, for he sat down on the edge of the porch, got out the makings, and rolled a cigarette. I asked him how he had caught the trout.

"Grasshoppers," he told me. "They're the best."

"He's got a private pool of his own back there in the willows," Mrs. Keough added.

I learned that as a young fellow, fresh from Canada, George had driven stagecoach, carrying mail, bullion, express, and passengers over the southern deserts. He had also, for a time, traversed that lonesome area by muleback carrying dispatches from one isolated outpost to another and camping out at night en route.

Mining booms had been routine affairs to him—Austin, Belmont, Candelaria, Delamar, Eureka, and so on, through the rest of the alphabet.

This ranch was his heaven. It hadn't been much to look

at when he first moved on it with his radiant young wife and a mortgage. That was long before its verdant meadows had replaced the raw, sage-grown acreage, unfenced for the most part. Whether it was judgment or luck, he had picked the ideal spot at the right time. Where could he have duplicated the range conditions prevailing right there, and when was there a more opportune time to get into the cattle business, when a cow and a calf could be had for a mere eight dollars?

Tea and chocolate cake, delightful companionship, and incomparable surroundings—what kind of prospecting was this anyway? I asked myself.

Mrs. Keough spotted a "dust" far off to the northwest, and she was sure it was Charlie returning home.

"You might as well spend the night here," George said. "Better unpack and put your packs in the barn and then turn your stock in the corral."

Such unheard-of hospitality! It just seemed these extraordinary people considered it nothing short of a privilege to share the good things of their felicitous existence with the stranger within their gates. They didn't let you feel like a guest. They just about adopted you. No one asked questions —had I ever gone through bankruptcy, ever been rejected for a surety bond, ever been turned down for life insurance? How did they know, or, for that matter, did they give a hoot if I was on the up and up? Preachers, gamblers, or what-nots looked alike to them as long as they acted "regular." It seemed they could spot the other kind at sight, instinctively. Even then, no one was turned away hungry or hurt.

The big trout dinner was ready out there on the porch when Charlie and Goodrich arrived. Mrs. Keough was an absolutely effortless cook. Food, dishes, everything, seemed to appear spontaneously out of the air—a true culinary magician! She announced that there was more of everything on the kitchen stove where we could help ourselves when the table supply was exhausted. It was a species of buffet, ranch style.

Charlie was far and away the most prodigious eater while at the same time he did more than the rest of us combined to keep up the flow of conversation. He had a faculty of seeing the funny side of practically everything—incidents and sayings he had run across in his ramblings—and he had the true story-teller's knack of relating them. He should have been a scribbler by profession.

As he helped himself to another of his mother's hot biscuits, he told of the time old Jimmie Graham's biscuits, instead of rising while baking, took a nose dive in the bake pan, which so riled him that he took the hot pan to the door of his cabin, gave it a hefty kick which sent biscuits, pan, and all flying in every direction, while he shouted, "I'll raise ye, ye 'lowlifed' sons of"—well, let's say—"biscuits!"

Ed Goodrich ate sparingly and spoke even less, being about as sphinxlike at the table as when he was dealing faro bank in the Tonopah Club. There was no mistaking the fact that he stood ace-high with these good people, and why not? He was known to be a man of his word. Selah.

There wouldn't be much doing for the next month or so while the hay was ripening. Later the ranch would be overrun with Paiutes, their squaws and papooses. All through the haying time things would hum from dawn till dusk. For the present the cowboys lived up in the hills with the cattle. That was what Charlie was going to do for a few weeks of riding, fishing, and sage-hen shooting. He asked me to join him, for which I thanked him, but I told him I felt I should look into that Becker Canyon strike.

85

"Maybe that's your best bet right now," he agreed. "That Ward showing didn't look a bit bad."

True to his word, Charlie fixed me up with a first-rate bed and told me to hang on to it as long as I wished. It had been left there on the ranch by a young Englishman who had done a spot of prospecting around there and then had suddenly decided to try his luck in West Australia. It seems his father was putting up for him—anything to keep him out of Merrie England.

I thought how easy it would have been to yield to temptation and stay on a while at the ranch as I had been invited to do. I could have fished, trailed along after George on horseback while he irrigated, or just plain loafed. Besides, in the parlor was a large assortment of good books and a brand new upright piano on which I could amuse myself. No, I couldn't see it any other way—it was my move!

So, with Charlie's help, I packed to leave for Becker Canyon. I was spoiled, hated the thought of leaving, and I could tell that my animals weren't too happy about giving up those mangers filled with sweet-smelling hay.

I was sent on my way with a parting gift brought out by sweet young Miss Inez. It was a cardboard box in which reposed a whole chocolate layer cake. Charlie and I fastened it carefully to the top of Old Gal's pack, she being the most velvety-footed of my burros.

10

THE WARD BOYS, Jim, aged sixty-five, and Frank, seventy-two, were doing a job of prospecting up there in Becker Canyon that should make Hanchett crawl in his hole and hide, if he could see it.

These old lads were on the square, not only legitimate prospectors but seasoned hard-rock miners. They were not just shooting off their faces but shooting away at the face of their drift with hammer, steel, and giant powder. There was no fanfare, no ore-sacks filled with worthless waste, said to be high-grade ore, piled around their workings, no barbed-wire fence with warning notice for trespassers to keep out. Here visitors were welcome, and there was no attempt to pressure them into seeing what wasn't there. The boys were running a tunnel into the mountain five hundred feet up from the floor of the canyon, following a very narrow, but rich, stringer of quartz.

"It's an in-and-out son of a bitch," Jim Ward allowed. "Now you've got it, and now you ain't. The country's faulted like all hell. I've seen these knife-blade seams open up to big chambers o' high grade, an' then again, I've saw 'em plumb peter out." With that, he relieved himself of a great blob of tobacco juice which splattered all over the country rock around his boots.

His brother, Frank, handed me a specimen about the size of a pigeon egg. It was sugar quartz, one side of it being spottily encrusted with gold. Later he pounded up some pieces that hadn't shown any free gold, and it panned big— a lazy, inch-long trail of the yellow metal.

Of course the country round about was staked solid. The Wards, however, had not exercised their prerogative to make claim-hogs of themselves. Two claims, end to end, were all they had taken up.

"Two's a-plenty," Jim Ward said. "If she's any good we'll be fixed for the rest of our life," and he cut himself a fresh liberal chew from his plug of "Horseshoe" brand tobacco.

Certain others, though, had not emulated the Wards' commendable example. Down at the mouth of the canyon I met a man—there's one wherever you go—who knew all about what was going on around there. He honored me with a visit while I was unpacking my outfit and laying out my camp. As he approached, I noticed out of the corner of my eye that he was carrying a walking stick and limped slightly. Aside from that, he was a sprightly little chap, bright eyed, clean shaven, one of those baffling individuals of the great outdoors who usually turns out to be years older than he looks. With a friendly greeting, he introduced himself as Jake Gooding.

"But just call me Uncle Jake," he said. "That's what they all call me."

Ah, Uncle Jake, I reflected. Charlie Keough had spoken of him to me. According to Charlie, Uncle Jake was without question the most fastidious, elegant, and refined prospector in the state. His familiar house-on-wheels with its lace curtains and its snow-white bedspread had once been given a big write-up in the *Reese River Reveille*, that famed old Nevada newspaper which was founded in the days of the Pony Express and had never once missed a single weekly issue.

As soon as the introductory prelims were out of the way, Uncle Jake began a tirade against that despicable breed, the "claim-hog."

"Now you take that fellow Gopher Dan," he said. "Do you happen to know him by any chance?"

"I can't say as I do," I said.

"Well then," said he, "seein's he's no friend o'yours, how many claims do you reckon that big hog's got located up there?"

"I wouldn't rightly know," I begged off.

"Nineteen!" he practically screamed, his face contorted with rage.

"Must keep him pretty busy doing location work," I remarked.

"Location work, your granny!" he sneered. "If a hen was drug backwards across those claims she'd scratch up more dirt than all the work he's done on 'em. I know, 'cause I been all over the ground, an' yet he's got the gall to stand up an' swear he's done the full legal amount."

"That being the case," I said, "how does he expect to hold them?"

"Can't, if it ever comes to a showdown," Uncle Jake declared. "You see, some of those claims are right up agin' the Wards' an' you just let them bring in a bonanza an' there'll be some claim jumpin' up there, or I'll miss my guess. Then's when the trouble'll start, mark my word!"

Next Uncle Jake tackled the townsite situation. He had it in for the townsite man—the chap who'd staked it out.

"Those townsite fellers are a lot of lazy grafters," he said. "Wherever there's any excitement, they horn in by takin' up the surface rights. I no sooner got here'n this slicker tried to hold me up for the price of a lot—twenty-five dollars, no less! I told him I wasn't in the market for no lot just then, an' with that he ordered me to move my wagon off'n *his* townsite. I told him I'd move whenever I got good'n ready. That's been over a month ago now, an' there I still am, right on the same identical spot," and he pointed to the scene of his triumph.

I counted something like fifteen tents scattered haphazardly around the infant town. One of them was exceptionally large.

"That's a tent saloon," Uncle Jake volunteered, anticipating my query.

"Have any of these people bought lots?" I asked.

"Nary a one," he replied. "The townsite feller claims he sold the one the saloon's on. If he did, he's taken it out in trade. I don't believe he's drew a sober breath since that place opened up."

It was a mighty pretty townsite, and it had what I thought was an equally pretty name—ULLAINE—plagiarized from a can of kerosene oil of a brand then widely in use.

Uncle Jake was reputed to be an all-round expert—expert this, and expert that. He was said to have delved into both law and medicine quite a bit. I was glad to know the latter, because Charlie Keough had told me the place was infested with rattlesnakes.

Ullaine was definitely taking the play away from Grantsville. The Wards still hadn't hit ore in quantity by the end of my first month in Becker Canyon, but their in-and-out streak was staying with them and they were making better than day's wages on it. By close sorting they had accumulated at least a ton of high grade which was all sacked and ready for shipment. They figured to get around two thousand dollars net for it from the smelter.

Prospectors were arriving every day, and despite the protests of the townsite man, they were camping wherever they liked. Result: a white-canvas metropolis was springing up on the erstwhile jack rabbit reservation which sloped gently downward from the mouth of the canyon. The squatters proclaimed Uncle Jake their mayor. When he told the boys to stand pat, they did just that. Uncle Jake was the law.

Sure enough it happened, just as Uncle Jake had foretold. A wiry little fellow named Riggs, who had been a soldier in the Philippines, jumped a pair of Gopher Dan's locations. There had been considerable drinking going on in the tent saloon one afternoon. Riggs was setting them up for the house, which numbered just seven thirsty individuals, one of whom was Doc Fulkerson, a former Missouri practicing M.D. who had chucked his profession and taken up prospecting. Several rounds had been imbibed, and the stuff was of high potency. Riggs had stood up under the tarantula juice better than the others present, and just as he raised his glass to wish the gang good luck, Gopher Dan reached in under the tent flap, grabbed him by the collar of his shirt, and pulled him outside.

"You're coming along with me," Gopher Dan yelled.

"What for?" Riggs demanded, defiantly.

"You're going to knock down your monuments on my claims and tear up your location notices!" Gopher Dan shouted for all to hear. "Maybe this will teach some people a lesson."

Riggs suddenly twisted his body violently around, tearing himself free, and leaving most of his shirt in the grasp of Gopher Dan's big fist. The latter now charged in with his huge bulk while Riggs, with a swift motion, got out a knife and plunged the blade all the way in the side of his assailant's abdomen. Letting out a cry of pain and delirium, the big fellow doubled up, his hands clapped over his wound which was hemorrhaging profusely, drenching the front of his tan-colored pants. He sank to the ground, groaning and grimacing, clearly afraid he was about to die. In all probability he would have succumbed on the spot if Doc Fulkerson hadn't stepped out with the rest to see what was up. Doc, high as he was at the moment and far below par, instinctively rose to the occasion, and with such makeshift facilities as were at his disposal he somehow got the patient ready for the sixty-mile trip to the county hospital at Austin. Gopher Dan recovered completely, but the hospital doctor gave full credit to Doc Fulkerson for his prompt and efficient first aid. Unfortunately I had missed the show. My account of it is based on what witnesses told me. At the time, I was 'way up in the canyon working on my claims.

Yes, I'm not joking. I had some claims of my own, two to be exact. One I had named "Little Emily" for little Miss

Emily Stevens of Castle Point, Hoboken, New Jersey, and the other "Lady Maud" after Miss Maud Eden, Emily's charming English governess, a cousin of Sir Anthony's. Neither claim, alas, was worthy of its namesake.

I wish I could have seen Doc Fulkerson in action on that momentous occasion out there in front of the tent saloon, for afterwards he and I became the closest of friends. That evening, when I referred to the matter and voiced my admiration of his part in it, he brushed it off as being hardly worth mentioning. When I asked him if he thought Gopher Dan would pull through, he said, "Yes, unless infection gets him, which it might, but sometimes plain orneryness'll pull a fellow like him through where a decent one'll keel over dead."

No charges were preferred against Riggs. The verdict was that he had acted in self-defense.

Doc Fulkerson belonged to that picturesque quartet, the placer kings of Manhattan Gulch. His three confreres were Jeff Auxier, Snowshoe Charlie Ravenscroft, and Happy Jack Barrier. These four gentlemen—and I use the term advisedly —batched together in the same cabin and worked their diggings as harmoniously as they did their drinking, attending strictly to business in either case.

Jeff Auxier was the oldest and the heaviest drinker of the four, quiet and reserved. Liquor never put him under the table. He could carry it in unbelievable amount without batting an eye. He had discovered the Stray Dog mine in Manhattan, the richest of them all, and cleaned up a fortune from it, which, like others he had made before, soon slipped through his fingers like so much water.

Snowshoe Charlie Ravenscroft was the acknowledged king-pin of the desert's unconscious humorists. He made more people laugh than all the rest of them put together, though his own face never lost its somber mien. One day some missionaries dropped by the cabin and asked if they could leave some tracts. "Tracks?" Snowshoe exclaimed, "You sure can, and see that they lead away from here!"

Snowshoe's closest competitor as a humorist was his friend and companion, Happy Jack Barrier. The two were usually linked together when humor was the topic of conversation. One day Happy Jack was driving his team of mules up the gulch with a heavy load of green, mine-lagging. One of the mules had been soldiering most of the way and finally balked entirely. Happy Jack got down from his seat and, according to Sam Carter who was riding with him, he stepped up to and faced the mule. "Look here, Jehoshaphat," he said, without raising his voice, "I've been watchin' you all afternoon. Not one pound have you pulled to date. For the love of Christian charity make up your mind if you'll have oats for supper tonight or go to bed on an empty stomach!" Then Happy Jack went back to his seat, picked up the reins, clucked his tongue, and Jehoshaphat threw all his weight against his collar and pulled as he had never pulled before, all the way to the cabin.

Happy Jack Barrier got himself elected sheriff of Nye County, Nevada, a few years later. He had campaigned on a platform of "It's an easy job, the pay's good, and you voters could do worse."

As for Doc Fulkerson, it was hard for me to picture him garbed in white, surgically clean, performing an intricate operation surrounded by nurses and attendants. Yet such was his background. Husky and rawboned, he looked more like a mule skinner than the man of science that he was.

I had been slaving it on my claims. It was a long, steep pull to the top of the mountain, lugging steel, water, and powder, but the sheer joy of loading such holes as I somehow managed to drill, spitting the fuses, and then hurrying down the mountain to the stirring music of those earth-shaking Boom! Boom! Booms! made the whole enterprise pay off handsomely in dividends of true self-satisfaction. Meanwhile, good old Uncle Jake was tutoring me in the intricate art of tool dressing. He had a small anvil, a blower, and a sack of expensive blacksmith coal. I hadn't known there was anything special about blacksmith coal to distinguish it from ordinary kitchen-stove coal. Actually, to this day I don't know what it is, but it seems that blacksmith coal is the aristocrat of the coal family. Tempering the steel bits after they had been shaped was the trickiest part of the operation. It's like cooking, in a way. You have to know instinctively when it's done. To see the straw color which Uncle Jake drew down on his bits was like witnessing a miracle of beauty. It spelled exactly the right degree of hardness for the steel.

One morning on my way up the canyon I noticed that my beautiful Daisy mare was not with my burros. Till then she had strung right along with them. I had never put hobbles on her dainty ankles. She was gone the next day and the next. No doubt Uncle Jake was right as usual. He said a mustang stallion must have run her off into his band of mares. I figured it was good-by my Daisy and that I'd never see her again. Then, to complicate matters even more, I found when I returned to camp a few afternoons later that I was being paged by a deputy constable and a very peeved gent from Grantsville, one Ed Kiefer.

"That's him!" cried Kiefer, pointing me out to the peace officer as I came around to the side of Uncle Jake's wagon where they had been sitting on empty powder boxes. Kiefer had the look of a snarling Yorkshire feist, all set to snap and bite, but the deputy looked to me like a decent sort. He took a folded paper out of his inside coat pocket and handed it to me.

"Ever see that before?" he asked quietly.

Sure enough I had, and I said so. It was the check I had given the circus fellow for Daisy. It was stamped NSF, and I spelled the letters out aloud. I wondered what had gone amiss.

"Know what that means, don't you?" the deputy asked.

"Why yes, yes, of course I do," I replied, "but I've never had it thrown at me before, and this notice of protest is a new one on me too. Seven dollars protest fees—wow!"

"Have you got eighty-two bucks?" Kiefer barked at me.

"What for?" I asked, just to gain time while I could think. I was trying to figure out what had made the check bounce. What could have happened? I simply couldn't imagine.

"To make good on that there check," Kiefer shot back, "an' the seven bucks they went an' soaked me for turnin' it down."

"Where do you come in on this?" I demanded—but of course the answer was obvious. He had cashed the check for the circus chap, doubtless at a usurious discount.

"That's none o'your damn business, you crook!" he replied.

"Easy there, Ed," the deputy warned. "That kind of talk won't get you anywhere."

The whole thing had caught me off guard. No doubt the little sawed-off rooster had the goods on me.

"Whatcha goin' to do about it?" he crowed. All I could do was shrug my shoulders. I was at a loss what to say or do. That seemed to give Kiefer his cue.

"If he ain't got the dough," he said, turning to the deputy, "I'll take the mare an' let him keep his bum check." That gave me an inspiration.

"Suppose I don't want to sell her to you?" I said, to egg him on.

Uncle Jake came along and joined us. I introduced him

briefly, catching his eye, and made a covert sign for him to keep his mouth shut. I was afraid he'd spill the beans about Daisy.

"Suit yourself," Kiefer warned. "If you don't settle one way or another I'll have you put in jail. You can take your pick."

That was too much for Uncle Jake. His curiosity got the better of him.

"What's this all about anyway?" he demanded. Kiefer spoke up before I could say anything.

"This young feller bought a mare in Grantsville with a bum check," he said. Uncle Jake turned a puzzled look on me.

"Please wait till I'm through, Uncle Jake," I entreated him. "It's all a mistake. You'll see." Then turning to Kiefer I said, "Well, I haven't got the money, and I certainly don't want to go to jail, so I guess I'll have to take you up on your proposition. I'll take the check and the mare's yours. Is that it?"

"You're on," he snapped. "Give him the check, Bob," he instructed the deputy, "an' remember, you're a witness, an' you too," he added, addressing Uncle Jake.

"Sold!" I hollered, taking the check and attached paper the deputy handed me and tearing them to bits.

"Okay," said Kiefer, triumphantly. "Where's the mare at?"

"I don't know," I replied. "She's yours now, isn't she? Go and find her."

"What d'ya mean?" Kiefer sputtered. Uncle Jake broke out with his cackling laugh, but the deputy frowned.

"I mean go ahead and find her, and good luck to you," I replied. "And while you're at it go right ahead and help yourself to the rest of the mustangs she ran off with, if you like."

"Grab that crook, Bob!" Kiefer fairly screamed. "I thought

they was sump'n funny about this. Grab him an' put him in jail!"

"No so fast, Ed," the deputy advised.

"Yes," I offered gratuitously, "that's what it said on the check. Not so fast—NSF—quite a coincidence, I must say."

"This is no joking matter," said the deputy, frowning, "but Ed, I don't see there's much of anything I can do about this. Looks as if he's put one over on us. You bought the mare sight unseen. I'm afraid you're stuck."

"Pig in a poke," Uncle Jake threw in, likewise gratuitously, while Kiefer let loose with a defamation of my character in language that would have broken up a mule skinners' convention. I took it in silence. When he had finished in exhaustion and was literally drooling at the mouth, the deputy turned to me.

"Young feller," he began in deadly earnest, "I believe you'll bear watching. You're too smart for your own good. I'd take you along right now on general principles, but I've got to admit I haven't got a warrant."

I considered it a right manly speech.

"Will you let me say something now?" I asked.

"I don't want to hear no more," Kiefer shouted. "If you ain't goin' to pinch him we might as well get the hell outer here. I'll get him one o' these days. Don't worry."

"You'll be sorry," I warned.

"Can't you keep your shirt on a minute, Ed?" the deputy begged. "Let's hear what he's got to say."

I told my story, explaining that the check bouncing was all just a mistake. However, I felt I wasn't being believed.

"When you get back to Tonopah," I said to the deputy, "I wish you'd drop in and see Tom Tennant in Kenneth Donnellan's brokerage office. Ask Tom if he sold my Bonnie Clare stock, and if not, why not. I gave him an order to sell it before I left Tonopah, and there should be close to a thousand dollars either in his office or in the bank belonging to me. He promised to deposit the money right away. I can't imagine what happened there."

"I'll look into it," the deputy promised.

"And another thing," I continued, "the next time you're in the Tonopah Banking Corporation, please tell Bob Moore he's made a crook out of me in these parts by turning down my check when a little overdraft would have protected me. I want him to remember that. When I said good-by to him, he wished me all kinds of luck, and he even asked me to stake him out a claim if I made a strike. I promised him I would, and what's more I'll keep my word, but I know what I'll name that claim, just wait."

"All right feller, I'll tell him. I believe you're telling the truth," the deputy said, holding out his hand.

"Just one more thing," I added, as I held his hand. "I'll buy that mare back from our friend here if he wants to sell her."

"With another bum check?" Kiefer jeered, witless chump that he was.

"No," I said, ignoring the jibe. "I'll give you my note for the eighty-two dollars, with interest, and as soon as this mess is all straightened out, I'll pay it up in full."

"Might as well go you on that," he conceded. "I'm stuck anyway."

"There's just one condition," I added.

"What the hell you got up your sleeve now?" he sneered.

"First, you've got to apologize for calling me a crook," I said.

"I'll do that whenever I see the color of your money," he hedged.

"It's now or never," I insisted. I was about fed up with the nasty little rat.

"Okay, okay," he said, impatiently. "I'll take it all back."

"That's the ticket," Uncle Jake chimed in. "Shake hands on it, boys."

We did just that. I wrote out a note, and everything was settled, even though Kiefer still wore a dubious look on his face as he pocketed my note.

"Next time you're in Grantsville, drop in," he said. "I'll buy you a drink. So long."

II

VISITORS CAME EVERY DAY to Ullaine. There were scoffers to be sure—they're a universal breed. Goldfield had its share of them, and Tonopah was turned down cold by a no less eminent authority than John Hays Hammond, who, it is said, received a handsome fee for his classic opinion, which, fortunately, was not heeded.

One day a youngish mining engineer by the name of Whipple rode over from the gold camp of Berlin, where the J. G. Phelps Stokes interests of New York owned a mine in full operation. Whipple mentioned in passing that he could use a few more miners, muckers, mill hands, and roustabouts.

"I don't suppose you'd be interested in a job over there," he said to me.

I hesitated a bit before replying. "I'm not so sure I wouldn't be," I said. "Tell me about it."

He said the accommodations were nothing to brag about. I'd have to bring along my own bed, but there were cabins to sleep in. He was proud of the company boardinghouse where I'd pay $40.00 a month for my three squares a day. Surface jobs paid $3.50 per eight-hour shift, and miners got $4.00.

It didn't sound at all like a bad deal to me. As a matter of fact, I'd been trying to figure out a way to adjust my tangled finances without having to go clear back to Tonopah. Besides, maybe Tom Tennant had neglected to sell my stock after all, and meanwhile the bottom could have fallen out of it, making my trip worse than futile. I concluded my best bet was to stay out there in the hills, work a while for Whipple, pay off my note, and put a few extra shekels in my pocket besides.

I asked Whipple if he'd hold a surface job open for me a few days so as to give me a chance to find a place for my outfit before I settled down in Berlin. I explained the fix I was in, and that I'd only want to work long enough to get out of it. He said he understood how those things were, and that I could work as long or as short a time as I wanted, and that he'd be looking for me.

I might as well admit that I had already decided to call it deep enough on my claims. Uncle Jake never came right out and said so, but I could pretty well tell that he thought I was just wasting my time and energy up there on top of world. Actually, it was a nice-looking little streak of pure white quartz I had been flirting with, and in gold-mining, quartz always commands respect. However, my stringer didn't pan any better at the modest depth to which I had explored it than it did at the start. That is to say, frankly, that it didn't pan at all.

So, I might as well give back my claims to Uncle Sam and call it a day. Why keep on pecking away at that majestic mountain top? Why hasten the natural erosion which, so the geologists tell us, is taking place all over the surface of the earth at the alarming rate of an inch every seven hundred years? All too swiftly that day is bearing down on us when all the earth's crust will be under water and arks'll be back in style.

It seemed I had the good fates on my side in arriving at my momentous decision to take the job at Berlin. A well-known rancher named Warner, who did a bit of mining on the side, told me I could turn my burros out to pasture and store my packs on his place in Indian Valley, which is a tributary of the upper reaches of Reese River. Not one cent did Warner ask for the accommodation. I accepted gratefully, expressing the hope that I might some day be able to do as much for him.

Now I was afoot, since all three of my burros, Dan, Rickey, and Old Gal were required to pack my outfit to Warner's some twenty miles, and I hadn't yet figured out how I was going to get from there to Berlin with my bed. I just made up my mind I wouldn't let that, or anything in future, worry me.

Berlin was over the range a few miles south of Ione. I got there in time for my date with Whipple, and my first impulse was to call the whole thing off and go back to Reese River with Juan Nava, the Mexicano *vaquero* who had brought me over with a load of beef from the Keough ranch. I felt as if I were bidding farewell to my glorious freedom and entering some penal institution of which Whipple was the warden. I had to brace myself to submit to my self-imposed sentence, consoling myself as best I could with the thought that the hills would still be there and waiting for me when I got out.

How had I come to get that ride with Nava to Berlin? It goes back to the afternoon I arrived at the Warner ranch and began to unpack my burros and store my things in his shed. Who should come riding down the trail from the big L. H. Sly ranch in upper Indian Valley but Charlie Keough and the aforesaid Nava. They were driving a few head of whitefaced steers which they forthwith penned up in one of Warner's corrals to be left there that night. They had meant to continue right on to the Keough ranch, but both Warner and his wife insisted that they wait till after supper, which they showed no reluctance to do, Mrs. Warner being esteemed as a cook par excellence. Of course I, too, was in on that supper. Now, to anyone looking askance at my propensity for playing the game of hospitality on the receiving end, I should like to put the question, just what would you have done under the circumstances? These wonderful people seemed to feel that you were bestowing a blessing on them instead of vice versa.

A special bonus came with that splendid supper. I was going to have my Daisy mare back! In the morning Charlie would come back with an extra horse for me to ride. We'd take my bed along in two rolls tied behind our saddles, and we'd drive the steers the rest of the way. That would give Nava a chance to shoe his horse, and in the evening they'd butcher one of the steers.

"We owe about everybody on the river a quarter of beef," Charlie said. It seems the custom was to share butcherings among neighboring ranches. The plan now was to have Nava take care of distributing the beef while Charlie and I would ride up into the hills and recapture Daisy.

It sounded fantastic to me. What earthly use could I be? I wanted to know.

"You'll see," said Charlie.

In the morning all worked out as per schedule. By noon the steers were corralled on the Keough place. Toward evening, when supper was over, Charlie and Nava started across the wide ranch yard on what to them was just a routine affair, namely, a butchering, but to me, trailing along after them, seemed like going to witness an execution. I wasn't at all sure I wanted to see it, especially right after the hearty meal I had just eaten, but, having accepted Charlie's invitation, I couldn't very well back out.

The white-faced steer stood wonderingly in the little pen

back of the slaughterhouse. Not yet full grown, he was in fine condition, looking trim and firm around the belly and hips, a product of the mountain grasses and clear snow-water around the head of Reese River. In his dumb, brute way he must have enjoyed those high meadows and the free life of the rugged canyons where he had spent the summer months ever since his half-wild mother had calved him up there, three years before. There, as a baby, she had licked him till the white of his face and along his flanks gleamed like the snowbanks around him, and the red portions of his thick coat glistened in the sun like silk while he impetuously butted his head against her underside to make the elixir flow faster from her warm body. All the while she stood guard over him against all comers, even to mountain lions.

Here he stood now, uncomprehending, but instinctively defiant. Man he had always distrusted, feared, hated. Once he had made the mistake of charging a rider. Next thing he knew he was tossing on the ground, two men on horseback pulling him from opposite directions, his horns and one hind leg held tight by rawhide riatas which, for all his strength, he couldn't snap. As they rolled him over and over one of his horns got banged on a rock and since then it had pointed downwards over his left eye. When at last they loosened the ropes and let him up, he had learned his lesson and struck out at a trot through the brush and rocks.

Of course he had long forgotten that episode, but what, now, was that man up to there? Was he coming over the fence after him with that shiny black thing held over his shoulder? Let him dare!

He fell with a heavy, thudding sound on the hard-packed dried dung of the pen. Nava had hit him between the eyes with the ball from a twenty-two rifle. Now he was mer-chandise, and there was work to be done.

The boys worked lightning fast. Even during the bleeding the skinning knives flashed. The carcass, ripped open at a single slash, was hoisted gradually off the ground as the offal rolled out, warm and fresh, and the hide fell away. As the big pulley slowly turned, Nava ripped through the length of the spine with an ordinary carpenter's saw. There they hung now—two halves of beef, surprisingly long. Sponged off with fresh cold water, they were left suspended there to cool through the night in the open air, for the blowflies had already gone to roost, and that was why the butchering took place after sundown. At daybreak the beef would be covered with fly-proof canvas bags before the blowflies got thawed out.

Nava didn't go along when Charlie and I set out to the rescue of Daisy from the harem of that infamous sultan of a stallion who had abducted her. Nava stayed behind. No busman's holiday for him. He was on vacation and in the mood for *dolce far niente*.

Charlie, mounted on Snip, the big, powerful animal I had seen him on at Grantsville, assigned a smaller animal to me. His name was Steel, and his color was a steel-gray, and he was as tough and springy as Damascus steel. He was perfectly gentle and tractable but a little fire-eater who would kill himself running away with one unless he were constantly curbed and held back. I was fitted out with a pair of orange-colored chaps while Charlie wore his black angoras. Chaps, I found, glue one down to the saddle and keep one from bouncing around. Steel's headgear consisted of a bridle with a Mexican spade bit and a hackamore across his face above the nostrils. Attached to Charlie's saddle was his rawhide riata, made by himself, honda and all. It would have been nonsense for me, who knew nothing of roping, to have one on my saddle.

Instead of going up Becker Canyon, as I had expected,

Charlie chose another one which opened five miles closer by. He knew every foot of the country where the wild horses we were after ranged. This particular canyon was beyond a doubt as miserable a place for a horseback ride as one could find anywhere. It was narrow and steep; its lower reaches were choked with willows and wild rosebushes, and up above the loose rocks afforded such insecure footing for the horses that it was a wonder they had the heart to struggle on.

Charlie, in the lead, came to a halt directly below the mahoganies close to the top. Both horses were sweating freely, and though pretty well blown they were still as fretful as ever and eager to keep going.

Now we were to separate. I was to wait right there till I saw Charlie disappear over the next spur to the north, a mile or so off, when I was to continue on to the summit. If there were no mustangs up there, I was to work down a half mile or so on the other slope cutting through the mountain meadows and cottonwoods while I swung around to the north. By strictly following those instructions, Charlie said, I was sure to scare up the mustangs. The instant they caught sight of me they'd break for the canyon, where he'd be lying in wait for them.

"Don't run after 'em," he cautioned. "Just keep follerin' 'em at a walk. They'll run a ways an' stop. Every time they see you comin' they'll lead you right around to me."

There it came, the snort defiant! No need to ride down to the cottonwoods. Steel went hard against the bit, prancing excitedly. All I saw was a thin veil of dust. How could I have missed seeing the band? Steel fought hard for his head, dipping and swinging it from side to side. It was nothing new to him to have the spade bit cut into his jaw and tongue till blood dripped from his mouth, but the harmless-looking hackamore was what made him give in. It closed his nostrils, cutting off his breath, for a horse cannot breathe through its mouth. To have lost control of him just then would have meant dashing us to perdition in his chase after his wild cousins. It took work to hold him back to a walk.

I reached the far end of the hogback where the dust had risen. Ahead lay a deep saddle, the broad rim of a canyon whose walls converged several hundred feet below. Down there I caught my first glimpse of the band. Numerically it was a disappointment. The stallion, of course, was a picture. Any stallion, no matter how small his harem, is prima facie a champion of sorts. This one probably would have been no match for the black one farther up the range, although his color, a golden buckskin, denoted toughness aplenty. He stood poised for but an instant after he spotted me. Then, with a snort that echoed around the basin, he wheeled and chased his mares and colts on down into the canyon proper. In all there seemed to be about twenty mares and half a dozen colts. They were all of five hundred yards away, and while I was fairly sure I had spotted Daisy among them, I couldn't have sworn to her identity. They were all excitingly pretty to me.

Again they were out of sight. Down through the slide rock I put Steel. At times he was practically on his haunches in the treacherous going. He wasn't trying to show off now. Neither of us enjoyed that descent. It was so steep that I kept expecting to find Steel's tail drapped about my shoulders. But soon we were out of it and back on solid ground, and now the canyon closed around us and we struck a well-worn trail. At first the straight stretches were very short, and it was only after rounding many bends that I could see any appreciable distance ahead.

Then, just as I had about despaired of ever again seeing the mustangs, there they were! This time I was really close to them—within a hundred yards. I was now sure it was Daisy I had seen. But I wondered why they were so abruptly veering off, tearing at breakneck speed up along the sides of the canyon. On the instant I had the answer. This was a real show! There was Charlie, out of nowhere, his rope twirling in a great loop over his head as his big bay horse bore him magnificently into the very midst of the frantic band. Suddenly the rope lengthened out ahead of him, and now there was a queer sight. One lone animal, my Daisy, stood meekly still, left to her fate, forsaken, while her heartless former associates melted away over the hillside and quickly disappeared from view.

I couldn't help feeling sorry for her standing there, caught by the neck after Charlie had brought her up with a jerk when he took his turns on the horn of his saddle. All the wildness had gone out of her. Blithely she led along after us as though nothing unusual had happened. She seemed quite indifferent about the whole thing, even to forsaking her brief gypsy life. She had forgotten it already.

Her memory might be short, but her foal, conceived under circumstances of such high romance, would certainly be a beauty when it arrived.

I didn't say anything to Charlie about what I had in mind, but when we got back to the ranch a few hours later I told his little sister that Daisy was hers. She thanked me very simply, very sweetly.

12

THE STOKES INTERESTS owned the Berlin properties by virtue of a corporation named The Nevada Company, which also operated a store at the mine in which there was a fourth-class post office.

Indians and their squaws were the store's main outside

customers. To them the stock of claptrap which the company slanted to their artless cravings was a source of wonder and fascination. The company was in no way to blame. It had to stock those items or face the risk of Indian boycott by grunting and grumbling shoppers, braves and squaws.

Of course, there were the good, solid things of life—tobacco, flour, axle grease, salt—an altogether respectable line of frontier groceries. The outstanding value, though, was the Reese River beef. A thick porterhouse steak was yours for four bits, and anyone even mentioning sales tax, income tax, luxury tax, or withholding tax in those days would have been tarred and feathered.

The morning after the day of Daisy's thrilling recapture Sly's boss *vaguero*, Juan Nava, took me and my outfit to Berlin along with the side of beef he was delivering to the company there.

Whipple happened to be underground when I arrived at the mine. Meanwhile, I went over to where a man was working with pick and shovel. He was a six-footer, straight, lean, and altogether fit-looking. I guessed him to be about thirty. He had a brown mustache and his eyes, too, were brown, with a forthright, searching look. He was not averse to stopping for a chat with me. We shook hands, introducing ourselves. His name was Gaston Ashe. Here was a soft-spoken man of culture of whom I was to see and learn considerably more in the days ahead. He liked Whipple very much and said he had heard from him that I was expected. Also, he told me that Whipple would probably offer me the position of powder monkey and tool nipper in the mine, which sounded interesting, to say the least. But Ashe said I needn't take it unless I wanted to, and that Whipple would doubtless put me to work on the surface if I preferred. I asked him what that job was like—that powder-monkey, tool-nipping thing. He explained I'd just be a kind of errand boy for the miners. The duties were light enough to be sure. I'd pack drill steel to and fro, lugging the dull drills and picks to the blacksmith shop on top and returning with newly sharpened ones, which didn't sound like bad nipping, so far. Near the end of the shift, I'd have to furnish each miner whatever he might order in the shape of powder, fuse, and caps. That didn't sound like bad monkeying to me, either. But, Ashe said, I hadn't yet heard the worst. There was one extra function to the job. I'd be expected to round up those dirt boxes used by the miners in cases of extreme personal emergency and see to it that they were sent on top to be disposed of over the brink of the waste dump. I fully agreed with Gaston Ashe. Somebody else was welcome to juggle those underground bedpans around.

Whipple, however, bless his soul, never mentioned that job to me at all. He had kept his word—saved a surface job for me.

Poor old Berlin! It was just an in-between so-and-so, neither a big low-grade proposition nor a small high-grade one. Hence, it was hardly a mine at all. The wealthy Stokeses could afford to toy with Berlin a while. They even erected a tall rock castle on a prominent hillside nearby, which amazed all who saw the incongruous pile for the first time. Berlin was an excuse for Anson Phelps Stokes to make periodical inspection tours over his ninety-three-mile Nevada Central Railroad which made tri-weekly trips between Battle Mountain and Austin. After roughing it a day or two at Berlin, Stokes would return to his socialist spouse in New York, the former Rose Pastor, to be regaled by her with anti-capitalist, humanitarian preachments. It might be said that by financing these profitless operations he was sparing others the anguish of going broke on them, thus dividing up, à la socialism.

I became a beneficiary of all this largess on the payroll of The Nevada Company in the capacity of assistant surface roustabout at $3.50 a day. Down below I'd get $4.00, but I'd have to inhale powder gas and dust—bad for the lungs. God's fresh air was good enough for me.

Up there on top I helped on such jobs as laying tracks for mine cars, unloading lumber and supplies for the company store hauled in by freight teams, digging ditches and sundry excavations with pick and shovel, and sawing stulls with a six-foot crosscut saw. Also, I was enabled to practice with a single jack, for there was quite a bit of foundation work where the bedrock had to be drilled and blasted.

Mostly, Gaston Ashe and I worked together on these projects. By his invitation I moved into his cabin with him. It was called "The Bucket of Blood." It had a washstand, water bucket, pitcher, and basin, and an extra bedstead with springs for my bedding, all quite luxurious for me. The shack's murderous name derived from the color it was painted—a glaring, carmine red.

Of course, I wondered what had brought Ashe to Berlin. In all the six weeks I was there I never asked him, nor did he ever tell me. He never displayed any curiosity about my affairs either. All I know and can say is that his presence there was a godsend to me. Possibly he was there to get away from this, that, or the other thing. If so, he had picked the right place, the tail end of nowhere.

Yet, he wasn't reticent regarding his background. He was a Harvard man, had graduated in law, and had practiced in San Francisco. His connections were of the very best on the coast. A brother, Porter Ashe, had been one of the leading social, political, and intellectual figures of the old pre-fire-and-earthquake San Francisco. Gaston always spoke of him with pride and affection. He told some choice anecdotes laid in that lavish social era, one of which tied in with the horse races which used to draw the elite of San Francisco society—of course along with the riffraff—down the peninsula to San Jose, where extravagant banquets and brilliant balls were quite the order of the day.

One night, so the story went, Gaston's brother Porter was host at an elaborate party in the town's most fashionable hotel. While the guests were in the midst of the dinner the headwaiter laid a note beside Porter's plate. Not one of the guests ever learned what that note was about, and no one saw what Porter had put in the envelope he handed back to the headwaiter. All they had seen was his smile as he excused himself, extracted the note from its envelope, read it, and tucked it into his pocket.

Later, though, he showed the note to Gaston. It had been scribbled at the door of the banquet hall by one of Porter's Harvard classmates, a brilliant, likable fellow who had fallen by the wayside and had sought solace in the bottle. The note read: "My dear Ashe: Ancient Pistol says 'Base is the slave that pays.' If you will be so good as to accommodate me yet again with a loan of five dollars I will indeed make every effort to incur the Pistolian stigma." It was signed with the writer's campus nickname.

I had been in Berlin a couple of weeks when I got a letter from my broker in Tonopah stating that my stock had been sold but that through an oversight the proceeds had not been deposited in the bank. He enclosed a duplicate deposit slip showing that some eight hundred dollars had been placed to my credit as of the date of his letter. I believe I got out of that stock at the very top. What a break! Now I could pay

Kiefer and take up my note, quit my job, and pick up the trail of my prospecting where I had left off. However, after a little reflection I decided against quitting immediately. I'd let that money lie in the bank as a reserve and work on till I had enough coming over and above what was due Kiefer to keep me in funds for a while. Fifty dollars would supply my wants for weeks to come.

If it hadn't been for Ashe I probably would have called it a day. We hit it off very well together, and besides I was taking lessons from him in the manly art of self-defense.

One of the first things he had asked me after I had gotten settled in the cabin with him was if I had ever done any boxing. I told him I had had the gloves on a time or two, but had done nothing worth mentioning.

"Let me have a look," he said, "while you just stand up here a minute."

I did as he directed, putting up my dukes the best I knew as I faced him. Very seriously he looked me over from head to foot and ended by shaking his head negatively in manifest disapproval.

"Do you know what?" he said. "I could send you flying through that door without moving my fist more than an inch."

Where did he get that stuff? I said to myself. Why, I was fit and solid and weighed a good two hundred. I must have edged him at least twenty pounds, though in height he topped me a couple of inches.

"All right," I said. "Let's see you do it."

"We'd better step outside," he said. "You might get hurt going backwards through the door."

We went out front on the level roadway and squared off. His left fist was extended to within an inch of my chest.

"Lead!" he cried. Before I could get going, I found myself

reeling backwards faster than my feet could keep up with. They just seemed to drop out of the race, as I went tail over teakettle down on the hard gravel. Ashe trotted over and grabbed my hand to help me up.

"Nice work!" I said. "I wish I knew how you did it."

"I'll be glad to show you," he said. "Some day it might come in handy for you."

He was prophetic. There did come a day when I was glad that Gaston Ashe had stood up with me day after day in front of our little red cabin there in Berlin patiently drilling me in the proper stance and how to put every ounce of my weigh behind a left hook. Ashe had held the amateur heavyweight boxing championship of the United States while at Harvard. He had often sparred with Teddy Roosevelt, who, he said, was more willing and anxious than effective.

I left some fine fellows behind at Berlin when I climbed aboard the Keough beef wagon en route back to Reese River. To me, naturally, Ashe stood out above the rest, probably because I was with him the most. Some twenty years later I dropped in at his law offices in San Francisco where he was back practicing. He was trying a big criminal case at the time, defending one Blackie Ford who had been mixed up with the murder of Governor Stunenberg of Idaho during labor troubles. Ashe seemed just as glad to see me again as I was to see him. He had lost his lithe figure and had become very heavy; he moved about with a cane.

Before dropping the subject of my stay at Berlin, I want to put in a plug for Whipple. He was more like a pal than a boss, and the whole gang was all for him, at least while I was at Berlin, and all of them gave him the best they had. I don't want to overlook good old man Watson. He ran the store, was postmaster, kept the books, made out the payroll, managed the boardinghouse, and was like a daddy to us all.

Never a foul word passed his lips, though he spoke five languages, not counting Paiute.

13

AH, REESE RIVER! Haying was in full swing on my return. It's a joyous season, harvesting the sweet wild hay, Indians sweeping the meadows with buckrakes, pushing great loads to the rising stacks, squaws a-bustle around the wickiups and helping out in the ranch kitchens, youngsters at play, ponies tethered out, dogs a-scratch, all suggesting a carnival rather than the serious business it was.

On my way to the Warner ranch to retrieve my burro outfit I stopped with my bed at the Keough ranch to join Charlie in his favorite boudoir on the roof of the horseshed. In the morning I went along to the hay fields where I had a chance to show what I could do with a pitchfork. I wasn't altogether green at that sort of thing. I was glad to be a little useful while waiting for a lift up to Warner's with anyone happening by.

What a jolly life! In the evening Charlie and I would take a dip in the deep pool of the river back of the corrals. All was so fine and dandy! But my conscience bothered me. It didn't come under the head of prospecting. Still, I couldn't strike out without my burros, and I couldn't go after those critters without my bed, and there I was, in a pickle, and a sweet one at that.

All too soon, on one of Mr. Warner's weekly trips to pick up mail and what not, we met at the stage stop down the river where the horses were changed for the long pull up the Ione grade; I rode back to his ranch with him.

I couldn't rightly make Warner out. He wouldn't take anything, not even my proffered help with his haying, in return for pasturing my burros. As a rancher, he seemed quite the amateur, running what is loosely described as a baling-wire outfit. He had two Indians helping him, one of them a very elderly, long-haired fellow who played the fiddle, and not too badly.

I learned more about Warner after leaving his pretty little mountain ranch. For one thing, he was said to be a dead shot with the pistol—could keep a tin can rolling along the ground as he poured six fast ones after it, fanning the hammer with the palm of his hand while the trigger was held down. Also, I was told that he had worked as an accountant in his younger days and had given that up on account of his health. He spent a lot of time away from his ranch following up rumors of new mining strikes, and he kept working on claims he had held for years, never losing faith in their ultimately making him a fortune.

To the very last, Charlie Keough did his best to talk me into joining him on a trip to hunt bighorns around Arc Dome at the head of the river. The way I looked at it was this: if I just kept mooching around there having a good time, I'd never, never amount to a damn. My pesky conscience kept telling me to get out and make a stake. After that, I could get myself a layout like that beautiful Keough ranch and settle down to a life of hunting, fishing, and dreaming.

I wanted to get up into the northern part of Nevada. There's where they seemed to be striking it right and left. A rash of new names was spreading all over the map—Rosebud, Seven Troughs, Rochester, Kimberly, Gold Circle, Jarbidge —just to cite a few. The farther away the place, the richer the strike was reputed to be. Poor old gold! The way the boys were carrying on about their discoveries it did seem it might have to surrender its supremacy as the world's chosen standard of value, so plentiful, so common, was it becoming!

I hoped, and I prayed, that I wouldn't turn into a mere road runner, never lighting anywhere for long, always itching to be somewhere else than where I was.

My first night away from Warner's I made camp at the base of a bold cropping in the foothills well up from the floor of the valley. I had covered a good twenty-five miles, about half of it afoot and the rest astride sturdy old Dan. I had cut down the outfit to what I could pack on Rickey and Old Gal, leaving Dan available for riding, and I still had Jennie B's saddlebags and crosstrees, if I should want to use Dan for a pack animal.

The big dike which I had spotted from a distance was disappointing in the extreme when I reached it—just a hopeless pile-up of shattered rhyolite not worth bothering with. There's where I would spend the night notwithstanding, and never did I sleep more soundly than I did right there against that friendly, sheltering dike.

When finally the sun over the Toiyabes routed me out of bed, I could see my burros a long way off down on the flat where the river road ran. No doubt they had been lured there by the green meadowland through which the river flowed, but on arrival there they had found themselves cut off from access by a barbed-wire fence. It was the Wholey (pronounced Hooley) ranch down there.

I particularly wanted to meet Mr. John Wholey, quite a remarkable man according to what I had been told. Perhaps I should be able to after breakfast, when I'd go down after my burros.

Down there by the river as I was stooped over removing Dan's hobbles, I noticed what I took to be a stick lying across the road just about spanning the distance between the wagon tracks. Just a stick, so what? Next I started on Rickey's hobbles, and just as I straightened up I saw another "stick" wind itself out of the brush and pause halfway across the road, a few feet from the other.

There they were at last, the first real live rattlesnakes I had ever seen in their native habitat! They were big ones, too, with thick bodies, flat triangular heads, and some two to three inches of rattles on their tails. For a moment I was seized with a kind of paralysis. I felt as if I couldn't move. Then I sort of came to and decided I must kill them, but with what? There wasn't a rock nor a stick in sight and my pistol was back up there in camp. Down the road a short way stood the ranch house and across from it was a corral, and now I saw two young fellows leaving the house, and I whistled and waved at them. "Rattlesnakes!" I yelled, motioning toward the ground.

Up came the boys on the run, one of them armed with a shovel, and the other with a willow sapling. The reptiles were polished off in jig time.

These were the Wholey boys, Jimmie and Willie, and on their young shoulders rested the responsibility of keeping the ranch running while their father busied himself at his more specialized calling, which was that of a stonemason. As it happened, Mr. Wholey was at home just then resting up for a few days, and when I said that I had wanted to meet their father, the boys practically herded me toward the house.

John Wholey was tall and gaunt. A black full beard gave him a scholarly look. Stonemason Wholey strikingly resembled Stonewall Jackson, and, like the latter, he was a man of sterling character and deep religious conviction. Most cordial of manner, he insisted that I take a seat while his wife went after a cup of hot coffee for me, the breakfast table having not yet been cleared. Meanwhile the boys told their father about the rattlesnakes.

"Yes," said Mr. Wholey, his voice deep and musically

modulated with a brogue, "we've lots of them here. The boys keep killing them pretty nearly every day when the weather's warm, but I'd just as soon they wouldn't. They do more good than harm, keeping down the ground squirrels and gophers. That big rock up above here, that's where they mostly come from. There's a den of them up there."

All of which confirmed what the boys had already told me, namely, that my camp was smack up against a rattlesnakes' den. To think that I must go back up there for my outfit!

John Wholey was a latter-day Leonardo da Vinci. Besides having his skill as a mason attested by scores of stone buildings, rock foundations, pillars, arches, culverts, and tall brick chimneys, I discovered that he was an artist at wood carving and had even made some good violins. As if that weren't enough, Jimmie spoke up and said that his dad was a champion checkers player.

"Tut, tut," Mr. Wholey deprecated, " 'tis not becoming to be boasting. I've no doubt this young man plays a far better game than I do."

"Mr. Wholey," I protested, "I'm the world's worst checkers player. The game's 'way over my head."

"Come now, don't be giving me that," he said good-naturedly. "We'll just have a game right now whilst you're drinking your coffee. Jimmie, go fetch the board."

In three games I just managed to get through to the king row once. Fortunately Mr. Wholey had had enough, and he didn't seem to be a bit pleased. I felt that he thought I was taking a dive to him so as not to show him up before his family, but, of course, he refrained from saying as much, he being too much of a gentleman to impugn my motives. I'm sure he would have been delighted if I had licked the stuffing out of him, for then he might have learned a thing or two and improved his game.

I had played a bit at Tonopah with a very wealthy but very sick young man named Stuart Hills who had come out there from New York for his health. He belonged to the Hills clan, importers of dates, whose coat of arms was a dromedary, symbolical no doubt of the fact that they had surmounted the financial hump in a big way. Young Hills, by way of improving his time and demonstrating his business acumen, managed to drop what would have amounted to a good-sized fortune to anyone in less opulent circumstances by plunging into the Greenwater boom of sorrowful memory. He was a Yale man and at one time had held some big checkers championship. I learned a couple of opening moves from him— that was all. Never, however, had I succeeded in getting a king with him. Now I was wishing I could have put him up against Mr. Wholey. Probably Hills would have come out on top, but at least he wouldn't have sneered at Mr. Wholey as he had at me. The last time Hills mopped up on me he stared ominously at me across the table and said, "Why couldn't my head have been on your body?" I agreed that such a switch would result on the one hand in an exceptionally endowed individual, and just the opposite on the other, and then I began to fear he might think of a scheme to bring about that catastrophe. Thereafter I made it a point to avoid him.

Mr. Wholey was a powerful man who feared neither man, devil, nor beast—in broad daylight, that is. However, it was common knowledge thereabouts that he was deathly afraid of ghosts and that he wouldn't venture alone outside the house after dark for all the money in the world.

Once again, it was all very well, and extremely pleasant, to be sitting there and visiting with the Wholeys, but it wasn't getting my outfit moved away from that snake-infested rock. Probably by now several of the sociable creatures had crawled inside my bed to warm the reptilian counterpart of their tootsies. No doubt others were slithering about in my packs, darting their tongues at my beans, sugar, and flour.

"How do you account for the fact that I didn't see any snakes all the time I was up there?" I asked.

" 'Tis a mystery sure," said Mr. Wholey. "The good Lord must love you. But if you'd like to see more, just have a look around in back of that rock. I'll promise you'll see all you want and more besides. There's some long poles the cowboys took up there to kill them. For me, I'll have no part of it."

Right then and there I resolved that if I once got clear of that rock without being snake-bit, I'd leave well enough alone and not go hunting for trouble with a pole. The reptiles had been kind enough to leave me alone, and, besides, even a rattlesnake has its rights.

When I had gotten all packed up without having run across a single snake, I began to wonder if I was really at the right rock, the one the Wholeys had been referring to. I left my burros standing in their packs while I went around one end of the dike and climbed up the bank of a draw on the rim of which I found myself behind the jutting pile.

Sure enough, about fifty feet ahead of me lay a long willow pole on the loose rocks, and as I continued on I counted three or four others. I felt safe enough in my high laced boots, but, even so, I searched out each step before putting my foot down. What I had expected to find on reaching the nearest pole was some sort of pit, or maybe a cave, for the place had been spoken of as a den. There was neither. It was just a jumble of loose rocks. True, there might have been a fissure underneath where the snakes hibernated, all intertwined and rolled up in a big ball.

As I reached for the pole, I became vaguely aware of a slight movement among the rocks in front of me. I straightened up, and what had been only a fleeting impression a second before was now not only a fleeting impression but also an aural reality. There it was now, in full view, the thing I had seen move. Cursed from the days of Eden, hate and defiance incarnate, its horn-ringed tail erect and whirring in fair, and in this case suicidal, warning, snugly curled there on a rock, it was deluding itself that like all other animate beings it had met in its peregrinations, this one, too, would give it a wide berth. Instead, I gave it cause a-plenty to change its mind. Down came the pole upon it to the accompaniment of a popping report as its belly burst asunder and the contents of its entrails spattered the adjacent rocks. Instantly it sank its fangs into its own body where the hurt was, surely in the belief that it had caught its assailant. With the pole I finished the job on it before realizing that almost wherever I looked I could see portions of snakes winding and undulating between rocks, offering good targets as they dragged themselves out of one crevice and into another. I was evidently in the vicinity of their den, the chimney up which the ill-smelling creatures crept out of their underground lair. I whacked away wherever a head or a stiffly-rattling tail showed up. The place was beginning to take on the activity of an anthill, and the movements of the snakes struck me as being just as aimless appearing as the comings and goings of scurrying pissants. I soon had laid out upwards of a dozen of the crawlers but couldn't manipulate the pole fast enough to scotch every one that I saw. What's more, I wasn't relishing the pastime. The bursting of that first victim had left me with a sickening qualm which failed to subside as I grew more and more sensible of the stench the reptiles exuded. My decision to call it quits was hastened by the sudden discovery that I was almost on top of one fellow that had assumed its challenging attitude at my feet while my attention was directed elsewhere.

I got to thinking as I pulled away from that abominable rock that the whole experience might have seemed more like a nightmare than an actuality had it not been for the stink. It was not till several hours later that the last trace of it left my nostrils. At least there is this to be said for nightmares: they don't smell.

As I poked along I tried to picture what those underground caverns were like, and I thought what a satisfaction it would be to set off a case of giant powder in one of them.

14

MY ROUTE FOR THE NEXT FEW DAYS took me along the foothills of the Shoshones with side excursions into some canyons on the way. I was becoming a fancier of pretty, unusual rocks. I enjoyed picking them up and examining their structures through my magnifying glass, always, of course, on the alert for a speck of gold. What if it did slow me up? Prospecting isn't supposed to set any records for speed. By now I was firmly convinced that a prospector should walk, not ride. It made for closer observation, for keener awareness of the sermons that are said to exist in stones.

One day, around noon, I noticed some odd-shaped buttes off to the west where the Shoshones broke off sharply and the valley spread out to double its width in the foreground. The setting was remarkably similar to Goldfield's. Doubtless those buttes had been investigated by keen-eyed prospectors, but just suppose that everybody else had said the same thing about them! That could actually be the case, which would mean that they were virgin ground. Sure, I'd give those bare grayish hills a lick and a promise if nothing more. They looked 100 per cent dry. I'd take in ten gallons of water and see about the advisability of setting up camp there.

About sundown, I reached the break in the hills I'd been

aiming at. Except for the water in my cans, the region was as dry as a W.C.T.U. convention. For feed and fuel there was only a straggly growth of greasewood. A man would spend an hour gathering enough of the stunted plant for a fire to cook his supper. It is made up of clusters of inch-long stickers, sharp as needles and stiff as steel. The only way to harvest it is with a shovel. Imagine, then, my amazement to find that my burros went wild over it. I couldn't believe my eyes when I saw all three of them, Dan, Rickey, and Old Gal, browsing and munching on that barbed wire of the vegetable kingdom. It was a far better show than the man in the circus who merely eats glass and swallows razor blades.

I gave two full days of this transitory life—as the Episcopalians say—to those otherwise lifeless hills. Pan as I would, with my precious little water supply, not the tiniest speck of gold rewarded my efforts. That, of course, proves absolutely nothing. Sometimes, out of innate modesty, the richest gold ore won't show a color in the pan, its precious secret being locked up in some baser mineral. Thus, the efficacy of the gold pan has its definite limitations. Hence, there still could be gold in those dratted hills. If so, it can stay there as far as I'm concerned.

Once again, I struck out in the general direction of the North Pole. Some ocher-tinted hills were all a-shimmer in the heat waves off in the far distance, giving them the appearance of being afire, a possible outcrop of hell itself. They were not for me. I was quite warm enough as it was. About midway, I could see a faded greenish area with a group of low structures and a compact clump of cottonwoods, clearly a ranch of some kind, though it lay far off the course of the river. It seemed an inviting spot to spend that night and to refill my water cans for whatever dry camps might lie ahead of me out there in the unknown.

Foxy little Rickey! He could smell a stack of hay ten miles off. We pulled up at that oasis which turned out to be the Ryan ranch. On my honor, I hadn't meant to mooch on Mr. and Mrs. Ryan for supper, though I must say that the evidence against me was nothing short of monumental. I seemed to be a specialist at arriving on ranch after ranch at mealtime. I was just going to ask for water—that's all. But Mr. Ryan didn't invite, he ordered me to come into the house and sit in with them as soon as I'd be ready with my camping arrangements.

These fine people were living in retirement on the fruits of their past industry and thrift. They were within striking distance of a golden wedding anniversary, yet young at heart and with minds undimmed by the passage of time. Ryan still ran a few hundred head of cattle, from force of habit no doubt, and ranged them out with the vast herds of his good friend and neighbor, that fiery septuagenarian Pat Walsh. Ryan employed a year-round cowhand who assisted during roundups, brandings, and related activities.

Entering the house with my stocky, white-haired host, I discovered I was not to be the only supper guest. Mrs. Ryan, active and trim in her summer dress and bibbed apron, was bustling about the table, and it was evident she was setting an extra place. A man, seated on a couch beside the door by which we had entered, must have warned her that it seemed her husband had invited another guest for supper. She smiled pleasantly as Ryan introduced me, and I felt a genuine welcome as she frankly looked me over with her cheery blue eyes.

The other man had a name that sounded like *la Boo*, but I later found it was spelled *le Beau*. He was about forty and good looking, and he lived on a distant ranch in a canyon known as le Beau Creek. His people were old-time settlers in that part of Nevada. Henry—that was his first name—was on a cattle-buying mission. He had a considerable butchering business and was supplying beef to the new boom camp of Rawhide.

"You ought to go over there," Henry said to me, "even if it's only to see the camp. It beats anything you ever saw."

Well, I rather questioned that. I had seen Goldfield at its peak, when Messrs. Hayes and Monette were hoisting fifty thousand dollars' worth of gold every twenty-four hours out of their rapidly expiring lease on the Mohawk claim. I had sat through the thirty-odd rounds of the Gans-Nelson prize fight on Labor Day, 1906, when the camp was swarming with crowds from all over the United States. I had seen gold ore worth one hundred dollars a pound and bogus "assayers" buying it from high-grading miners for half of its intrinsic value, mining stocks spurt from a nickel to twenty dollars a share, Tex Rickard the fight-promoter, Diamondfield Jack Davis the braggadocio two-gun "bad man" everyone advised leaving alone, skittles played in the luxurious Goldfield Hotel with tall brass cuspidors for pins and bottles of champagne for balls, the I.W.W. (I Won't Work) wobblies, and George (the Great) Wingfield who let the five-dollar poker chips fall where they willed and scooped up the whole shebang in one big pot!

Nevertheless, there was something about Rawhide that put its boom in a class by itself in the estimation of many connoisseurs. Its gold output was insignificant compared with Goldfield's. Its mines were rich but pockety, spectacular but short-lived. It was a one-act drama which worked itself up to its climax in the funeral of a noted sports figure and gambler named Riley Grannan.

That funeral was attended by every living soul in the camp. Certain chroniclers who merely dish up journalistic rehash have seen fit to belittle the remarkable impromptu eulogy

125

spoken over the bier on that uniquely solemn occasion out there on the silent desert under cloudless blue skies when the air was hardly stirred by the gentlest of warm breezes. The speaker consulted no notes. Each word he uttered flowed easily and naturally from his lips. As he laid his simple bouquet of wild desert flowers inside the open casket and bade good-by on behalf of everyone present, a mighty sigh swept through the crowd. There were few standing there with dry eyes or concealment of emotions.

Who was this khaki-clad Ingersolian orator? Few knew at the moment that his name was Herman Knickerbocker, that he was an ex-clergyman from somewhere in the deep south who had turned to skepticism. No one in that audience would have surmised that before long his pristine faith would prevail over his temporary doubts and that he would resume preaching Christ, "And Him Crucified."

I missed all that. To my deep, lasting regret I ignored Henry le Beau's advice and by-passed Rawhide. Afterwards I couldn't hear enough about it from those that had been fortunate enough to be on the ground while the drama was playing. I missed seeing the natty Nat Goodwin in that incongruous setting and Eleanor Glynn, whose "Three Weeks" was regarded as the real tabasco in those innocent days. At Rawhide she was cavaliered by none other than the redoubtable Ray Baker who was never one to shy away from a chance to shine in reflected glory. Ray, with his red silk neckerchief and jaunty pose, later became a luminary in the administration of Woodrow Wilson who appointed him Director of the Mint. Ray didn't know a mint from a julep, but he did know enough to switch from Republican to Democrat in time to snare the fat job. From there he went on to even greater fame, accompanying Ambassador Marye to Russia as secretary, which equipped him to enter the social lists in Reno and Washington. There just seemed to be no stopping that Ray, at least not till after marrying into two or three staggering fortunes, and he up and ran for United States senator from Nevada. That high honor the electorate of the Sagebrush State bestowed, in the eloquent language of the polls, on his opponent, the Honorable Tasker Lowndes Oddie, yes, Tonopah's very own Oddie!

Indeed, I'm sorry to have missed Rawhide, in spite of good old Ray of whom I had seen a'plenty, and then some, around Tonopah. No, Henry le Beau, wherever you may be now, I can't say you didn't tell me—that night on the Ryan ranch on Reese River.

15

Although burro-men were by no means an uncommon sight in those days, my outfit and myself drew the curious gaze of a big crowd in front of the International Hotel in Austin, where I had gone to replenish my dwindling larder. I had been piecing out with jack rabbit along the way, an entrée not too highly esteemed even by prospectors. That saltatory hare, when done to a nice brown in bacon drippings, is to southern fried chicken about as home-brew used to be to real, imported Pilsner. It was my good fortune never to run across one of those revolting grubs, of which Hot Steam had spoken, under a jack rabbit's pelt.

The Austin populace seemed friendly and sociable. Instinct told me they were all curious to know from what planet I had come, and if I had heard any good stories lately—stories about mining strikes, that is.

Their principal spokesman was a pleasant-faced young man of about my own age who was neatly attired in contrast to most of the others there, who appeared to be old-timers putting in their time just being old-timers. He turned out to be the county auditor, Bert Acree, who was destined to fill that office in the county seat of Lander County for many years to come.

I left my outfit at the hitching rail in front of the old hotel and walked up the steep street a half block with Acree, who took a great interest in my prospecting and advised me by all means to go to a place called New Pass, in the mountains about twenty-six miles west of Austin, along the old Pony Express Trail. He led me to the Austin Commercial Company's store and introduced me to its manager, Billy Christian, a brisk, affable man, with whom I placed my order. While it was being done up, I slipped up street to the post office and got off a card to Kiefer at Grantsville, telling him that I had left the money with Charlie Keough to take up my note and that he should get in touch with him. I had a nice chat with Charlie Littrell, the postmaster, who was also county treasurer, and a fine type of pioneer of Austin's hectic bonanza days.

I don't see how anyone could help liking Austin, that picturesque old camp on the historic Pony Express Trail. I had a premonition that I'd be seeing more of it some time.

With New Pass filed away in my mind for future reference, I first wanted to take in a country on the opposite side of the valley and some distance below Austin—a district known as Ravenswood, which the postmaster had highly recommended for prospecting.

Ravenswood is a desolate plateau in the foothills. No houses there, not even a tent. I had the whole place to myself. It did look mighty interesting. Location monuments stood everywhere, and yet the whole district was open to location. I fished out many faded, stained old location notices from rusty tin cans tucked in among the rocks. The writing in many cases was too faded to decipher.

But heavens, what veins there were, wide strong ones, fissures filled with solid white quartz! Shafts abounded some fifty to a hundred feet deep, their collars ringed with dumps of gleaming quartz speckled with pyrites and hematite which in any other environment might be pay ore. Here it lay abandoned to its wretched sterility. Surely many a dollar had been hopefully spent having it fire assayed, only to be rewarded with a certificate of *nulla bona.*

One day's sojourn at Ravenswood convinced me that there was nothing I could add to the work of exploration performed by the hardy crew whose hopes had been blasted and gone up in powder smoke there years before.

Ravenswood may yet come into its own. Who can tell? But it's going to take money, gumption, and perhaps some mineralogical enlightenment, of which this generation is as yet in the dark. Diamond drilling may give the answer. I departed, blessing those old-timers who had spared me the task of drilling and shooting those beautiful, but damned, veins, and all in vain. (A purely accidental pun for which I humbly apologize.)

Off to the west I saw a peak that looked enough like Tonopah's Mount Oddie to be its twin brother. In that general direction lay New Pass. I decided to take them both in while I was at it; en route there might be some good-looking outcrops worthy of my attention.

Before I knew it, I was on a road in the lowlands sloping gently upwards for miles from the river bottom. It headed about to where I wanted to go, and Rickey seemed all for it too. Good old scout, Rickey! Farther on, the road came out on a broad mud flat now caked and dried, and there my poor animals had a real foretaste of hell. It was infested with botflies! All the way across that flat, the bloodthirsty, relentless pests goaded and tortured their helpless victims and so demoralized them that I feared they'd go completely loco. We were a good half hour getting the hell out of that inferno, and strangely enough the minute we hit higher ground we had left the botflies behind. What bound them to that flat is a mystery of nature too deep for me to fathom.

Finally, in the early afternoon, there we were at the base of our objective, Mount Airy.

How did I know its name? I got it direct from Gilbert Joe. There he stood waiting for me. There's where he lived, he and the remnants of his tribe. Gilbert Joe was a Paiute chief. His first great concern as I drew near was to ascertain if I had any whisky aboard. Fortunately, such was not the case, and I could truthfully tell him so. In any event, he wouldn't have got any from me short of massacring me. It was bad business giving, selling, or in any way furnishing whisky to Indians, and I was aware of that fact. Just let Sheriff Mike Ryan of Lander County catch you at it. Ryan had an obsession on the subject, so much so that he set traps for offenders, and the penalty was severe. Ryan was slight of build and of medium height. He dressed and looked more like a school principal than a peace officer, and his quiet, reserved manner was something else to throw the uninitiated off guard. His fanaticism about whisky and Indians was the outgrowth of his having been forced to kill an Indian crazed with firewater who had attacked him with a knife when he went to apprehend him on the streets of Austin.

Gilbert Joe, for all that, was prepared to barter a squaw for a bottle of whisky; nevertheless, he had a considerable natural dignity about him. I could see at a glance that the old fellow was wont to take life easy, for a short way back from the road a bevy of noisy squaws were hoeing and digging away in a small potato patch. They were setting up a loud, raucous chorus. Naturally I understood nary a word of their nasal, guttural grunt, and yet I knew they were making merry over me, for they kept brazenly looking my way and laughing their heads off. It would have made a good scene for a play, the way that troupe of actresses was supported by a score or more of barking, yapping, mongrel dogs. To me it was quite understandable that Chief Gilbert Joe should be wanting a drink.

This headquarters camp of the tribe was a jumble of non-descript huts built of scraps of this and that, sheets of discarded corrugated iron, weathered boards, salvaged bits of tar paper, burlap, willow twigs, and mud clay. Most of the able-bodied males and squaws were away working on the Pat Walsh ranch at that particular time. When not doing that they could be found camped here or there, sometimes in the high canyons of the Shoshones or the Toiyabes, cutting cord-wood, hunting, harvesting pine nuts, always just Injuns, free, not cursed with ambition, not looking for a job with a future. They lived off the country as they found it, strictly hand-to-mouth, with nothing laid by except perhaps some pine nuts and a pack of dogs which went into the pot when the going got rough.

Though I well knew it was useless, I asked Gilbert Joe if there was any gold around there.

"Maybe so," he shrugged. "You no got'um whisky?"

"No whisky," I replied, extending my open palms in a gesture of futility.

His expression became so utterly glum as to be ludicrous.

"Maybe so you got'um vanilla exwak," he suggested, hopefully and brightening a bit.

"No vanilla extract," I doefully replied.

He pondered that calamity a moment and then said, "Lemon exwak?"

I shook my head negatively. Surely he must have sensed

that I really felt for him. Finally I had an idea. I loosened Old Gal's pack and produced a bottle of Worcestershire sauce, nearly full, and placed it in his eager hands. Without so much as a look at the label, he pulled out the stopper, raised the bottle to his lips, and swallowed a big mouthful. A look of dubious pleasure spread over his face and without further delay he took another big swig, which was followed by a grunt of ersatz satisfaction.

"How's that?" I asked, hoping it wouldn't make him sick.

"Uh," he uh'd. "Skookum—whisky more better."

Once again, still not hopefully, I asked if he knew any good places to look for gold. He merely kept eyeing the bottle as if he were pondering whether he should finish it off at once or to save a dash or two for a rainy day. Now the sharp-eyed squaws, who knew a bent elbow when they saw one, came swooping down en masse as if determined not to be left out of the party. That decided it for Joe. No ladies first for him. He hastily drained the bottle, and the protests that went up sounded like a herd of yelping sea lions. Joe tossed the empty bottle at their feet, and in the most guttural lingo I had ever listened to he was either decrying the impotency of what it had contained or else he was denouncing me for a weak sister of a paleface for not packing anything with a bigger wallop than that insipid sauce, concocted from the recipe of a gentleman in the country as the label proclaimed.

An elderly female brave took over. A protracted exchange between her and Joe ensued.

"She say you got'um chewing tobacco?" Joe finally stated.

My reply in the negative was the last straw. The squaws, thoroughly disgusted, turned and trudged off, muttering to themselves.

I hadn't done myself much good around there. My one desire was to get away from that gang as fast as possible before making camp for the night. Just as I started off Joe seemed to have a change of heart.

"You want find'um mining rock you go big mountain," he said, pointing westward. "Big mountain," he repeated. He could only have meant the roundish bald peak which loomed there ahead, pretty much by itself, a true landmark.

"Which side?" I asked.

"This side," he replied. "You over there, you see'um."

Naturally I had no idea of making it clear "over there" that afternoon, but one thing was sure, I was getting away from Mount Airy, and at once.

There was a wide level stretch of sagebrush through the Mount Airy pass. I wondered what kind of depression would greet me beyond. How sharply would it break off, and would there be a dry lake with a surface of white alkali?

There was no alkali flat, but a bowl-shaped valley, six miles or so in diameter, burst into view. On the far side, where the foothills began, I saw the exact spot where I would camp that night. It was a little ranch, looking parched and deserted but with a clump of cottonwoods which spelled water. I could make out some sprawling sheds, corrals, a low ranch house, and some kind of structure standing off by itself in one corner of the meadow. It looked like the bridge of a steamboat with a black smokestack.

A little-used wagon road led down the gentle slope through the sagebrush making for the place in a virtual beeline. Rickey had instantly descried the layout, and under his inspired leadership we swung along down that grade at a clip that called for some smart stepping on my part. Right there I decided I had the smartest, packingest, travelingest trio of burros in the business. As for Dan, he could, and did, outbray any politician that ever ran for office.

It was a miniature ranch we had come to, and it was deserted. It was a dream place—and still is, for me. "Oft' in the stilly night" I'm back there. I can hear the plaintive cry of the kildee running on his pipestem legs along the thin water-course in that little meadow, and often I bathe in the velvety softness of its warm spring and rinse my clothes and hang them to dry, and oh, how peaceful and sweet it all is with the doves cooing in the rocks nearby—"Cooie coo, coo coo!"

It didn't take me long to move into the ranch house, bag-gage and all. Devoid of doors and windows, the big main room was fresh and airy. I wished I owned the pretty little place. How busy I'd get making a real Garden of Eden of it! The surrounding terrain, its gentle slopes dotted with scrub piñon pines and junipers, all so peaceful and silent—what more could any man ask? What a spot for a prospector's honeymoon with his long-haired partner! Cooie coo, coo coo!

I decided to make a rice pudding on the old kitchen stove. I had all the makings—rice, sugar, salt, raisins, canned milk, and a whale of an appetite. One thing was dead sure—no matter how my pudding might turn out, it wouldn't be wasted. Down there in the meadow were three gourmets who knew good cooking when they sniffed it.

Things were coming along nicely. Pancakes were piling up on a warm plate on the back of the stove, bacon was siz-zling in the pan, teapot was steaming, and pudding was swelling and browning.

I stepped to the doorway on one of those inexplicable hunches—call them ESP or whatever, that often give a fellow pause—and was I in for a surprise! Someone was coming—white man or Indian—I couldn't tell. He was over a mile off, riding in a wagon drawn by two horses, or perhaps mules, moving leisurely at a walk. He was on a different road from the one by which I had come. It entered the bowl farther to the southwest where the encircling rim was broken by a narrow gap.

Well, whoever he might be, Indian or white, friend or foe, he would be just in time for supper. What luck that my pudding was turning out a grand success! I'd cook more bacon and cakes after my guest arrived.

I didn't have long to wait. The rig, a buckboard, pulled up in the yard close to the house, and a splendid span of mules stood heads erect while their driver tied their reins to the rim of a wheel. Could this be the owner of the place, and would he order me off? No matter what, I'd ask him to sup with me anyway.

We called out mutual greetings. His "Good evening" didn't sound quite so cordial as I should have liked. He came on, felt hat in hand, wiping his forehead with a blue bandanna. His shoulders were somewhat stooped, and his hair and mustache were a steel gray. As we shook hands, I knew that all was well by the firmness of his grip and the look in his keen blue eyes, somewhat cynical, quizzical, yet not entirely without warmth and amiability.

No softie was my guest, Daniel Webster Morgan, who introduced himself. He didn't rave over my supper, not even the rice pudding of which he had two good-sized helpings. He merely said, with a twinkle, that it was nice to eat out for a change. I'm sure that the old desert rat had me spotted for a rank tenderfoot, and he meant to maintain a certain distance between us till he had a better line on me. There was to be no snap judgment about taking me on as an accredited member of his profession. Well, and why not? I still had most of my illusions, whereas his had, no doubt, long since gone with the wind. Hard realities had become his daily fare. I really liked the man, and I believe that in his way he didn't dislike me. I enjoyed hearing him talk, and he doubtless appreciated a good listener. He appeared to be an "Appeal to Reason" devotee, the great class-strife-rousing sheet of that day, published at Girard, Kansas. I didn't care two cents about his socialism, one way or another, though I couldn't make sense out of his being so anti-private property on the one hand, and out looking for mines on the other.

I've forgotten what it was that I had said which drew a mild rebuke from him—or was it so mild?

"Young fellow," he retorted, "God Almighty gave you a set of brains, and, by God, he intended for you to use them!"

After all, isn't that exactly what Christ tried to convey in his parable of the three stewards and their talents? I thank Daniel Webster Morgan for having driven home to me that lesson out there on the little desert ranch that wonderful Indian summer evening.

All the while, I wasn't learning the one thing I was most interested in, namely, what had brought Morgan to that spot at that particular time? Whenever there seemed to be an opening for him to speak up on that point he managed to veer off on some other topic, such as Tom Paine, deceased, his for-all-time idol, or Eugene V. Debs, much alive at the time, his extravagantly admired hero of the labor front.

There just was no way to figure him out. Here he was, dead opposed to capitalism, and at the same time freely boasting of his friendship with a man like Daniel C. Jackling, the copper magnate.

Finally I came right out with it. I asked him point blank how he had happened to come there.

"Tell me," he countered, "what do you know about that old mill over there?"

"Not a thing," I replied. "I didn't even know it was a mill till I took a close look and saw all the machinery and things."

"Then you didn't come here to clean it up, did you?" he asked.

"I'm afraid I don't understand," I replied. "What do you mean?"

"Well," he said, "I'll take your word for it."

He went on to explain that the little old mill had run on ore from the New Pass mine which was situated in the hills above the ranch. The mine had been shut down a number of years back. The ranch and the mill belonged to a prominent cattleman named Frank Byers who lived in Dixie Valley across the range from New Pass.

By cleaning up the mill, Morgan had meant recovering any amalgam that leaked from the sluice boxes below the copper plates or elsewhere about the plant. He said it might take him a little time to locate what he called the main outlet, but that once it was found there ought to be a good stake in it. He said he had cleaned up old gold mills here and there, on and off, for a number of years and had done pretty well at it. He generously invited me to join him in this venture, offering to share the recoveries fifty-fifty with me.

I begged off with the excuse that I didn't believe I'd be any real help to him as I knew absolutely nothing about that kind of work, and besides, I wanted to prospect in the hills above.

Pretty good socialism, I thought. Here he was quite willing to divide not only his own wealth with me, but other peoples' too, for if the mill and ground belonged to Mr. Frank Byers, so also must the gold. Later I got out of Morgan that he had obtained Byers' permission to help himself to any amalgam he might find, so long as he didn't do any damage to the property.

Even with that assurance, the thing didn't appeal to me

at all. I feared it might be just a waste of time, not that time meant a great deal to me just then.

I was wrong again. Morgan worked there less than four days. He located the "main outlet" all right, and he took out something over two hundred dollars' worth of amalgam, as he roughly estimated it—a round lump, heavy as lead, the size of a tennis ball.

Half of that would have been mine had I accepted.

16

CHARLIE BRAY, A CORNISHMAN, delighted in telling stories about his countrymen, the Cousin Jacks. It wasn't that the stories themselves amounted to so much. It was the way he told them that made them so much fun to listen to.

I wish I could set down his "Cousin Jack Funeral" tale exactly as he related it, h'accent and h'all. It was about poor old Cousin Bill Polhemus who had given up the ghost at a ripe old age off in the hills where there was no preacher. His mates had built him a coffin, dug his grave, and one of their number, Cousin Pendry, had been drafted to say a few words in old Bill's behalf. So, as they all stood by, bareheaded, Pendry stepped forward.

"Boys," he began, "there's not much as h'I can say for h'our poor friend 'ere. 'Owever, h'Ill say this: 'E were a good miner, fair on timbers n'done a bit o'bossin'. Now let's h'all bow h'our eads while we give 'im three bells 'n lower the bloody bucket."

I also learned some quaint mining terms from Charlie Bray, for the Cornish have a word for it if it has anything to do with mining. I knew that each hole in a round of shots had its own specific name. I knew what a "lifter" was and a "breast hole," but it remained for Charlie Bray to enrich my vocabulary with "cundert-side-tosser," which one may rest assured is something very, very special in the way of a hole.

Little old Charlie was a first-rate watchman. He had spotted me from 'way up at the New Pass mine the minute I hove in sight on the hogback a mile or so below.

He was a Cousin Jack from 'way back, short and dumpy, and he put me in mind of an Airedale terrier, because he happened to be hard pressed for a shave. His face was all a'bristle with sandy gray stubble. Beneath it all, however, I detected a kindly spirit lurking behind those hazel eyes peering out at me from the depths of his shaggy countenance.

The mine, shut down and idle, was at the base of the big mountain Gilbert Joe had pointed out to me. The openings consisted of a series of tunnels at different levels, each with its waste dump hanging like a chin whisker at its mouth. There also was an incline shaft with gallows frame and hoist house. Mine buildings, shops, office, bunkhouses, and sheds were strung out both ways from that shaft.

The office was Bray's living quarters, all cozily equipped. It had a kitchen range, tables, chairs, cupboards, rugs, and against the back wall was a bunk in which a man could snugly ride out a blizzard on a cold winter's night. With such ideal bachelor's quarters, I didn't wonder that Charlie Bray fairly radiated contentment.

Actually, he wasn't a bachelor as I had thought. He had a wife and son in Austin whom he visited about once a month, weather permitting, and for that purpose he kept a team of gentle horses browsing around the mine until the snows drove them down on the flat. On each of his trips he came back from Austin loaded with all manner of good things to eat, which his wife had cooked for him. These included pasties, scones, poor man's pudding, saffron cake, and just about the entire gamut of cookery pleasing to the palate of a Cornishman.

Bray's salary, whatever it was, was just that much velvet. Everything was furnished to him free, except his food and clothes. His job had other perquisites of which, it struck me, he wasn't availing himself to the fullest. What an opportunity it offered for reading! Yet, old Charlie, like Daniel Webster Morgan, read the "Appeal to Reason" almost exclusively. Both men, I observed, referred endearingly to that hypnotic sheet simply as "The Appeal."

Charlie was greatly interested to learn from me that there was a kindred spirit in the vicinity and vowed he must drop down to the little ranch for a visit with Morgan. He asked me to stay for lunch, which consisted of tea, bread, cheese, and apple sauce. It was excellent, and it set me to wondering if there mightn't be something to socialism after all. Here were Morgan and Bray, as radical as they come yet not bad eggs at all. On the contrary, they were excellent company when practicing, rather than preaching, the tenets of their cult. I enjoyed the sharing.

Charlie had a mail-order fiddle and bow. He asked me if I played. I told him he'd laugh if he saw me playing a violin, because I held the instrument upside-down on my lap like a 'cello. He wouldn't let me back out. I positively must play. No, he couldn't play at all. He was just starting to take it up, practicing an hour a day out of a book.

"I want to hear how she sounds," he urged. "I paid thirty-two dollars for her—fiddle, bow, and box. She's pretty, ain't she? See that curly maple neck! Now go ahead. Maybe she ain't tuned right."

I really had no technique at all, but holding a violin the way I have described, it's easy to draw a big, round tone out of it, equal to anything Fritz Kreisler could dish up. I could play all the old favorites by ear—"Love's Old Sweet Song," "Silver Threads Among the Gold," and even classics, like "Meditation from Thais." The great Kreisler never had a more appreciative audience than I had in Charlie Bray. In fact, I was appreciating myself come to think of it. I was actually tone starved and needed no urging to keep a'going. Charlie wouldn't let me stop, and it was a good thing he didn't try to. However, the artist in me finally chose the peak moment of my triumph to bow out.

"I could listen to that all day," said Charlie, which proved that he was not hard to please, and so a bond was established between the genial Cornishman and myself for which I had reason to be grateful during the coming winter months.

With the fiddle back in its box, I finally was able to steer the conversation away from the subject of music and have Charlie Bray tell me something about the New Pass district. He had been there a good many years and had worked in the mine up to the time of its closing.

"Narrow veins, low grade," was how he summed it up. Still, he was convinced there was another mother vein, or lode, which had not yet been discovered around there.

"Have you any idea where it might be?" I asked, hopefully.

"It could be over in Bull Canyon," he replied. "I'm doing some work in there. It's over on the other side of the hill."

Then he told me about a man who had some claims about a mile from there, an old fellow I shall simply refer to as John.

"He's looking for a partner," Charlie said. I gathered from the way he spoke that what was wanted was someone who would put up the grub, powder, and other expenses, in addition to working on the ground.

"What do you think of his ground?" I asked. "Does it look good to you?"

"Not bad," he replied. Of course, here again, the rich float legend reared its alluring head. "You never can tell. That could be the very place. It wouldn't surprise me."

"What about this John?" I asked. "What's he like?"

"Seems like a sociable old fellow," Charlie replied. "I've only seen him a time or two. When he first came here he had a partner with a team of broncos, a fellow name of Evans. I understand they've split up, and Evans is going in for catching mustangs. He's no miner anyway—been a cowboy all his life."

"Well, doesn't he own a half interest in the claims?" I asked.

"Sure," Charlie replied, "but he offered to sell out to John for a hundred dollars."

"Might pay me to look into it," I said. "I'd like to get located somewhere for the winter. Who can tell? You might have me for a neighbor."

We sat for a while on the steps of the old office while Charlie Bray smoked his pipe and reeled off yarns about the early days of Austin. A peaceful, pleasant spot, New Pass, with its pine nut trees and water holes high above the surrounding desert. Off to the east were chains of slumbering hills, more country than ten men could prospect in a lifetime. There they were, practically coaxing to be prospected.

I got back to the little ranch in time to help Morgan get supper ready. It was to be his last night there. He said he was practically finished with his cleanup, with just a small area to be panned. He had saved, in addition to his amalgam, about fifty pounds of quicksilver which he had squeezed out in the process through a chamois skin.

Morgan listened as I told him about my visit with Charlie Bray and what he had told me about old John and his claims around the hill from the New Pass mine. I mentioned that

I was going to look up the old fellow and maybe tie up with him for the winter, if his setup struck me right.

"Seems to me I've heard about that old fellow," Morgan said, wryly. "If he's the same John I saw down around Searchlight a year or so ago he's the worst old crank and blowhard in the country. You're crazy if you pay a cent for an interest in the ground. Who ever heard of a prospector buying ground? Better make sure what his game is before you waste any time and money with him."

I found out later how right Morgan was. He invited me to pack my burros and go along with him. We'd find us a good lease—lots of good opportunities around the new districts—fellows you never hear about making big money right from the grass roots. And that was the truth. The records proved it. Maybe I should have taken him up. He knew prospecting and mining—a hard man to fool in the hills.

But I had gone hook, sinker, and all out for New Pass. I was sold on it, and it would have taken plenty to dissuade me.

A sense of loneliness possessed me as I watched Morgan drive away.

I never got around to asking old John if he had ever been at Searchlight. I couldn't believe this jovial old-timer with the pink cheeks and twinkling blue eyes, the ready smile, and ingratiating address, was the man Morgan had referred to as having such a vile disposition. This John was easygoing, heart o'gold, the ideal type to hole up with for the winter. He'd wear well, improve on acquaintance as the days rolled by.

Such was John in Act I, when he was enticing me into his web.

I found him in his cabin sewing a button on a woolen undershirt. The first thing I noticed about him was his low, receding forehead. He was exceptionally handsome. His hair was thick and snowy white. He had a neat white mustache free of any tobacco stain, being a non-smoker. His smile was uninhibited, for he had teeth to be proud of, seemingly flawless. I still feel it was only natural for me to have fallen for the old codger.

He had a dandy little cabin. It was solid, cozy, and clean, and it was furnished with all the comforts and conveniences a prospector could ask for, complete with tomcat. Woodchoppers had built the cabin for their own use when the New Pass mine was running. It was handy to a good little spring. All John had had to do on his arrival was move in.

He had six claims. They were called the Eagles.

"Good names for good claims," was how he put it. As I look back on it now, it was pretty good versification for an old duffer who could neither read nor write, not even so much as to sign his own name.

The Eagles started about a hundred yards back of the cabin and ran two abreast clear across the crest of the big hill which loomed so imposingly above. It was a steep climb to get up there. But John insisted on my seeing everything. It was remarkable how the old fellow rambled over those rugged slopes. He was about three times my age, and yet I really had to step to keep up with him. It was plain that he wanted me to buy out his partner Evans' half interest for one hundred dollars, just as Charlie Bray had said.

John's plan was to run a tunnel into the mountain on the chance, which he considered excellent, of cutting at depth some of the quartz veins that cropped higher up. It sounded to me like a good gamble at the time, but mining men that know their ABC's don't play it blind like that. John showed me a block of float, solid quartz, so big he couldn't even budge it. He claimed he had broken off a representative sample of it, had it assayed, and that it had run eighty dollars a ton in gold. Boy, if we could find the source of that boulder we'd be fixed! John was sure we could. He had it all doped out, just where to start tunneling, and exactly how far in we'd have to drive to cut the vein.

"I believe it'll make another Camp Bird," he declared, the reference being to a famous gold mine in his native state, Colorado.

So it came to pass that I bought Mr. Evans' half interest in the Eagles, paying that gentleman with my check for one hundred dollars. The next I heard about him was that he had gone to Rawhide and got himself killed in a dance hall there.

Now, what to do for a place to sleep. I couldn't move in with John. There wasn't an inch of space to spare in the cabin. I examined the ruin of what might once have served as a shelter for mules, just a few steps back of the cabin. It was roofless, and all that remained of it was a corner formed by two crumbling mud-and-brush walls. I fashioned a low platform of rocks and dirt, spread a deep cushion of rabbit brush over it, and laid my bed on top of that. With some scraps of canvas flap salvaged from the old mill, I rigged me up a lean-to roof. John pronounced it a good job and predicted I'd sleep like a log there because, to quote him, I was "as hearty as a hog." In truth, no one ever slept more soundly than I did all through the following winter, even though many a morning I shook a foot of snow off my bed-canvas on arising. It was an ideal bedroom for a fresh-air fiend.

In a few days we were ready to start operations. Charlie Bray brought us a bill of goods from Austin. The kind little Cornishman did all our hauling and never a penny would he accept for his trouble. I placed a standing order for ten pounds of pork sausage from Johnny Murphy's butcher shop and a gallon of eight-year-old Belmont whisky, which cost five dollars at Cooper's saloon and which was drawn right out of the barrel as shipped from a bonded warehouse in Kentucky. We could always induce Charlie to join us in a hot toddy. Just one—that was all he'd accept. John and I had one every evening after we came down off the hill cold, tired, and dirty. A jigger of Belmont in a cup with a spoonful of sugar, then poured full with hot water, made the world look brighter to me even after my old partner and I had ceased to be on speaking terms.

Sausage grease poured over sourdough hotcakes, a dab of sausage, and plenty of coffee, was our regulation breakfast, and mighty good did it taste. John always cooked it, and a few raps on a tin pan warned me it was nearly ready. I washed inside, wiping on our common towel which was laundered every Sunday at the little spring. I always said good morning when I entered the cabin and in return got a muffled grunt from the old chap.

The break between us came in the first month of our partnership. We had started our tunnel, and when we got under cover the bedrock was so hard that we couldn't make so much as a foot a day. Drill bits broke right and left. There was something radically wrong with John's tempering technique. How I wished for Uncle Jake! John never deviated from his fixed, erroneous method. All he would let me do in our blacksmith shop was crank the blower. Finally I asked him to let me have a try at it. He sulked and muttered under his breath. I still wanted him to dress the steel. His bits were fair, better at least than I could turn out. To my delight I found that I could draw down Uncle Jake's pretty straw color just as I had seen him do it by dipping the hot bits briefly in the water tub.

Breakages now dropped to a minimum. John showed that he felt he had been humiliated. He sulked and wouldn't answer when I spoke to him. I tried in vain to convince him that all I cared about was our common good. It only made matters worse. He remained adamant.

Still, that wasn't the worst. After we had pounded away two and sometimes three days drilling a round of holes, John invariably took it upon himself to do the loading. He was so awkward about it that it was disheartening and dangerous to stand by while he was at it. Once drilled, a hole is a thing of value. I don't know how many times John broke the tamping stick after it had become jammed in a hole. As there was no way of extracting the broken end, it simply meant good-by hole and whatever powder was loaded into it. Then a duplicate had to be drilled alongside making sure to point it so as not to impinge on the original and possibly set it off.

Then we had an epidemic of missed holes. Something would go haywire during the loading. Old John always used his teeth to crimp the blasting cap on the fuse. Those caps, charged with fulminate of mercury, were so sensitive that even just jarring one could set it off, and a misbite was all it would have taken to blow off the top of John's head.

One afternoon at the end of our shift we stood outside the tunnel to count as the blasts went off. Again a hole had missed. I made up my mind that the very next time it happened I would have a showdown with John. We went down to the cabin, had our toddy, ate our supper in silence, and afterwards I settled down as usual to read by the light of the candle flickering on the table. What ailed the poor fellow anyway? Was it just hypersensitiveness or the Oriental's aversion to losing face? My taking over the steel tempering had put a deep scar in the shell of his pride. Also, I sensed that he resented my resorting to reading a book when my attempts to engage him in conversation ended in failure. Here's about the way they went:

"Were you born in Colorado, John?"

Slight hesitation, business of stroking cat in double time. "Yes," grudgingly.

"What place in Colorado?"

"Rifle." Business of shifting foot in irritation.

"Live there till you left Colorado?"

"No." Business of addressing cat. "There, Tommy, nice Tommy."

"Do you plan to go back there after we've struck it here?"

Business of pretending not to have heard, pushing cat off his lap, clicking his tongue, and bending over to stroke cat's arched back. Prolonged silence.

"Well, guess I'll turn in." Put away my book, push back chair, stretch, yawn. "Good night, John."

"Good night."

There was a peculiar side light to the situation. Let Charlie Bray, or, as once happened, Frank Byers drop in on us, and John's attitude toward me in their presence would miraculously change to one of almost excessive affability. He would turn to me for corroboration of this and that and address his conversation, his jokes, and stories as much to me as to them. The first time that happened I came near hugging him on the spot, thinking that at last the clouds had all rolled by. Then, the minute we were alone again John froze up tight, and I was thoroughly deflated.

The hole that had missed fire that afternoon had been partly wrecked by the blasts around it. Most of it was still intact and had the end of a stick of 40 per cent powder hanging out of it. All it would have needed was a fresh detonator on a short fuse and it could still have been set off and saved. Instead, however, John commenced picking around it with the point of his candlestick, and the result was that the paper wrapping, and then the powder itself, caught fire from the flame of his candle. I yelled at John to run, and I rushed to get out of there alive expecting at every instant to be blown out through the mouth of the tunnel by the concussion of a ground-shaking blast. John, however, stuck to what he evidently regarded as his post and watched the powder burn till the stench drove him out. No doubt what had saved his life was the fact that he had neglected to insert a blasting cap in his primer when he loaded the hole.

Now I was primed for him when he emerged from the scene of his near demise. I was in a state of high excitement mingled with intense relief that I didn't have an undertaker's job on my hands. Heatedly I proclaimed that I was taking over the loading from then on, that I was fed up with missed holes, that he, John, could continue to thaw out the powder and cut the fuse, but that I would crimp on the caps, using the regular crimping tool and not my teeth, and, finally, that I was going to spit the fuses in future.

Now, all this sounds pretty rotten of me, I know, and so it was. If poor old John were here I'd be glad to give him space to tell his side of the matter. Maybe he could pin most of the fault on me. As we descended the hill on our trail through four feet of snow I cooled off and felt sorry, what with Christmas only a week off. We were both loaded down with dull drills and picks, John coming along behind me. I knew he wouldn't bash in my cranium with a drill, that he was as harmless as Tommy, the cat, for all of his former bluster and bragging about his marksmanship with a pistol. Now for the first time in many a day he was following me in absolute silence entirely devoid of the usual curses which I could always distinctly hear, even though they were muttered under his breath. He was really crushed for the time being, wouldn't take a toddy when we got back to the cabin, and precious little did I enjoy mine.

Next morning when we arrived at the tunnel, John suddenly found his tongue.

"Well, boss," he bellowed, "what are my orders for today?"

"Listen, John," I said, "nobody's boss around here. If my plan doesn't work, we'll try another. That's fair enough, isn't it?"

Under the new arrangement things ran along more smoothly than before. Once again John began cursing sweetly and purringly as we worked side by side, and he started calling someone the most fearful names, *sotto voce*, and I knew the old boy was back to normal again.

17

THE LATCH STRING WAS ALWAYS OUT for me at Charlie Bray's, and for John too, for that matter. I often walked over there for an evening of sociability and fiddle practice, but John always stayed home with nothing to do but hold Tommy the cat on his lap. Evans had told me that the poor old fellow could neither read nor write and signed his name with a cross which had to be witnessed. I could have taught him that winter—at least got him started—and would have been only too happy to do it, but I wasn't supposed to know about that deficiency of his, which was just another sheet of ice between us that I couldn't break. What does a man think of, I wondered, shut off by himself that way, shielding his secret self with a thin make-believe of know-it-all?

Two nights before Christmas I wandered over to Charlie Bray's through the snow. The walk along the dead-silent hills all a'glisten in the starlight was a joy. Charlie said he was going home for Christmas, leaving the next day, and he said he'd be glad to take John and me along. I accepted with enthusiasm and promised to do my best to talk John into going. John promptly declined. I knew it was because he didn't have any money to pay his hotel and other expenses in Austin.

"Look here, John," I said, "if you're a little shy of cash for the trip I'll lend you some and you can pay me back after we've struck it. How about it?"

He lied bravely, said he had plenty of money but didn't care to make the trip "nohow."

"Well, then I won't go either," I said.

"You don't need to stay on account of me," he said. "I'll make out same's ever."

"Come to think of it I can't go anyway," I said. "I haven't got a decent pair of pants to wear." We had just finished breakfast and Charlie Bray was due any minute. I had just said it for an excuse. My old pants wouldn't have deterred me. It was the thought of leaving the old cuss there all alone at Christmas when everybody else was having a high old time.

John fished under his bed and dragged out an old valise from which he took a pair of trousers—very good-looking gray ones.

"Here," he said, "wear these. They'll just about fit you. They're a mite too big for me anyway."

What was I to do? My excuse hadn't gone over. It was all too clear that he wanted me to go—for my sake, or for his? There was just no deciphering him.

Austin! Such a time as I had there! What a Christmas! There'll never be another like it—not for me at least.

Charlie Bray took me right to his home. I had a fine hot bath, after which I dressed up in John's trousers and then sat down to a dinner in which Mrs. Bray's pasties were the chef-d'œuvre. That marvelous Cornish repast will always occupy a special niche in my memory.

'Twas Christmas Eve. Charlie was anxious for us to get going. He wanted to show me the sights and bright lights.

For a starter, we visited Cooper's saloon. We got no farther that night.

We had a drink at the bar where I was introduced to Mr. Cooper. Later we were joined by the district attorney and another man who was of most distinguished appearance, namely, Doctor Mann. The latter was the only man I had ever met that was not only a practicing physician and surgeon but a lawyer as well. He was a man of culture, a thinker, and a deist.

In the rear of the barroom a chap was playing softly and exquisitely on an upright piano. Charlie Bray informed me that he was the "professor" from Bull Con Alice's parlor house. He didn't look the part, and his playing was anything but honky-tonk.

"Ah," Charlie Bray said to Cooper for all to hear, "you ought to hear this young fellow play the violin!" Golly, what did he want to bring that up for? I thought.

"Why say," said Cooper, "I've got a violin back there in the closet. I let a fellow have twenty dollars on it about a year ago. He left the country and I've never heard of him since. Wait a second while I get it."

I was surprised when he came back with a real professional steel case, leather bound. He laid it on the bar and opened it while the crowd, which was getting bigger by the minute, gathered around to watch. Cooper lifted out the violin and handed it over to me.

"Here," he said, "see what you think of it." There were two bows in the case. He took one out and passed it to me. The E string was broken, but it was of double length; I drew it down and went over to the piano to tune up.

The professor's name—well, suffice it that he was known as "Red." He seemed very glad to have me join him and obligingly sounded his A on the piano for me. The district attorney had followed me. He seemed to be a sort of master-of-ceremonies that evening.

"Can you give us 'Schubert's Serenade'?" he asked.

Red said, "Sure," and he looked up at me inquiringly as he played the opening chords.

I fell in with the melody, and we were off as though we had been playing together for years.

Only twenty dollars for that violin, and the poor devil had never come back to redeem it! It practically played itself, and next to a genuine Strad, on which I used to play at Castle Point when the Stevens family lived there, it was far and away the best instrument I had ever gotten hold of. It was a Ruschenberg, made in Denver.

Everything came to a standstill while we played. New arrivals coming in at the door walked on tiptoe when they were given the hush sign. Red's accompaniment was masterful and at all times subordinated to the solo instrument. What a marvelous barroom audience we had—every man there a music-lover! No one seemed to see anything strange about my way of holding the violin.

Now to take stock of who all were there. Besides those already named there was venerable old Judge Weller, bank-president Joe Miller, Billie Easton, who owned the International Hotel (which dismantled structure had been moved to Austin from Virginia City), Charlie Littrell, the post-master, Bar Francis, the tamer of wild horses and sheriff-to-be, George Watt, handsomest man in Nevada and head of the big livestock company. Also present were miners, prospectors, cattlemen, cowboys, businessmen, stage-drivers, horse-shoers, and others, including mere hangers-on.

When the serenade was over, the applause was loud and long. I wondered what Doctor Mann really thought of the performance. He came forward and very deferentially asked if we would play the "Intermezzo" from *Cavalieria Rusticana*. A real gentleman! He hadn't asked if we *could*—he had used the more gracious *would*. As for Red and me, it was both. It's an easy one to play. I doubt if the famous aria had ever had a finer rendition—in Cooper's saloon, that is.

Naturally we didn't play continuously all through that marvelous impromptu Christmas party. After all, it wasn't a concert. Lots of the guests volunteered to treat Red and me to drinks. To my surprise, I found that Red was a teetotaler and would take nothing but mineral water. As I had no stomach for after-dinner drinking, I each time had the same. As a result, the orchestra remained plumb sober, while Cooper and his bartender had their hands full pouring out the orders that were pouring in on them. The district attorney was busy varying the acts. Skinny Williams, who only sang at his own request, the trick being to induce him to cease and desist, was at his best, that is to say worst, in his offering of a heartrending ballad, which, however, gained him tumultuous applause mingled with peals of laughter. The district attorney, not to be outdone, delivered a timely little dissertation, everyone according him respectful attention, though the import of his remarks was somewhat crepuscular.

It was an evening of gross profit for host Cooper.

After midnight two ladies from opposite ends of town arrived on the scene within a few minutes of each other, both definitely uninvited, unexpected, and unwelcome.

The first accosted the district attorney and pulled him out after her into the night. Poor man, he had a job of explaining on his hands. The Christmas-tree party which his wife had arranged for the members of her church guild, the minister, and his wife, had been obliged to struggle along as best it could without its male host.

The other lady made a more sedate, though equally dramatic entrance. In her sumptuous white furs, I at first took her for some famous diva, which would have been quite in keeping with the fact that she held a lighted cigarette in her bejeweled hand. In those days only actresses and such used the weed in public. Strange that the men kept their hats on in such a regal presence, I thought. The only man in the place who seemed to be at all awed was Red. Her highness made straight for the poor devil, who cowered on his stool like a dog that fears its master's lash.

"What are you doing here, you red-headed son of a bitch?" she screamed.

Red raised his hands in self-protection, against the onslaught he regarded as imminent, and kept cringing away from her.

"Listen, let me explain, will you?" he kept repeating, frantically trying to interrupt her tirade.

"Explain be goddamned!" she yelled. "You've loused up my Christmas Eve party! That's what you've done, you (unprintable), you!"

"Listen, Alice," Red finally managed to say. "I've told you I'd come back if you'd fire Genevieve."

"Say, just who do you think you are, running my house?" she cried. "I'd look pretty, wouldn't I, taking orders from a half-assed ivory-tickler!"

Just how it all ended I don't know. Charlie Bray took me home with him and fixed up a bed for me in his parlor. The best I could do was get in an odd wink or two here and there, for I found I wasn't house-broke any more. I needed the outdoor oxygen, and how!

Christmas afternoon Charlie Littrell had me up to his house for a bit of cheer, and I met his wife and two beautiful daughters. They had heard about me through their friends the Keoughs, up the river, and it made me wish I were going there instead of back to New Pass and old John on the morrow.

A big turkey dinner at the Bray's ended the festivities. We went to the Episcopal church that evening, and I recognized several members of the congregation. I felt sure I had seen some of them before, somewhere, especially the district attorney, who was one of the alms-plate passers. Everything was sweetness and light with him and his handsome wife. They held the same hymnal as they sang. The Littrell girls looked particularly stunning. I expected to hear the minister allude in his sermon to the evils of drink. But he completely fooled me.

Back at New Pass we fell into the same old routine. As for old John and me, our relations didn't improve one iota. And neither did our tunnel. I had no way of telling which way it was headed, because John had changed its course a dozen times to follow this seam or that fault plane, and neither of us possessed a compass. It wouldn't have surprised me a bit if with any round of shots we had broken through to daylight, back in the outside world where we had started. Not a sign of encouragement had we encountered in the hundred feet or more of work we had done.

By the first of May I had drawn my Tonopah bank account right down to the quick.

It was a beautiful day. John was doing his usual housework, washing, and mending. I went down to the little ranch, rounded up Dan, Rickey, and Old Gal, and drove them up to the cabin. John stood in his doorway with a decidedly forced smile on his face.

"Well, what's this?" he asked, shakily.

"John," I replied, "I'm pulling out. You can have my interest in the Eagles. I'll send you a quitclaim deed. Good luck! I hope you strike it."

He tried to say something, swallowed hard, but finally gave up. I rolled up my few belongings in my bed, lashed it snugly to Rickey's back, and steered for Charlie Bray's where the rest of my things were stored.

The last I saw of John he had his blue bandanna in his hand.

18

I WAS LIVING HIGH, literally, 'way up above timberline, with ten thousand feet of rough and rugged elevation under my feet. I was wearing a copper badge depicting a pine tree flanked by the awesome letters "U" and "S."

I had a powerful horse to ride, a beast with a diabolical disposition whose very name, Ravenswood, had the ring of doom about it. On the other hand, there was my reliable old Dan, every bit as stout-hearted, but with an angelic disposition, faithfully trudging along behind me, his back weighted down with my bed, pots, pans, pick, shovel, axe, mortar and pestle, blowpipe, acid, blank location notices, extra duds, soap, towel, and grub.

Rickey and Old Gal? Ah yes, they were taking it easy, rusticating on the Big Creek ranch, four thousand feet closer to sea level, in an alpine setting where a wild, blustering stream came dashing down out of the snowbanks high above, through the steep canyon, only to find itself trapped in a maze of dams, ditches, and gates that told it whither to run, and how, over the far-flung grass meadows.

I was now what you might call a subsidized prospector. The Toiyabe Range, from Austin to Arc Dome, was mine to search for gold, silver, copper, lead, zinc, and any other metals of value, to hunt and fish, and to enjoy in all its aspects for the whole summer. And for this I was being paid a hundred dollars a month by the long-suffering taxpayers of the United States of America.

On the side, I was supposed to be a kind of honorary sheepherder, that is, ride herd on the actual sheepherders, see that they kept up high in the rocks where they belonged and kept their destructive bands off the cattle ranges down below. In short, I was an embryo forest ranger, a guard, to be exact, and ex-officio game warden, on the Toiyabe National Forest.

Of course, as an official of the Forestry Service I was estopped from locating any mineral claims on a national reserve, but just let me find a rich outcrop and see how fast my resignation would be in and my monuments up. Sound like a shady deal? Well, actually, it wasn't at all. Only such time as would otherwise be spent in complete idleness would be allocated to prospecting, fishing, sage hen hunting, and such. Besides, it was all understood beforehand, at the outset. I had served fair warning of my intentions. How had all this come to pass?

They were trying to stir up a boom in some volcanic hills lying to the west of Austin a matter of twenty miles or so. The place was named Skookum, which is a Paiute name meaning skookum, for all I could ascertain then. But "skookum" in colloquial jargon means "mighty good," I have since found out.

Skookum boasted a population of about fifty boosters and road-running prospectors. The only structure in the camp that didn't have a dirt floor was the saloon. I came by there on my way out from New Pass and stopped to look the district over but soon decided to move on. On my last night there I met a man in the saloon, an old-time resident of Austin. He said he understood that the forest supervisor, a young man named Benedict, was about to put on some extra guards for duty on the sheep ranges, and he suggested that I have a talk with him. It sounded good to me; it was becoming imperative that I get my name inscribed on some sort of payroll in order to relieve the stringency of my financial state—an empty pocketbook.

Benedict was friendly, modest, and very much the gentleman. I told him my story, ulterior motives and all, and on the payroll I went. But I must have a horse, and a good one, before going to work. At first it seemed like poor business to invest the price of a horse in any job, but on second thought I decided that I probably could sell the animal when the job was over and so get a good part of my money back. So I started right in making inquiries. One of the first persons I spoke to said he had just the horse for me, a chestnut gelding sixteen hands high, weighing around fourteen hundred, rangy, tough, and fourteen years old.

"He's fast and furious," the young man said, "but handle him right and you'll have no trouble with him. He kicks, but you can watch out for that. I'll sell him for fifty dollars."

I asked him if he'd trust me till I got my first check from Uncle Sam.

"Yes," he replied, "but if you take him you'll have to keep him and pay me whether you like him or not—no turning him back to me."

The horse was on a ranch thirty miles north of Austin. We drove out in the young man's spring wagon, and I took my saddle along in case I bought him.

He looked like a lot of horse to get for fifty dollars but he had a surly look in his eyes. I wondered if I could handle him. I noted that he had a far-from-ingratiating mannerism with his tail. Even when standing still, he'd give it a petulant whisk, and when he trotted, snorting, around the corral, he carried it arched menacingly. Of course there was something fishy about him. No one had to tell me that. Still, there was no doubt that he was sound as a dollar in wind and limb. With fingers crossed, I bought Ravenswood.

In my flimsy old army saddle I little realized that I was astride an animal that the best of broncho busters would find it anything but child's play to stay aboard. Either I had fooled him with my audacity, or else the old scoundrel was deliberately deceiving me for future delivery into the ether. Just hold his head up, I had been cautioned. When we got down on the flat and the road stretched ahead straight and level I let him run a good mile, and when I pulled him up he fought for more of the same.

"What's the catch?" Benedict asked. He seemed to think I had struck a wonderful bargain. So did Riley Patton, the ranger with whom I was sent out on my maiden trip over the range.

Twenty bands of sheep were entering the forest reserve, twenty-five hundred head to the band, ewes and wethers, to spend the next three months grazing on the high mountain herbage of the Toiyabes, fattening on the succulent wild sunflower and the sweet bunch grass growing among the rocks.

So now I was to find out about sheepherders. Perhaps I'd learn why that term of contempt had supplanted the noble, poetical designation *shepherd*. Could be the cattlemen were to blame. To them, sheep are nothing but range-destroying vermin, and the sorry crew that tend them are anything but romantic.

I must admit there was little about the first sheepherder I met face to face that suggested the remotest kinship with the Shepherd kings, the Hyksos, of biblical days. Then, what was there about this sturdy fellow that seemed to compel my admiration? Well, it was because dirty, unkempt, unshaved as he was, understanding hardly a word of English, as out of touch with world affairs, almost as if he were on the moon, he definitely was an expert in his own field, one of which I was abysmally ignorant. To me every one of the baa-ing, bleating, stupid creatures that he watched over looked exactly like the next one, only more so, but not to him. He knew them all apart, like so many people. There was no end to what he would continue to learn about them, even though he spent the rest of his days working with them and observing their insane antics. "Sheepcraft," if there is such a word, ran in his veins, handed down from father to son through the centuries in the Basque country on both sides of the Pyrenees. This one happened to be a Spanish Basque. Later I would meet French Basques whom, as a rule, I found more affable. Besides Spanish or French, as the case might be, the herders all spoke the Basque language of mysterious origin.

This young Spanish Basque sheepherder, as I saw him that day, was a far more important member of society than I. At the moment his job was yielding him only forty dollars a month and found. But it would be well to keep an eye on him. In another season or two he might have a thousand ewes of his own. What, on forty dollars a month? Heavens, no. He'd borrow the money to buy them, like as not from old Billy Sciuchetti, who knew sheep and men and was living in retired opulence in Austin. That's how the Bordas, Ypparraguires, Arenas, Laxagues, Alustizas, and the rest of the big Basque sheepmen had worked it. They made their fortunes the hardest of ways, then sold out, settled down to a life of ease while their offspring went to college and earned sheepskins of a different texture and were assimilated and contributed their ruggedness of body and spirit to America's lifestream.

Riley Patton, my mentor, was a little fellow physically, smiling and full of fun, but definitely no man to trifle with. He had been up against the bolos of the Philippinos and had a zealot's regard for authority. He was neither "sheep" nor "cattle." That's what made him a good, fair ranger on a grazing reserve, such as the Toiyabe.

I rode up to the head of Washington Canyon with him. The peaks before us looked like Switzerland. Big snowbanks still clung to their northern slopes. Halfway up the almost perpendicular face of the mountain that loomed ahead I saw what looked like a great grayish sail, rippling in the breeze. It was a band of sheep being pushed up, inch by inch as it seemed, the helmsman being the herder, and the wind the incredible performance of his dogs, three of them, warping the big sail thus and so as willed their master by merely signalling with his arm. Twenty-five hundred sheep completely cowed and controlled by three medium-sized, amazing dogs!

Riley, in the lead, pulled up for a word with the herder. He spoke to him in English, but all he got in response was the old reliable, "No sabe." Then Riley suddenly switched to Spanish, taking the fellow by surprise and cutting his subterfuge right out from under him. He commenced to "sabe" plenty and in English what's more. Riley gave him a few pointers on range regulations. He was at all times to keep above the red markers he would see at intervals. Being an alien, he was to abstain from fishing unless he felt disposed to pay fifty dollars for a non-citizen license. Of course he would shoot no deer, bighorn, grouse, sage hen, or quail, and would use his rifle solely for coyotes and catamounts, sometimes known as mountain lions.

By noon we were on top of the range and had caught up with another band which was at rest in the heat of the day. When the sun beats down straight the sheep huddle in whatever patches of shade they can find. The herder then unpacks his burro and cooks his noonday meal, which is the same from day to day, namely, strips of mutton in his frying pan with a can of tomatoes, an inordinate quantity of garlic, and a terrific dousing of black pepper. Meanwhile, a pot of villainously strong tea is brewing, and, when all is ready, he brings forth a round loaf of bread from his pack, baked in loaves two feet in diameter by the camp tenders who follow the bands with provisions and stay down in the canyons with their pack trains. The herder holds the loaf under his arm while he cuts off thick slices with his sharp carving knife. That rich sourdough bread and tea with sugar in it is a marvelous meal in itself.

At dusk the sheep bed down for the night. It is then that the herder cooks some more of the same for his supper, just enough so there'll be a little left over for his dogs. He must keep them on edge so that they'll nip at the sheep's legs while working them. It keeps the sheep afraid of them. At times a dog will run over the tightly jammed backs of the sheep, nipping them en route, much like a lumberjack at work on a log jam. Sheep dogs must not be overfed.

I had a good many meals with the herders that summer, having soon become inured to their manner of living. In one instance, at least, I found there was no myth about their letting the dogs wash the frying pan after supper. I got around that by eating just bread and tea for breakfast the next morning.

At night I would crawl in with my host, and we would both sleep the sleep of the just—and dirty. In a week I'd be as dirty as the best of 'em, only I'd contrive to get a bath and a change of underwear now and then, whereas those hardened pros continued to cake up in good shape, taking it out in dreaming of the hot bath they'd take at a cost of fifty cents in the barbershop tub as soon as they got to town to celebrate the season's end.

One night I supped with a quite superior French Basque. He was very fastidious. His dishes were clean, as nearly as I could determine by applying the smell test and feeling them over for dried food particles and grease. Monsieur made me feel most welcome and professed himself highly honored to have me as his guest. While I was at it, I worked him for a French lesson. He was delighted. As a special mark of his esteem for me he brought out a brick of exceptional cheese for our dessert, giving me a liberal slab which I spread on my bread. I vowed that never had I tasted its equal. Leave it to a Frenchman, I remarked, to serve *fromage* like that! Ah, but I must have some more, *mais oui*? Well, just *un petit, merci*, but that definitely would be all. Man alive, I could easily have devoured his whole visible supply of the stuff!

In due season we retired. Even his bed seemed rather less dingy than those I had been sharing with some of his colleagues. Naturally I had breakfast with Pierre. I wondered if he was going to trot out some more of that ambrosial cheese.

He did, but actually it could have trotted out by itself without his assistance. By the light of day I saw what gave it that smooth, creamy texture. It was alive with skippers! When my poor stomach stopped looping the loop I explained to Pierre that cheese, be it ever so delectable, was something I never could eat for breakfast.

Riley Patton and I passed four more bands on the way to their respective ranges on that first day's patrolling of my territory. It was a vast region, and there were some precipitous gaps that made hard going for the sheep and called for everything the herders had to offer in the way of ingenuity. More than once I saw a ewe drop a lamb on the trail though the lambing season had long been past. The procession could not be held up for a late-born, helpless lamblet. The herder simply picked it up by the hind legs and bashed it against the rocks, flinging it away and prodding the baa-ing ewe onward with his stick.

The next day, along about sundown, Riley and I wound up at the head of Reese River, where Ranger Archie Bell had a permanent summer camp.

Archie, born and raised on his father's ranch in the very shadow of Arc Dome, was an all-round buckaroo and, like Charlie Keough, he had graduated from the State University. Archie, who liked to do things in style, had brought a big string of horses with him. There were lots more of them down on the T. J. Bell ranch, which took in a long stretch of the finest, loveliest part of Reese River.

We supped that night out of three big Dutch ovens which yielded biscuits, sage hen, frijoles, respectively.

The new-born river, fresh out of the snowbanks, rushed by the camp with a tumult which lulled me to sleep about as soon as I had gotten settled in the bed Archie improvised for me, while Riley and he shared his own.

Next morning I was awakened by something wet and cold flapping in my face. There stood Riley, grinning down at me. He had caught a fine trout and was dangling it, still fast to the hook, so as to give me the benefit of its frantic efforts to free itself. There was no further delay about my getting up. When next I saw Mr. Fish he was sizzling in the pan alongside two of his mates. At any altitude a breakfast of trout, flapjacks, and coffee is well worth being fish-tailed out of bed for.

We had gone out there without pack outfits since the trip was just a trial spin for me. I was to go back with Riley, pack a ranger's outfit on my Dan, and strike out for myself. I had a fair general idea of what it was all about.

Archie Bell had begged Riley to let me take over in his place right then, for a few days, while he went down to

Golden to arrest a man. There had been a destructive brush fire in upper Cloverdale Canyon. Word had reached Archie that the man who had set the fire was hanging around Golden and had bragged that he'd never be taken alive by any forest ranger that might try to arrest him. Riley was all attention while Archie spoke.

"Can't let anybody get away with that kind of talk," Archie concluded. "Bad thing for the service."

"You're right," said Riley, "but you don't have to go. The fellow's in jail right now."

"You don't say!" Archie exclaimed. "Who arrested him?"

"Somebody Benny (Benedict) deputized down there," Riley replied.

"Well, whoever it was did a good job," Archie said. "He was a bad customer. I'm mighty glad it's over and nobody got hurt."

We shook hands with Archie and started back for Austin. About noon we were up above Ophir. We dropped down off the range, and where should we end up an hour or so later but on the Keough ranch!

The family were all at home. They did their best to have us stay there that night, but I was under orders to return to Austin without delay, and Riley had a special commission to attend to before going back.

Mrs. Keough and pretty little Miss Inez set a nice lunch for us. Before long I was on Ravenswood riding down the river by myself. I reached Austin by noon the next day. I couldn't enlighten Benedict about Riley's activities other than that he had told me he expected to clean up the business in hand in two or three days.

It turned out that Riley had ridden to the Cloverdale ranch that night and early the next morning he had gone up to Golden, arrested the fire-bug, the would-be-ranger-killer, lugged him to Manhattan where he was jailed awaiting the arrival of the federal marshal who would see that he got what was coming to him.

The next time Archie Bell saw Riley he called him everything he could think of.

"You little so-and-so!" he said, "if anything had happened to you, it would have been my fault."

Which only served to widen Riley's grin.

There's a little family plot on a knoll near the upper end of the Bell ranch on Reese River. There's where they laid Archie who died of an infection a few years after these events took place. In him I lost a sincerely treasured friend, but there I know he is content to lie, while the river glides noiselessly by, and the lowing of cattle in the distant canyons mingles faintly with the saucy cry of the bluejays in the nearer junipers.

19

THE NEXT THREE MONTHS as I look back on them were nothing but one glorious vacation with pay. With Ravenswood and Dan, I shuttled between the Big Creek ranch at one end of my range, and Archie Bell's camp at Arc Dome on the other.

Up there in the mountains Ravenswood became a veritable pet. I could freely walk around his heels, mount him from either side, and even stand up in the saddle to tack a notice on a tree. He was indeed a mountain horse as the young man from whom I bought him had said. The mountains had been his home till, when he was ten years old, his free life in them had been cruelly interrupted by his capture and subsequent castration and "busting." He would have been better off had he been shot instead, and maybe in his equine way that is what he felt about it.

Often I dropped into this or that canyon and in no time at

all I'd have half a dozen splendid trout, which I sometimes gave to the sheepherders who were profuse in their thanks for them.

I found some of the herders good company to sit and chat with on occasion. John Laxague and I became first-rate friends. He branched out for himself that fall, sent to the old country for his fiancée, and on the night of his wedding he gave a big banquet at the International Hotel in Austin at which Riley Patton and I were guests. The hall was filled with Basques. John insisted that I make a speech. It was an easy assignment. The gallons of red wine they had drunk, coupled with their limited comprehension of the English language, presented an opportunity of which I took every unfair advantage. What they got was words, big fat ones, and gestures, the one as meaningless as the other. It went over big. John and his healthy, rosy bride beamed delightedly.

My well-tailored, olive-green uniform enabled me to put up a fairly presentable appearance at such affairs as the all-night ranch dances in Smoky Valley which brought together all the cowboy sons-of-ranchers and schoolma'ams from distances up to and more than a hundred miles away. Many were the maidens who came to teach and remained to wed some eligible cattleman's heir apparent. Judging from what I saw of them, the boys could have done lots worse—the girls ditto, I thought.

I heard that some honest-to-God prospecting was going on around the head of Clear Creek. A man named Hales had a fair showing in a tunnel he was running by himself. He had piled up a few tons of gold ore that was rich enough to sack and ship even from that inaccessible location where pack trains would have to be employed. Close by, two partners, Simmons and Rolles, were working in an open cut on a strong dike. I got there just in time one day, after they had blasted to a fracture. The whole face of the cut was splotched with free gold. Simmons, an erratic and excitable sort anyway, went completely beside himself. He wondered if he was just seeing things. Rolles, his partner, was just the opposite, cool and equable. Simmons wanted to rip into the showing without an instant's delay. Rolles was for leaving it in *status quo* and for seeing what kind of deal they could make on it for cash. In the end Simmons had his way. The spectacular showing vanished with the next round of shots. It was a case of beauty being literally only skin deep. Not so much as a sack of ore did they realize from what the moment before had seemed to hold such thrilling promise. They put down a forty-foot shaft along the crack. No luck! Nature had played a mean trick on them.

Up in Broad Canyon four men were taking out better than daywages on a placer claim, using a hand rocker. Down in Ophir Canyon the excellent showing of the Murphy mine had been cut off slick and clean by a fault. It would be worth a fortune to anyone lucky enough to pick up its extension.

George Gooding, the Clear Creek rancher, offered me the use of a big easy-riding jack. "Try him out for a couple of weeks," he urged. "Turn your Ravenswood horse out in my pasture. Give him a rest. He deserves it."

It seemed like a good idea, and I was sure that Tony, the jack, would get along perfectly with my Dan, and so he did. I rigged a breeching on my saddle, and now I could ride straight down a mountain if need be. Tony was a marvel, and I was guilty of coveting my neighbor's ass—Gooding's, that is, but that good neighbor informed me in no uncertain terms that Tony was not for sale.

I rode Tony to Austin, where I was to take the civil service examination for forest ranger. I put Tony and Dan in John Recend's corral.

Twenty-six candidates presented themselves for the two-day test. We all went up to the courthouse and sat in a big room. Examination papers were passed out to us, and it took me over four hours to answer the questions in writing, such as, "Name the different types of forest fires. How does one combat each?" There were questions about range conservation, erosion, reforestation, contamination, forest regulations, trailmaking, range rights, free-use permits, mineral rights, eminent domain, detainer, fish-and-game open seasons, patrol, care of horses, packing equipment, preparation of camp meals, and many others that have escaped me. I had boned up for the thing. Riley had lent me a book which dealt with most of it. Only for that I couldn't possibly have answered many of the questions.

Next morning came the field tests. We assembled on the flats below town. There we were tried out on setting up a surveyor's transit and level and were told to step off the dimensions of a big staked area. We had to saddle a horse, mount, ride, dismount. Then came the packing test. There stood the naked mule beside a dismaying assortment of dunnage, a full-rigged packsaddle, padding, ropes, canvas, all jumbled up in disarray. This operation was timed with a stop watch. On and off went the stuff, and each time it was messed up again for the next fellow. Several of the boys displayed plenty of skill here, but it wasn't enough to win them a passing grade.

The outcome of the whole thing was a great surprise to me for two reasons. First, that whole bunch of cowboys had flunked, and several of them I felt sure would have made excellent rangers. Secondly, I was one of the two that had passed. Brown, the other successful candidate, was even more astounded than I. It seemed we were the only two with college training, which had taught us the trick of cramming in a hurry—and forgetting with equal rapidity. However, in talking it over, we two threw that out as the real reason for our phenomenal success as soon as it developed that we both enjoyed playing the fiddle.

We got the sheep off the range late in August. The wether lambs were fat as butterballs and ready to adorn the butchers' meat blocks. I hated to think of leaving the Toiyabe wonderland, but I was working now.

My next assignment was to be out from the gold camp of Manhattan. That really didn't sound too bad, and, besides, there was at least a semblance of timber over there, stunted though it was and only fit to be burned under the boilers of the quartz mills. With my own three burros, and riding Tony, I stopped at the Gooding ranch to change mounts—Tony for Ravenswood.

Gooding's little boy jumped on a horse and ran my big chestnut in from the pasture. I saw at once that something was up. The tone of Ravenswood's snort was disquieting and his eyes were ablaze. Never had I seen him like that. I tried to soothe him while putting on the saddle, but he kept his ears pinned back in an altogether antisocial manner. As I started to tighten the cinch his body tautened in protest. It was time indeed that the old boy were taken in hand. His vacation in the lush pasture had gone to his head. Well, we'd see about that. I hoped he didn't think for a moment that I was scared of him.

I stuck my foot into the stirrup and swung aboard. The corral gate was wide open. Shaking his head from side to side to dislodge the abominable bit in his mouth Ravenswood trotted majestically out into the open. The ground there was gritty and hard and his hoofbeats were noisy and scratchy. His headtossing became more determined. The brutal Mexican bit failed to deter him. If kept up, it most surely break his jaw. I decided to ease up a bit, believing that would tend to quiet him. That was where I made a mistake. Down went his head, clear out of sight. His back became a lofty pinnacle affording a grand view of the countryside. Now came an appalling seismic upheaval. My spine felt as if it was being telescoped. Miraculously, I retained my seat on the rebound. I was sure I was headed for the bottom of the bottomless pit, when abruptly I was popped right back up where I had just come from with a fancy lateral twist thrown in at no extra cost. I couldn't see Ravenswood at all, though I had a strong suspicion he was down there somewhere underneath me giving me his interpretation of an earthquake. The next rebound doubled me over. My head came near snapping off as for a fleeting second I glimpsed Ravenswood's snorting nostrils down between his stiff forelegs. The upthrust which immediately followed decided the issue. Off into outer space I was launched. Up, up I zoomed till I wondered if I was going into orbit, first man in space. My old saddle, its cinch busted, had followed me up. It fell on one side of Ravenswood while I hit the dirt on the other, and I distinctly heard the whistle of his iron-shod left hoof as it barely missed my cranium in passing.

"You got off pretty lucky," George Gooding said, helping me up. I didn't have to be told that. His pretty wife had a fine big dinner ready, and though I was plenty shook up, it was a big relief to find that my appetite, at any rate, had come through unimpaired.

After dinner a husky, rawboned cowboy named Eli Hardy offered to "set" Ravenswood. Eli had a stout Visalia saddle, and there was no danger of its cinch breaking. While he wasn't a fancy contest rider who observed all the niceties of form, he nevertheless generally managed to maintain his equilibrium when superimposed on agitated horseflesh.

So Eli rode my Ravenswood to a standstill, not fairly and squarely according to accepted standards but by dint of pulling plenty of leather all the way, all of which was pointed out to me by Bert Virden, an exhibition rider who happened to be on hand. To hear Bert tell it, Eli's ride had been something akin to shooting quail on the ground.

Bert Virden begged me to lend him Ravenswood to ride in the Labor Day bronco-riding contests at Goldfield. He was welcome to him as far as I was concerned, but when he mounted Ravenswood a few days later for tryout, the big, noble equine dogged it. Eli Hardy's ride had taken the heart out of him. Myself, I would never again grace his back. I sold him cheap to Dave Stevens who wanted him for a work horse down on the Cloverdale ranch. After some preliminary practice, he put Ravenswood in a three-horse plow team. He worked splendidly till the conclusion of his first morning's plowing, when he dropped dead in his harness.

Every horse meets its rider, and every rider meets his horse. Thus runs an old cowboy's adage. I thought that would do very aptly for an epitaph on Ravenswood's headstone should there be one. I have always felt that the doughty old boy never got an even break out of life.

I dropped in at the Keough ranch to say good-by. There was a hush about the place. Grandpa Bowler was breathing his last. He had come up there to visit and became ill. The doctor had been brought out from Austin and was at the bedside holding the aged man's wrist, counting the slowing beats of his moribund heart. The word came finally. Grandpa was gone.

We were sitting on the veranda, Charlie, his father, and I. They left me out there with the doctor while they went inside where Mrs. Keough sat alone beside the lifeless form of her father. Young Inez would learn of it when she got back from the little schoolhouse over across the meadows.

Soon Charlie came back out. I could read in his face that he was wrestling with the problem which had been visited on the household. It all devolved on him—the funeral arrangements, the complexity and immediacy of the details that must be attended to. In a helpless sort of way he mentioned that he had to take the doctor back to Austin, fifty miles away, and return with the undertaker and a coffin. It meant a big two-day trip at least, and he felt that his presence was particularly needed right there at home at that critical time. At first he wouldn't listen when I offered to go in his place. He feared that I might think he had been hinting at just that, but the upshot of it all was that I set out in the spring wagon with the best team of horses on the ranch, the doctor sharing the seat with me. We had a change of horses at the Pat Walsh ranch and reached Austin in the small hours of the morning. I took a room in the International Hotel where I passed the word of Grandpa Bowler's death to Billy Easton, his staunch old friend, who assured me he would look after everything at that end.

After an early breakfast I reported to Benedict, who put the stamp of approval on what I had done and told me to go ahead and see the matter through.

Then I hunted up Humphrey Kearns, the undertaker, but learned he was off in the hills somewhere. Bar Francis got on a horse and went after him. It was noon before Bar returned with Kearns, but the latter immediately got into action. He knew the exact coffin to take for he kept a comprehensive record of the approximate measurements of all potential candidates for his ministrations. At two o'clock Kearns and I started on the return trip up the river. We had dinner at Pat

174

Walsh's, and it was after eight o'clock before we continued on from there.

Meanwhile, a real manhunt had gotten under way. They were looking for one Carl Flasch, an enigmatic, Mephistophelean character who never stayed put very long in any one place. He was wanted for questioning in regard to the disappearance of a bar of gold bullion from the mill of the Round Mountain Mining Company, which operated a rich lode and placer property in the foothills of the Toquima Range about fifteen miles north of Manhattan.

I knew Flasch slightly. He was wiry and agile. One of his eyes was decidedly walled. Men, generally, left him pretty much alone regarding him as flighty and unpredictable, likely to go off on a tangent and start something that someone else might have to finish. On the other hand, he got himself into the good graces of the ranch wives by volunteering to go into their kitchens and bake fancy layer cakes.

The sheriff at Austin had deputized Louis Lees, a bartender, to go after Flasch, who was believed to be headed down Ione Valley in his buckboard drawn by a team of horses. Lees, in turn, deputized a cowboy by the name of Jack Bryan to join him in the chase.

At about eleven o'clock Kearns and I, transporting Grandpa Bowler's coffin, reached a point some ten miles below the Keough ranch. A lopsided waning moon hung grotesquely over the ridge of the Toiyabes and cast a weird glow across the valley. In the road ahead, I made out a team coming toward us. It turned abruptly off as far out of the road as it could get. I was sure it was Flasch, who had come to a stop over against the barbed-wire fence, and that he had deliberately placed himself there at bay in the brush, believing that we were after him.

A couple of miles farther up the road we were suddenly confronted by a pair of horsemen armed with rifles. They were Lees and Bryan. They asked if we had seen anything of Flasch's outfit and where. We told them what we had seen, and they were off at a gallop while Kearns and I kept on towards Keough's.

Kearns went right to work on Grandpa Bowler's corpse so as to have it in readiness for an early start for Austin in the morning, where burial would take place.

Shortly after dawn the procession started. Several neighbors were on hand to make the long trip and others fell in along the road. I drove the wagon bearing the body in its coffin; Kearns sat beside me again. We were in the lead and, funeral or no funeral, we had to trot the horses wherever the road permitted if we were to make Austin by nightfall.

Directly in front of the entrance to Grandpa Bowler's ranch we were forced to turn out for an obstruction in the road. A horse stood there in harness, hitched to a buckboard which was loaded with an assortment of packs and gear. Another horse lay dead on the other side of the wagon tongue. Lying face down in the roadway a few feet from the wagon was the body of Flasch, the butt of his rifle just beyond the reach of his outstretched arm. Over around the bunkhouse I caught a glimpse of a group of ranch hands and Indians holding some sort of confab. Our procession kept right on till we reached Pat Walsh's where we went in for refreshments. At four-thirty we were in Austin, and the following afternoon Grandpa Bowler was buried.

To this day no one knows for sure who killed Flasch. Jack Bryan, a thoroughly trustworthy young man, told me that he and Lees had caught up with Flasch about a mile above the Bowler place and had called out to him to stop. Instead he whipped up his team and started shooting at them with his rifle over the back of his seat, and then there had been a running fight till Bryan circled around in the brush and shot one of the horses. Evidently Flasch had jumped off the buckboard the instant it came to a stop. He refused to give himself up and kept right on firing, so Bryan declared, until he was dropped. Bryan remained on the scene to see that nothing was molested, while Lees rode on to Austin to report the affair, as I was informed.

What became of the bar of bullion still remains a mystery. If Flasch actually was the man that stole it, there is a bar of gold cached away somewhere in the hills around there which some prospector might stumble across some day.

As for me, it was time to finish the good-bys and get on back to my new job.

I bought a tough, fidgety little gelding very reasonably from a buckaroo who had caught him as a colt in the San Antonio Range west of Manhattan. I named him Ginger and rode him behind my pack train made up of Dan, Rickey, and Old Gal. I arrived at my destination the second day after my departure from Reese River. After getting settled in my cabin in Manhattan Gulch, I took a day off to drive my burros across Smoky Valley to the Peavine ranch where they could amuse themselves until our next move.

20

THEY CALLED IT the Pine Tree Camp, and it is little wonder that its original locators thought they had the richest mining area in all Nevada, as well as the prettiest, the way free gold was scattered around over its hills.

The story goes that Ed Seyler made a mental note of those hills while he was riding down Smoky Valley to get in on the Tonopah boom. From a distance they struck him as a likely district in which to find a mine. After he had settled himself in the saloon business in Tonopah, his thoughts kept reverting to those hills. Unable to go back there himself, being too busy behind his bar, he finally persuaded a cowboy, Jack Humphrey, to undertake the journey. He had shown Humphrey a chunk of rock speckled with coarse gold and told him he had picked it up in that vicinity. In reality, it had come from a rich pocket in the Berlin mine. Humphrey, none the wiser, took Seyler at his word, followed his directions, and discovered the Seyler-Humphrey mine, which made them both a fortune.

I no sooner arrived in Manhattan than I commenced to figure on a way to get out. I didn't like the prospect of being cooped up there all winter in the snow. My job was to go out day after day and stamp trees for the woodcutters who kept the gold mills supplied with cordwood for their boilers. Not a tree must they touch unless it bore the imprint of my axhead—Uncle Sam's initials—in a blaze under the bark. The trees were small gnarled piñon pines and junipers and made a funny little forest. There wasn't a board foot of lumber in all of them combined. Some of the dead trees that had lain on the ground for untold years were as heavy as rocks and could hardly be dented with an ax. They were pure, solidified pitch and could be ignited with a match.

I had a yearning for warmer latitudes, come winter. The Death Valley region appealed to me as the ideal solution.

However, through a strange concatenation of events, I wound up at a little paradise called Benton, in the upper reaches of the Owens River Valley in California. Actually, geographically, it is an integral part of Nevada, yet is just over the state line, between the lofty White Mountains and the Sierra Nevadas.

Tonopah, being in the path of my southward trek, was a logical stop-over for a couple of days. As soon as I got uptown from the Headlight Corral where I had put up my livestock, I ran into George Badgett, just up from Ubehebe with big news a-plenty. He and Andy McCormick had been nosing around down there for over a year and had located me in on a group of copper claims that had the earmarks of rivalling the Nevada Consolidated at Ely. George Badgett was nobody's fool, especially when it came to mining, and when he said he had a mine you could bank on it. The question before the house was could I let him have a hundred dollars? He and Andy had about run out of grub and powder down there. I decided they were letting me off dirt cheap, considering the amount of work they had put in on the ground, opening up the veins and putting shipping ore in sight against the day when roads would be built into that region of impassable sand and rocky gorges over which the menace of furious cloudbursts constantly hangs.

George Badgett was a man of honor if God ever made one. A slight turn I had done for him, so slight that I actually had forgotten all about it, led to his remembering me with an interest in his important discovery. I didn't tell him that I had only eighty dollars to my name, but I promised that I'd have the hundred for him within the hour. So, back to the Headlight Corral I went to close a deal with Andy Roush. He had taken a fancy to Ginger, had gone all over him, from inspecting his teeth to lifting up his tail where, apparently, everything looked satisfactory to him, and he had offered me thirty dollars for him. We finally settled for that sum, plus two days' free keep for my burros, which meant that after giving George Badgett the hundred dollars I promised him, I could only stay in town ten dollars' worth. I doubted if I even wanted to stay that long.

Next I met Doc McLeod, that is, Doctor Percy deMille McLeod, a Bostonian of distinguished lineage, a top-notch surgeon, an all-round good fellow. Doc asked me to come as I was and have dinner at his house on the hill. He wanted me to meet his brother-in-law, Ralph Waldo Trine, a writer, and a good one, author of *In Tune With the Infinite*, and *The Open Road*, and more. I said I'd be up after checking in at the Mizpah Hotel, shaving, and bathing.

In the lobby of the hotel I met Cleve Baker, district attorney of Nye County, one of my best beloved friends who later became attorney general of Nevada. His charming wife, Pansy, was the daughter of United States Senator Perkins from California. Cleve told me that he and Pansy were also going to the McLeods' for dinner that night. It evidently was to be quite an affair. Cleve jokingly warned, "You must be careful what you say to Trine. His thoughts are so deep it takes them twenty minutes to come to the surface."

I found the great man, Ralph Waldo Trine, as easy to talk to as Uncle Jake, Doc Fulkerson, or Hot Steam Boyd. Once I got started telling him about the boys in the hills, he wouldn't let me stop. The whole idea of prospecting, he said, fascinated him. I have no doubt that but for his adoring wife—and needless to say, she was equally adored—he would have kicked over his literary traces for a chance to trail along with me a while.

I was still telling hill stories when Doc McLeod broke in on our conversation. Doc had a big white crystal in his hand. He said it was gypsum, "the purest ever analyzed by the government in Washington." The exceptional specimen had been given him by Bob Stewart, the "Mayor" of Sodaville, one day when Doc had stopped by there for a swim in the big pool of warm mineral water off there on the desert sixty miles west of Tonopah. Bob Stewart had gotten it from a prospector, who had been working in the hills back of Sodaville where he claimed to have found a big deposit of the stuff, but not knowing what it was, he had passed it up. Doc was very much interested. Plaster of Paris, of which he had used quantities in his surgical work, is made of gypsum.

"Whoever finds that deposit," said Doc, "will have a real gold mine." Then he cut loose with a long rigmarole on the manifold uses of gypsum, which left no doubt that its demand far exceeded the supply and that there was a pot of money in it and an eager market clamoring for every pound that was offered.

"Why don't you go after it?" Doc asked me. "Look," he added, all excited, "how about letting me stake you?" Trine wanted in on it too.

I told them that since Doc had put me on the trail of it he'd be entitled to an interest, if I were to find it, whether or not he grubstaked me. But no, they would have none of that. They both insisted that cash backing was strictly in order in a deal of that kind. I declined to argue the point but made the mistake of insisting that fifty dollars was all the cash I'd need to see it through. They would gladly have given me several times that amount.

Two days later, with a capacity stock of food, I was off again, riding Dan, with Rickey and Old Gal out front. I had meant to go south toward Death Valley. Now I was headed west, all because of a rumor that there was something that begins with *G* in the hills around Sodaville. Down to Ubehebe with Badgett and McCormick was where I rightly should have been headed. Ubehebe, across Death Valley, where winter is summer, and summer is but a few degrees from cremation!

Walking and riding by turns, I got as far as Crow Springs that day, a nice place to camp, though the water is brackish. The lights of Tonopah glitter like a great jewel at night, twenty-five miles distant across the broad open desert. I was certain that I was quite alone there, leastways I had been when I turned in soon after the twilight had faded and my feeble fire had burned itself out.

How was it then that I found myself abruptly awakened out of a sound sleep? Nothing had touched me. All was deep silence but for the intermittent faraway tinkle of Old Gal's bell. Prospectors don't travel at night. Yet, a sixth sense, something between seeing and hearing, an awareness which pressed at my temples, warned me that another presence hovered close by.

The night was clear and breathless. An ocean of desert showed up by starlight. I rolled over on my stomach, raising myself on my elbows to gain clear vision.

Out there, not ten feet in front of me, nonchalantly sitting on his haunches, looking straight at me as he panted, was a coyote. I knew at once what that meant. I knew that I could thank my lucky star for having been awakened before the beast had taken a nip at me. This fellow definitely was rabid —hydrophobic! All his normal traits were reversed. His natural timidity had been altered into boldness by his hideous malady. The mere sight of a rifle, even from a long distance, normally would have sent him slinking off through the brush because his breed has been educated to recognize and fear firearms. This one though kept stock still all the while I cautiously reached for my rifle and raised it in deliberate aim.

With the ensuing report whose exaggerated loudness rudely shattered the silence and peace of that balmy midnight, the sick wretch toppled over without so much as a kick that I could see.

He had spared me, and I had reciprocated by putting him out of his misery. Who is to say that wasn't precisely why he had come to me out of the night?

The low hills running north from Crow Springs have

lured many prospectors by their varicolored formations and crisscrossed quartz veins. Somewhere in their bowels lurks a fabulous mother lode, and lucky the man that uncovers it, for uncovered it will be one fine day. Jewelers in New York and other centers have, to a considerable extent, obtained their supplies of the finest turquoise from the deposits around Crow Springs. On the whole, right there at the back door of Tonopah was one of the likeliest-looking places to seek a mine in all the West, but I couldn't tarry there—not at that time. My backers were looking to me to find that gypsum mine, and I could not take any chances on having someone else beat me to it. Another day and a half and I figured I'd be in Sodaville.

I found Bob Stewart taking his comfort in the late afternoon sun outside the barroom of his two-story wooden hotel. Any description of Bob Stewart automatically begins with the unqualified assertion that he was a gentleman of the highest order. He looked more the part of a retired executive, a railroad or bank president, than the ex-prospector and miner he was, who after making his big stake in the hills had picked that spot, Sodaville, with its warm springs, as the place to pass his remaining years, instead of going back to his native Canada. He was a bachelor and a true lover of the desert. Sodaville was to be his last and permanent camp. In order to make it a rendezvous for desert rats of high and low degree, he put up his hotel with its big warm swimming pool and bathhouse nearby, a bar serving only such liquor as measured up to his own discriminating taste, and a dining room that was the end of the desert-freighter's rainbow. Billy Spainhower and his wife managed the establishment. They were a healthy young couple with a three-year-old girl baby who was on and off Bob's lap a thousand times a day. Fred Manheim, a gentle Jewish bachelor with a real Christlike kindness of soul, was general clerk. Bob, always faultlessly attired and groomed, was more a father to them all than their employer.

Since it was getting supper time, Bob ordered a place for me next to him at the big table in the dining room. Nothing but the best would do in his establishment for anyone coming in the name of Doc McLeod, for whom he had the greatest regard. There were seven of us at the table. Bob occupied the big chair. The others, besides myself, were Billy and his wife, and Fred, and two weather-beaten old-timers who were mining on their claims down at Marietta. I had struck a quiet evening when there were no freight teams on the premises. Only two other tables had customers. At one sat an old Irishman who, I was told, was watchman at the shutdown quartz mill across the way where there was a big bed of blood-red mill tailings of which the desert winds had swept away thousands of tons, reddening the country for miles around. At the other table, off in a corner, was a meek-looking, middle-aged man whose stooped shoulders and dour look betokened a soul weary and ill-at-ease. His name was Darms, and he had what was supposed to be a coal mine off a ways in the hills. From all reports it wasn't giving him much comfort.

Sitting opposite Darms, and apparently trying to cheer him up, was an old girl on the kittenish order who was on the eve of getting a divorce from some man who was to be congratulated. Gentle, polite Bob Stewart leaned toward me and in an undertone told me he couldn't stand her. He referred to her as "Old Mother Dingbat" and wished to goodness she'd get out. "We'll naver take in any more divorcees," he said. "Poor Darms better watch his step before she ropes him in."

After supper I had a good chance to sit and talk with Bob

in the barroom. He had only a vague, general idea where the gypsum had come from. He said it might be only five or six miles from there in the foothills. He suggested that I make my headquarters right there at Sodaville and offered me the free use of an old cabin that had been empty for some years. There were a lot of burros hanging around the place, enjoying the waters up by the swimming pool to say nothing of the garbage cans in back of the hotel. I could ride Dan up to the hills and back every day, tie him up while I prospected, and turn him loose at night to rustle with the rest of the "desert canaries."

I thanked Bob, cleaned out the old cabin, and moved in. It had a dilapidated but usable cookstove, a homemade table and bench, and an iron bedstead with serviceable springs. What more could a fellow ask? The cabin was only a hundred yards from the hotel. Between it and the track of the newly completed Tonopah & Goldfield Railroad was a more pretentious cabin with three rooms.

It was occupied by a widow, alone by herself. She invited me to visit her as soon as I finished getting settled. Indeed, yes, I'd be delighted, I told her.

A little storybook home she had. She sang me some of her own compositions, accompanying herself on a zither-like instrument known as an autoharp, very easy to play, with a tone both churchly and lovely. Next, she read me a number of her poems. I told her she ought to get somewhere with all that talent. She gave me one of her printed cards. It read, "Mrs. Clara Dunwoodie, Author and Composer."

For an hour I listened as she told me about her boy. He was a traveling minstrel—an artist on the guitar. She read me several of his letters and she was all agog over his coming visit for Christmas.

As I got up to leave and say good night she said, "Haven't

you noticed anything in particular about me?" She smiled expectantly as she awaited my reply.

I was floored. What could she be driving at? I had to think fast. If I said no, she'd be offended, and if I said yes, I'd have to be specific. One thing was sure—I had to say something.

"Indeed I have," I said, with all the conviction I could muster, all at sea about how to begin.

"Ah, ha!" she said, raising her face and smiling with unmistakable satisfaction. "Go ahead—say it. Don't be afraid. Come now—I'm listening!"

"It's just this," I floundered, "I've observed that you're a woman of exceptional mental attainments. How could anyone help noticing that?"

She looked disappointed. "It's sweet of you to say that," she said, "but you've misunderstood me entirely. Isn't there something of a physical nature about me that you've noticed, aside from the purely mental?"

Now what's up? I asked myself. She stood up and came a couple of steps closer. Her face took on a seriotragic expression. She turned to present her profile, clearly for me to study.

"Ah, yes, of course," I said, "your features! That's it, of course."

"But what about them?" she prodded. "Of whom do I remind you?"

Now I was truly up against it. She was far from pretty, and if I told her of whom her profile reminded me, she'd be insulted, for it bore a startling resemblance to a very homely man, the homeliest, and, at the same time, a man with the most divine, the most beloved face in American history—Abraham Lincoln!

"Think! What president?" she prompted.

Well here goes, I decided. She had asked for it. "Abraham

Lincoln," I blurted and awaited results. They were not long delayed.

"Why, of course," she said, heaving a sigh of relief. "I am Abraham Lincoln's illegitimate daughter!"

That's all I know about it. I only have her word for it, and she certainly did look the part, since she had mentioned it, any way you looked at her, sideways or head on.

For several days I skirted around the hills back of Sodaville and explored deep into the washes leading back into them, chipping rocks and studying them under my strong glass. I had to keep reminding myself that it was gypsum, not specks of gold, that I was pledged to hunt for.

One day I worked over to the east where a long sloping bench came down from a high ridge. Up above, where the break was, I noticed a conical blowout which suggested a miniature dead volcano. It was of a reddish gray color. I decided it was worth the climb for a look at it, especially since I could see that a little work had been done around its base and that there was a location monument above the open cut. The last thing I expected to find there was gypsum. Even when I was up there and saw the white streaks that ran through the country rock every which way, I still could only think of calcite. I went so far as to scratch the crystalline material with my knife to make sure it wasn't quartz. There were alternate seams of the water-clear stuff and the dull red gangue which looked like rhyolite. The white streaks measured up to six inches wide in places and their arrangement was on the order of a zebra's stripes.

So this was the gypsum, and someone *had* beaten me to it! However, the work in the cut was anything but fresh. The dump material was crumbly and slaked by weathering. I couldn't find any location notice in the monument. Whoever had built it hadn't stuck with his claim long enough to put up his corner posts nor done half the amount of the required location work. At several other spots on the hill I found shallow holes punched in the striated formation. It was all very puzzling to me. I had no difficulty prying out good-sized specimens as pure and clear as the one Doc McLeod had shown me.

This layout upset all my preconceived notions regarding the occurrence of gypsum. I thought it came in massive bodies, practically pure, all ready for loading on freight cars by means of power shovels. This striped conglomerate could readily enough be glory-holed, but it was at least half waste. Maybe that was the way with all gypsum mines. I just didn't know. It could even be that this was an exceptionally high-grade deposit, as such things go. Anyway, in nature, 'tis said, nothing comes pure. At all events, I couldn't dillydally, and I forthwith took up four claims to make sure I had the whole works corralled. I showed Bob Stewart some specimens from my find, and he pronounced them identical with what he had given Doc McLeod. He was convinced the specimens had all come from the same place.

All of this had taken several weeks to accomplish. Now I had a lot of work cut out for myself. The claims must be marked at each corner and side-center with a monument or post, and the location work had to be done within the next ninety days. Were the claims worth it all? Only digging would tell.

Now Rickey was drafted to pack powder and tools while I continued to ride Dan back and forth each day. It wasn't such a bad grind. Every day I had a swim in Bob's big pool. I enjoyed cooking and sleeping in my cabin and visiting with the boys in the hotel. Free firewood was delivered at my door, thanks to the goodness of a section boss on the railroad who had instructed his gang of Mexican track-workers to supply me at intervals with a "Harriman," by which he meant a worn-out or discarded crosstie.

I wrote a letter to Doc McLeod telling him I believed I had found where the gypsum specimen had come from. I sent him a few pounds of the crystals and promised he'd be hearing from me as soon as I knew for sure what was what.

Hear from me he sure did. Shortly before Christmas I sent him my final report concluding with, "She's deep enough. With the closest of sorting we could probably accumulate enough gypsum off our claims to make the amount of plaster of Paris it takes to put one medium-sized leg in a cast."

The fact was that those pretty streaks were hardly skin deep. I knew, because like the fellow before me I had drilled dozens of test holes into that blowout and they had all turned out blanks, bottoming in barren red rhyolite. The same was true of the twenty-foot tunnel I had run, only to find that the farther I got in the tighter the formation became.

Doc never answered my letter. I had done my best to give him and Trine a run for their money. He no doubt figured I'd be coming back to Tonopah, which could well have been the case but for the arrival in Sodaville of a gentleman—and he truly measured up to that appellation—by the name of Sam Musser.

That changed all my plans, just as I was preparing to vamoose.

21

THERE WAS PRECIOUS LITTLE stirring around my cabin the night before Christmas. Of cash I had exactly none. I was down to my last pot of beans, cooked without benefit of any ham or bacon to bolster the flavor a bit. There still was some sugar on hand and salt and pepper a-plenty, but no more flour. At that, my poverty gave me a strange feeling of revelry. I was poking fun at myself as I enjoyed my beans and tea, and it was nice and warm inside my Harriman-heated abode as I sat dreaming.

On the morrow, Christmas Day, I'd take my rifle and see about shooting me a jack rabbit or maybe a hawk. With leftover beans and tea, I'd hardly know it wasn't turkey. Maybe it wouldn't hurt me to go Injun for a while and get down to gophers and some of the crawling vertebrates.

There came a soft knock at my door. Must be the little lady next door, I thought, calling on me with her son, the guitarist. He had come in that morning on the caboose of a freight, having entertained the trainmen en route.

But I was wrong. My caller was Fred Manheim, the gentle Jew, whose smile didn't quite manage to hide something that lay deep in his heart, whatever it might be. We had become warm friends, and now he had a favor—that's what he called it—to ask of me. There was to be Christmas dinner, turkey and everything, at the hotel in the afternoon. Would I honor him by being his guest?

That's how it happened that the most enjoyable Christmas dinner this Gentile has ever eaten was provided by a Jew who, though he professed it not, practiced Christianity in its truest form.

The day after Christmas I was out betimes rounding up my burros. I was going to move on down the line to Mina. Maybe I could amass a few shekels by working a stretch in the railroad shops there before making a dash for the warmer climes of the southland.

I saw the train from San Francisco coming up the track and wanted to see if it was going to stop. It seldom did at Sodaville.

This time it did. A man got off with a pair of suitcases. He was big, husky, blond, and around thirty years old. He walked up to me and asked if I knew whether he could get a room at the hotel. I told him I was sure he could, but before going in he set down his bags and proceeded to ask a lot of questions. He expected to be there two or three weeks, sampling the red tailings over across the railroad track. Did I know of anyone around there he could get to help him?

Well, now, did I indeed!

Sam Musser was one of a group of young mining engineers who had gone in for working over old beds of mill tailings. If the Sodaville tailings warranted they would set up a small cyanide plant there to extract the remaining values of silver and gold from them.

Sam and I went right at the sampling. The bed was marked off in squares with cloth tags in each corner, all duly noted in his little black book. Day after day we went out there and churned holes through the bed with a length of two-inch pipe, saved the stuff we brought up, quartered it down to sample size, and sacked and labeled each sample separately. In two weeks' time we took something like two hundred samples. It was dirty enough work, especially if there was a wind. At the end of a shift we'd look like a couple of Paiutes, but a shower and a plunge soon transformed us back to palefaces.

Then we'd make for the hotel and take it easy till supper time. It became an established rite to have a little bracer before we sat down to eat. Bob Stewart always joined us on those occasions. We took turns in treating, but I never had any money with which to decorate the mahogany. My treats went on Sam's bill to be deducted later from my honorarium. It was a funny arrangement all around. I was to get three dollars a day and board—very good pay in those days, especially in view of the excellent table Mrs. Spainhower set. Sam had explained beforehand that I wouldn't see the color of any money until after the sampling and assaying job was completed. I was to take the samples down to Bishop, over the line in California, on the narrow-gauge railroad which ran from Mina, Nevada, through Sodaville, and across the Mount Montgomery Pass into the Owens River Valley. I was to buck the samples for the assayer and help in any way I could around the assay office. When finished, I was to come back up the valley to Benton, where the boys had a plant in operation on another bed of tailings. That's where I'd be paid what was owing me, and Sam said he could put me to work in the mill if I decided to stay on a while longer.

"What about my burros and outfit?" I asked him.

"You can come back for them as soon as you're through," he replied. "They'll be all right here for a while, and down at Benton there's a dandy little ranch where you can pasture the burros. Don't you worry."

We moved the samples over to the freight shed. Sam had to go back to San Francisco and left me in command of the situation—the loading of the samples in the baggage compartment of the railroad car and their safe delivery at the assayer's in Bishop.

"How about my fare on the train?" I asked. "I haven't got a cent, you know."

"That's right, by golly," he said. "I'm short of ready cash myself and I need all I've got for this trip to the city. You see, Billy Cahoone handles all the money end of this outfit, and he's down at Benton. Anyway, I'll fix you up for your fare on the train and your board and room in the hotel in Bishop."

With that, Sam sat down at a card table in the barroom, got out his fountain pen, tore a page from his little black book and wrote on it.

"Give this to the conductor on the train," he said, handing

me the slip. "This'll get you through to Bishop. Now I'll give you a note to Bert Rhine. He runs the Istalia Hotel in Bishop, and he'll take care of you in good shape."

I got the samples safely aboard the train the following morning. Then I took a seat in the passenger section of the combination car, got out Sam's slip of paper and waited for the conductor. All it said on the slip was, "Fred, IOU one fare Sodaville–Bishop. Sam."

The conductor came breezing down the aisle with a cheery, "Tickets please!" I gave him Sam's slip. He glanced at it an instant, folded it, punched a few holes in it, and stuffed it in his vest pocket. It was as simple as that. Surely Sam was a man of consequence; his credit was good on railroad trains! This was a funny little railroad anyway—utterly informal— whose crew thought nothing of stopping the train for a few shots at ducks along the right of way.

The assaying was a two-weeks' grind with long hours. When it was over, I was both glad and sorry—glad the dirty job was finished and sorry to leave the Istalia Hotel where Bert Rhine had seen to it that I had the best of everything, inasmuch as I was associated with Sam Musser.

"Wait till you get up to Benton," Bert said. "You'll see what a swell bunch of fellows they all are."

Billy Cahoone drove down from Benton to pick up the assay reports and take me back with him. I was surprised to see the number of people on hand when we drew up in front of the Wai Wera Hotel in Benton. It was a prosperous-look- ing gathering among which I noted two very attractive girls.

What was going on here at Benton, anyway? I wondered. In due time I learned they were going to re-open the old Comanche mine, up on Blind Spring Hill, which had pro- duced many millions of dollars in high-grade silver ore before it was shut down some thirty years before.

Old shutdown mines, alas, are not allowed to rest in peace. They are the innocent victims of wild, fantastic tales that increase in magnitude as they are passed along by gossip-mongers. Waking them up on the supposition that their old-time operators didn't know their business, or were crooked, or what not, never results in anything but disappointment. Now they were going to wake up the old Comanche.

There was plenty of money behind this Benton revival. This was no ordinary boom. It was quite an aristocratic affair. It was a privilege, not to say a social distinction, to be in on the deal. There definitely was not a share of stock for sale. In this game, Mr. and Mrs. Hoi Polloi couldn't even buy a lone white chip.

The old Wai Wera Hotel was all freshened up inside and out. Ancient dwellings, large and small, long ramshackle and empty, were now shiny bright and tenanted by the elect and their families. Boiling water gushed from the ground a stone's throw above the town and was piped into every bathroom. Bathtubs were everywhere and people spent hours in them. The miraculous water sparkled like a blue-white diamond, but there the resemblance ended, for it was so soft and velvety that one felt soapy all over on emerging from a soaking in it. It was so plentiful that one seldom bothered to turn it off, letting it circulate right on through the tub. The cold-water tap, fed from a big redwood cooling tank, was treated with more respect.

A good-sized general store and post office adjoined the hotel. It was a gathering place for Indians, sheepmen, and miners. Groceries and fresh meats were on sale along with hardware, guns, saddles, dry goods, boots, and gear of all kinds pertaining to the livestock and mining industries.

I had met an agreeable, conscientious fellow named Chal-

mers McCormick—Mac, for short. He was from the picturesque little town of Big Pine, down below Bishop. Mac
wanted me to go in with him on a lease in the mine adjoining
the Comanche, high up on Blind Spring Hill. The property
was in charge of an engineer by the name of Burroughs
Edsall, a man of high standing in his profession. Edsall was
making his headquarters at the Wai Wera Hotel. I spoke to
him about the matter. He thought it had good possibilities.
Another pair of leasers were already at work on a block of
the ground and Edsall expected a big demand to set in as
soon as the word got around that leases were available.

One of the insiders on the Comanche deal was an elderly
gentleman, a Mr. Pearce, who with his wife was enjoying
this little haven in its setting of snow-clad mountains. Mr.
Pearce was a retired magnate of some sort, a friendly, sociable
individual who liked to sit around smoking his pipe and
asking a lot of questions. He was keen to play along with
Mac and me for a third interest in the lease. He would foot
the bills for powder, grub, and other costs, while Mac and
I would do the actual mining. Presto! We signed a contract
of lease on a hundred-foot segment of the narrow streak of
ore exposed in the tunnel of the old mine workings. We
were to pay the owners of the mine a sliding-scale royalty
on the net smelter returns from any ore we shipped and
divide the remainder equally among us three partners.

Meanwhile, I had been up to Sodaville after my outfit.
Sam Musser had engaged a room for me in Benton's largest
dwelling, which must have been the abode of someone high
in authority during the active days of the camp. There was
a bathroom just off my big master bedroom. In it was an
enormous porcelain tub which would fill up in no time with
the azure water from the hot springs. I erroneously supposed
this was to be my private bath, till I stumbled into it one

afternoon and found a nymph disporting herself in what was probably the biggest tubful of the most delightful liquid warmth that had ever caressed her young body. I backed out softly. She hadn't seen me. I met her and her lucky young husband later that evening. Sam told me they were there on a semi-honeymoon—business combined with pleasure. Their wedding had been a society event on the coast.

The mayor of Los Angeles, Mr. Eaton, with his son and two alluring young daughters had been attracted to this glittering boomlet. They were all staying at the Wai Wera. Mr. Eaton, so I was given to understand, was the man responsible for that stupendous feat, the great aqueduct, three hundred miles in length, whose six-foot pipeline climbs like a monstrous python out of one canyon into the next along the base of the Sierra Nevadas and finally spills what had once been the lifeblood of the Owens River Valley into the reservoirs of the City of the Angels. Sam evinced somewhat more than a casual interest in one of the Eaton girls. I couldn't see why the interest should not have been mutual.

Once while preparations were in progress for a great banquet which I knew was to be quite formal, Sam and Billy Cahoone both invited me to the party.

"Clothes are no excuse," said Sam. "Everyone understands you're prospecting. I'll wear my khakis to keep you company at the shindig."

"So will I," said Billy. "I think this formality stuff is being overdone around here."

I thanked them both for their sporting gesture but made it plain to them that I couldn't possibly enjoy the party on any such terms as that.

Professor George Henry Maynard, one of the founders of the Columbia University School of Mines, paid a brief visit to Benton while I was there. He won instant popularity through his good-fellowship. He had studied at universities in Germany and was very much at home in the language of Goethe and Schiller. He had a fine assortment of stories and jingles dealing with his student days. They were all in the best of taste, even those reserved for the privacy of the smoking room. One of the latter was about the instructor who asked the class why the Kaiser couldn't use a gold chamber pot. As budding metallurgists they should have known the answer. But they had to give up, and he had to explain to them that it was because aqua regia (royal water) dissolves gold. This story sounds best as told in German.

Mac and I had our stuff hauled up the hill by company team. A barrel of water was included in the load; it was a dry camp we were going to. No more luxuriating in that big tub every day, but it was only a matter of six miles up to our aerie in the rocks, and it was a comfort to know that at least we were within striking distance of cleanliness, say, of a Saturday night, when at the same time we could rinse out our duds. Our worthy patron, Mr. Pearce, placed all his laundry and bath facilities at our disposal and set up an extra bed for us on the back porch of his house.

The little miner's cabin which Mac and I preempted on the hill seemed to cling to its moorings by its eyebrows. That side of the mountain was so steep that there wasn't any dump at the mouth of the long tunnel. Thousands of tons of waste rock and several dozens of mine cars which had hurtled over the brink of the dumping platform lay scattered in wrecked desolation a terrifying half mile below. It was going to be ticklish business dumping waste out of the one car that had survived the perilous operations of the old days. The old relic was too precious to risk losing, and we knew it. Every time it was rolled out of the tunnel it was hooked to a length of cable to hold it captive, even if it should go over. I must say I was scared to death of that car, and even though I dumped it several times daily for close to six months, I was always relieved when I saw it still upright on the edge of the track after being relieved of its load, which I could hear crashing down the mountainside. A slight misjudgment could send a man flying down there in a shower of waste.

The ore in the mine was tetrahedrite, beautiful stuff when you found it but as elusive as a wraith, leading one on and on in the hope that its thread of a streak would bulge into a lens good for forty or fifty tons of the solid, rubber-colored high grade worth from four to five dollars a pound for its silver content alone. Some such lenses had been extracted by the old-timers, but from the looks of things there had probably been more money put into the mine than was taken out of it.

Mac and I went to work where a small lens had been stoped and the streak was still from two to three inches wide where operations had ceased. At least we had values to start on, but we wondered why the other fellows had quit right there instead of driving on ahead. We thought up all kinds of excuses for them. Perhaps they had had a falling-out, or maybe one of them had followed a mine car down the mountainside to eternity. Anyway, they didn't know what was ahead of them any more than Mac and I did.

No such luck, however! We had burned up plenty of powder in our quest, and we had many barrels of water hauled up to our cabin, and what with our grub, candles, and incidentals, it all ran into money which Mr. Pearce ungrudgingly put up. Our pesky little streak would be three inches wide one day and pinch back to a squeak the next. We saved every last bit of the dullish black stuff we shot down and sacked it. Every day we'd beg the streak to open up like a good fellow, but it was a miser and remained obdurate.

There was another cabin not many yards from ours where another pair of leasers were living. They were nice neighbors. Night after night we'd go over there to play solo—sometimes called slough—with them. One of them, George, was an excellent cook and made pies that any woman would be proud to duplicate. Those boys were not doing too badly on their lease. They were making better than wages.

George also went in for trapping coyotes which were not uncommon on the hill. He caught from three to four every week and got three dollars and a half for their pelts, apiece, in addition to the bounty for each pair of ears. Often at night I would awaken to hear a trapped beast rattle the chain of its trap as it tried to free itself. The thought came over me that when man becomes truly civilized he'll quit trapping helpless animals and throwing live crabs and lobsters into cauldrons of boiling water.

I had been curious to have a look inside a drift which continued straight on from where ours branched off. No one had set foot in that part of the tunnel since the cessation of operations in the mine nearly half a century before. It was a risky thing to do, going in there, not only because the air was poisonous but because the timbers were supporting heavy ground. About fifty feet was all I could stomach, although the old maps showed that the tunnel extended some two hundred feet beyond. My candle flame shrank to a feeble flicker in there, a pretty reliable warning one should heed. The timbers were all dry-rotted to a leprous punk from which streamers and festoons of ghastly, dead-smelling fungus draped to the floor. I had to brush these aside with my free arm in order to get through step by step, until finally a qualm stole into the region of my stomach. That was all I needed by way of inducement to retreat from that sepulchral avenue before I was overcome or the roof caved in on me. Both were definite, imminent possibilities. I felt like a corpse groping around in my tomb.

One day a big party came up from Benton to look at the mine and were conducted by Sam Musser to where Mac and I were at work. I spoke of the fungus drift with its lace curtains and, naturally, the ladies in the party were all hell-bent for going in there to see the weird sight. Sam promptly talked them out of it by declaring that the least disturbance in there could cause a general cave-in. We showed them our cabin and for a long time everyone just stood and gazed at the wonderful view. Across the valley, deep and wide below us, rose the massive snowcapped White Mountains to a height of over fourteen thousand feet. Down there the ranches with their haystacks, corrals, houses, fences, irrigation ditches, and cattle, all so far off, inspired one of the young women to remark that it all looked like a toy Noah's Ark. How much better had she said nothing at all. I thought of the young guide at Grand Canyon who told about a couple of schoolma'ams who went straight to the rim for their first view of the great gorge. One of them turned to the other and said, according to the guide, "Well, if'n I'd a-knowed this was all there was to it, I never would have came."

What a priceless gift it is to know when to remain silent!

An inspector from the Post Office Department dropped in at Benton about that time for a routine examination of the little fourth-class post office. The handsome young man who was postmaster, as well as general factotum around the store and hotel, greeted the inspector with all the cordiality in the world and threw the place wide open to him. Then, stepping outside, whistling and gay, he stopped in front of the hotel and shot himself. It was something about postal money orders and gambling down at Bishop. It put a damper on the happy, carefree existence of the little community.

Toward the end of the summer, Mac and I decided to call it deep enough on our lease. By skimp and scrimp, we had hoarded enough ore to make a small shipment to the smelter. The returns amounted to a little over two hundred dollars net, after deducting the company's royalty, to be divided equally among Mr. Pearce, Mac, and myself. That, of course, didn't begin to amount to daywages for Mac and me, while it also left our financial backer holding the sack for a deficit which I estimated to be around three hundred dollars. Even so, good sport that he was, we had all we could do to make him accept his share.

The whole experience brought on a recurrence of my old malady, "itchibus pedibus," which is superinduced by lingering too long in any one locality.

Mac, too, was in bad shape. A new governor of California had just appointed a new warden for San Quentin prison and the appointee happened to be an old chum of Mac's. If there was one thing Mac yearned for above all others, it was to be a guard in the "big house." Mac had made a wonderful partner, and I wouldn't want a nicer guard standing watch over me.

I had a couple of hundred dollars in my pocket. Maybe now I'd get down to Ubehebe and see how George Badgett and Andy McCormick—no relation to Chalmers McCormick —were making out on our copper claims.

Maybe was right!

22

I MADE UP MY MIND to see some new country on my way south instead of going back through Tonopah. I wanted to get in behind old Pilot, that massive upthrust facing Soda-ville, which had a special charm for me, and on around to Petrified Spring, all on advice from Jim Plant of Marietta. He had sworn up and down that he had seen specimens from a lost mine back in there that ran five hundred ounces of gold to the ton.

I camped at Petrified Spring and hunted conscientiously for the lost mine, or any mine whatsoever, for a period of two weeks. It was a hard country to give up, a country of multi-farious formations and promising-appearing dikes. Acres of yellow and red ocher suggest the likelihood of vast copper deposits lying underneath.

From there I worked around through the rough Cedar Summit region till one afternoon I camped just below the old Liberty mine.

A big rugged-looking fellow came down off the hill while I was unpacking and setting up camp. He said his name was Fred Bowler—not related to the Reese River Bowlers. He just wanted to visit with me a bit, was interested in prospecting and wanted to know which way I was headed. I told him I was on my way to Ubehebe to join George Badgett and Andy McCormick.

"No use looking for them down there," Bowler said. "Badgett and McCormick left for Montana a couple of months ago." Bowler had seen Badgett in Tonopah before their departure, and he told Bowler that they planned to spend the winter in Montana developing a prospect they had gotten wind of.

That bit of intelligence left me high and dry. I said as much to Bowler.

"Then why don't you stick around here for the winter?" he asked me. "I'm mine super here and I'll put you to work."

I thanked him but said I didn't care to work underground.

I had a good pair of lungs, and I wasn't going to get them messed up with quartz dust.

He didn't blame me. I could have a surface job if I wanted it, at four dollars a day.

"We've got the world's finest boardinghouse here," he declared. "For a dollar a day they'll feed you three big squares. They dish up nothing but the finest, regardless of cost. Whenever you feel like it, you can take time out and go up in the hills back of here. It's as good a place as there is anywhere to prospect. We're in the same mineral belt as Tonopah and Goldfield."

Now, where could I hope to beat that? I was disappointed about Ubehebe. Surely the boys would be back as soon as they got through with that Montana deal. All right then, here I'd hibernate. A good offer like this one merits prompt acceptance. Man, I figured that by spring I'd have a real stake to start back up north on, and the burros would love it here—water and good feed and, no doubt, many a snack of garbage in back of the boardinghouse.

There were big goings on at Liberty. James G. Lindsay, a millionaire steel man from back East, was pouring his money into the venture. A completely integrated mine, mill, and power plant was nearing completion under the managership of his niece's husband who was a mechanical engineer, big handsome Bob Griswold.

I had a fine time there that winter. Griswold and I worked out a deal whereby I kept the books, made out the payroll, and plotted the surveys on the mine maps, all at five dollars a day instead of the four I had been getting as roustabout. I also moved up to the office building, where I shared a room with one of the mining engineers, Tom Carnahan. I ate at the staff table in the boardinghouse. We had the same food as the rest of the boys, only we went in after they had cleared out. It wasn't so snobbish as it sounds. The staff was as big as the working crew and there wasn't room for all of us at one time in the mess hall.

Also, there was a horse I could ride whenever I felt like it— a beautiful four-year-old named Curley. He was inclined to buck, but he never did so with me. Griswold rode horseback to Tonopah quite often to keep in touch by wire with Lindsay's office in the East. I frequently rode along with him on those trips, a fine ride of about thirty miles each way.

I spent much time exploring the high, rugged country back of the mine where quartz veins abounded and geological conditions appeared about the same as at Tonopah, in the same range. To date, however, no major discovery has been reported from up there.

The first clean-up, after the mill had run a few weeks, yielded a bar of metal which was more pig iron than bullion; it was not worth shipping. The sulphide-veined material they had been banking on, down below the water level, was base and below milling grade. It was a sad situation—a case of not looking before you leap. They had built a big plant before they were sure they had an ore body to warrant it.

Spring was just around the corner. I now had over seven hundred dollars cash on hand and in the bank. Nor did I owe any man a penny of it. My outfit was in tip-top shape, the hills were there up north more alluring than ever, and I had no boss to delay, hinder, or obstruct me in any way, shape, or manner. But my plans were again in for a complete reshuffling.

Fred Bowler had been to Tonopah and got back to Liberty just as I was preparing to leave. He announced that he had the biggest piece of news that ever fell on my ears.

"It's Gold Reef," he exclaimed, "the K. C. Fraction! I've got it sewed up in a lease and bond, and you're in on it fifty-fifty with me. Boy, pretty quick you're going to find out how it feels to be a millionaire!"

Gold Reef! Somehow I liked the sound of it. This could be it at last—the Big Thing—yes, indeed, could be!

Fred had had to pay for the option. How much, I didn't find out, but between that and a session with the chips and coppers of the faro bank, he had just about shot his wad.

We had to get busy. Time was of the essence. Outfit and I headed for Gold Reef nine miles south of Tonopah. By evening of the second day I was camped there on the claim known as the K. C. Fraction, where we were going to sink a shaft on a better surface-showing than Hayes and Monette had on their history-making lease on the Goldfield Mohawk. This thing really looked good, and it made the headlines.

Fred's idea was to whoop things up in town, keep the publicity at the boiling point, and make a play for a big, quick turn on our option, while I stayed on the ground and put down the shaft on our vein of ore with the help of an old miner named Sandy. I was to pay all expenses, including Sandy's wages, and it also fell to me to do the cooking for both of us.

One day Fred drove out with Jim Butler, discoverer of Tonopah. I had never met him before. When we shook hands he just about dislocated my knuckles in his huge paw. He said he had always believed in the country around there. His old Klondyke mine was but a short distance below where we were. He pulled a nugget out of his pocket, solid gold, about the size of a bantam hen's egg.

"I picked this up myself not far from here," he said, handing it to me to look at.

I expressed by admiration of the magnificent specimen, surely the finest I had ever seen.

"You like it?" he asked. "Put it in your pocket. You can have it."

No sir, I wouldn't accept it under any circumstances. He took it back reluctantly. That was Jim Butler's nature. Gentle and kind by nature yet, when aroused, he could, and did, kill a man. If it hadn't been for his good wife, he would have given away all of the four hundred thousand dollars he got for his Mizpah mine.

There were plenty of others besides Jim Butler that spoke highly of the new camp. L. C. Branson, fiery editor of the Tonopah Daily Sun, came out to our lease one Sunday and spent the day looking over the now solidly located district. The next night's edition of his paper carried big headlines across its front page, proclaiming the showings of Gold Reef as the "RICHEST ON SURFACE AND MOST EXTENSIVE OF ANY DISTRICT YET DISCOVERED IN SOUTHERN NEVADA—SITUATED AT BACK DOOR OF TONOPAH."

After devoting a couple of paragraphs to establishing his theme, Editor Branson, under the subhead "Great Strike In Bowler Lease," had the following to say: "The visit was just in time to see a new strike which if it had occurred at Goldfield or even in Tonopah would have created intense excitement and by this time have been telegraphed all over the country. The lease of Fred Bowler and H. W. Albert on the K. C. Fraction had rock with visible gold from the surface. But Saturday at a depth of less than forty feet the rock began to improve until for a width of three feet it gave values of $179. The rock that was hoisted Sunday was richer still and will average high in the hundreds per ton."

Branson was absolutely sincere about what he wrote. He was an editor of the widest experience around mining camps. Time has not yet proved him entirely wrong about Gold Reef. I am sure the stuff is there, plenty of it, even though we missed it, Bowler and I, in our lease on the K. C. Fraction. In its early stages Fred had laughed at offers up to as high as fifty thousand dollars for our option. Poor fellow, he was firmly convinced that we were going to be on "Easy Street," and then some, for the rest of our days, but . . . .

Something went wrong with our vein. Its values faded away to a whisper. Fred tried to pass it off lightly, said it was nothing at all, we had just run into a horse and as soon as we passed through it the values would come in again stronger than ever. Fred was good at putting on a front, but where was the money to come from to keep us going? My paltry pittance was just about shot to pieces. No more offers were forthcoming. People commenced shying away from the locality; even claim owners, leaving rings of empty tin cans, jars, and bottles around the spots where their tents had stood. They had all been banking on our lease to make good. Our ground was considered the cream of the district. Our success or failure was the signal they had all been waiting for.

The Gold Reef boom was over—but only temporarily!

Courageous to the last, Fred, observing the general exodus, remarked, "They'll all be back. Just wait and see." His words were prophetic. He foresaw the secondary rush, which set in a few years later and which went down in history as the "Divide Boom."

23

MY BUSINESS was prospecting. Yet, here I was, goaded by heartless Old Man Circumstance into wasting precious time on, of all things, a job!

"You'se done got yo'se'f flat busted," the old fellow gloated. "Now yo' kin jes' git in dar an' git yo'se'f mended, ha, ha, ha!"

"But why?" I protested. "I know an easier way. I'll get someone to grubstake me."

"Y'all c'd do dat, sho' 'nuf," he mockingly concurred, "an' den w'en yo' strikes it richer'n de Queen o'Sheba yo' kin divvy up wi' de odder feller. Whut fo' yo' wantin' to be beholden to anybody? Dey'll be pesticatin' yo' fo'ever'n ever, worl' 'thout end. Aaaaaaaaaaa-men!"

I could see his point. I gave in to him. When you let some-one stake you, you're in a sense taking on a boss. You've got to keep writing to him and sending him samples, and you're over-anxious to make good on his account, whereas, if it's just yourself you're answerable to you'll have no one looking over your shoulder and breathing down the back of your neck.

So I cast about for a job, just a short one—ugh! My quest ended in the shops of the Tonopah and Goldfield Railroad, at the lower end of Tonopah.

I soon concluded that Mr. Phillips, the master mechanic, had hired me to save wear and tear on his chain blocks and traveling cranes by switching their functions to my back and biceps. He had an impressive array of freight cars with flat wheels, six-foot locomotive driving wheels that were slightly out-of-round, connecting rods and eccentrics with worn bush-ings, and all kinds of links and trusses needing attention. Not an item in the place weighed less than a ton. Such were the baubles that he entrusted to my care with instructions to go easy on them. The wonder was that I didn't rupture myself in the course of bringing my physical powers to bear on those weighty problems. A hundred times a day someone invested with an aura of seniority would holler at me, "Hey, you, come over here and give us a lift!" I filled in odd moments wiping dust-covered locomotives and flushing astonishing quantities of scale out of their boilers with a hose. Another chore, which never failed to leave me looking like a negro minstrel, was shoveling coal from gondolas to engine tenders. Then there was the matter of keeping the ash-pits clear. That's where engines coming in off the road dumped their ashes so that the boilermakers could crawl into their scorching fireboxes to caulk leaky boiler-flues while steam was still up to full pressure, a hellish job to which those lads were more than welcome for all of me. Passengers riding comfortably and smoothly over the rails little realize the toil, devotion, and misery it takes to place that convenience and luxury at their command.

I had a room at the Celtic, a big lodging house uptown. At the Montana Cafe, I bought meal tickets which cost five dollars and were good for five-fifty in meals. My burros were at Frazer's Well, north of town in the San Antonios. Spring was a long time coming, even after I had been promoted to assistant hostler, whereby I became a sort of groom and stableman to the iron horses. The hostler, my immediate boss, was an ex-engineer who had lost his job on the New York Central due to a smashup. I got along fine with him. We took care of all locomotives in the yard, kept steam up in those that were to go out on the road, and saw that all were supplied with such essentials as lubricating oil, boiler compound, and cotton waste. We delivered fresh, clean engines to the depot and brought back spent, dirty ones to the roundhouse.

We also ran the switch engine, known as the "goat." Johnson, the hostler, was at the throttle; I served as fireman. We had to meet all incoming trains a mile below town to help them up the last steep grade. There was a bit of a trick to making a flying coupling while both engines were in motion. My part of it was to hold the goat's drawhead open till we were bumped, and then the little old goat would dig in for all she was worth while I scrambled back, grabbed my scoop, and heaved coal into the firebox as fast as the Lord would let me, fanning it out with a twist of the wrist the way Johnson had taught me, so as to spread it evenly over the roaring flames. Great volcano-like billows of black smoke would belch out of the stacks of the laboring behemoths, and every time we reached the top of the "Y" both engines finished in a state of complete exhaustion, having given their absolute all right down to the last asthmatic cough.

All of which was by way of breaking me in for a job as fireman. Now, that was truly nice of Mr. Phillips, and I did sincerely appreciate it. He had given me a manual on locomotives to study and told me to learn all about signals. Strange turn of fortune! Here I was actually in a position to realize the consuming ambition of my childhood—to be a railroad engineer! In fairness to myself, let me add that I did give the matter some serious thought; and just as soon as I had definitely decided against a career in railroading I so informed Mr. Phillips. I expected to be fired on the spot so that he could start grooming some other fellow for my soft berth. Instead, however, he told me to stay on as long as I chose, and that was right up to the moment when I was overcome by the first fumes of spring.

Four years almost to the day had passed since I first pulled out of Tonopah with Dan, Rickey, Old Gal, and—ah, yes— Jennie B, that blond she-devil. Again I was headed north, not, as then, into the unknown. I steered for the foothills of the Toiyabes to enter there by their southern gateway, Cloverdale, with its stately cottonwoods shielding the old ranch house. I couldn't wait to see the blackbirds, many with bright scarlet wings, clinging and swaying on the reeds along the water-ditches, and to rest my eyes on the dark green of the wild hay ripening in the long meadow. All of that, and even more so the country beyond, I had so completely taken to my heart that it amounted to a passion.

A night at Cloverdale, another in that big mountain-meadow, Indian Valley, where I lay in the lonely little cabin without windows or door, relishing the distant shrill yapping of coyotes cavorting in the moonlight, and then the next day the place I loved most of all, the George Keough ranch!

There I would have been happy to remain forever. There I had been made feel like one of the family. Years later, good-hearted Mrs. Keough, harking back to those blessed old days, remarked that she had raised three sons—a Dutchman, meaning me, an Irishman, meaning Charlie, and an Indian, meaning Johnny Boots who had come there as an orphan. Johnny Boots, she "bowlerized," was the best of the three!

It has been said of the mosquitoes that ply their trade along the tortuous Humboldt River, my route after leaving the Keough ranch, that they buzz in a deep baritone the while they pride themselves, as well they might, on their exquisite needlework. All I can personally vouch for is that they treated me with all the deference due a distinguished pincushion. My departure from their demesne, which I might add was a hasty one, was under full escort of the swarming hosts as far as the border, with sound effects no less impressive than police sirens.

It was out a ways from Oreana, a tank stop on the Southern Pacific, that I first ran into Bill Pfeifer. Bill was a carpenter by trade, and a mighty good one, but a prospector to the core, having made his quota of stakes in his time only to sink them all back into the ground again in search of bigger and better ones. He had a first-rate rig with an adjustable top, drawn by a span of tough-looking brown mules. Along with his prospecting gear he transported a complete set of carpenter's tools. Thus, the carpenter kept the prospector going when funds ran low.

At the moment, Bill was headed the same way I was,

namely, toward the new land of promise north of the Humboldt where so many camps were springing up that they were running out of names on the map.

Bill was an unconscious comedian. He spoke in the "Dutchified" jargon of Weber and Fields, and yet he was a native-born American, hailing from Milwaukee, and he had never been any closer to Germany than Cincinnati. He was in his late forties, of medium height and slight build; and affecting a trim mustache, there was a bit of cockiness about him. I gathered that he accounted himself not altogether unappealing to the gentler sex, for all of which he was a smart little fellow in many ways. I took quite a liking to him from the start, largely, I suspect, because I couldn't help laughing at practically everything he said, which seemed to be quite all right with him.

Bill, on the other hand, took to me too, at least enough so that he proposed we team up as partners. The man he had been knocking around with had but lately left him, having fallen heir to a big sheep outfit in Wyoming. Bill sincerely regretted the loss of Red, as he called him. Our partnership was a deal. We shook hands on it.

On carpentry jobs I would work along as Bill's helper. I started to say something about my lack of experience. Tut tut, all I had to do was "chust follow instrugshuns," and the prevailing wage was five dollars a day for carpenters' helpers! That laid the job spectre. Bill and I were an integrated, self-sustaining team. His cash was running low, but a job was, as he put it, "alretty in der bag." It was at Seven Troughs and called for a bunkhouse, a dry (miners' change room), a cabin or two with outhouses having artistic crescents cut into their gables for light and ventilation.

"In a couple mont' we got enough dough to brospect a whole year on," Bill said.

The Seven Troughs job was no myth. Bill started me off sawing rafters and joists he had previously marked with his big flat pencil and steel square. However, he had cautioned me strictly not to let anyone, especially the boss, observe me in the act.

"Veneffer you see him come aroundt," he warned, "you grab a two-by-four or anyding dot's handy and start walking away mit it." Sometimes he even suggested that I hide out for an hour or so while he was engrossed with some intricate operation like mortising a window frame. All in all though our patrons got full value for their money because Bill's great speed and efficiency more than made up for my ineptitude. He was as nimble as a cat and could drive a tenpenny nail all the way in with a single blow of his hammer and rip through a length of two-inch-plank with his saw as if it were so much cheese. Actually, my main function was to hand him things, which he miraculously transformed into floors, walls, and roofs.

Verily and indeed, by Bill's own admission, one would have to rise bright and early of a morning to get the better of him, no matter at what. Sure he could lick Jim Jeffries in a rough-and-tumble fight, or spot Willie Hoppe a whole string of points and still beat him at billiards. It was things like that that made him so funny, this sawed-off little Baron Munchausen who always came out on top in all his exploits— that is, to hear him tell it, and the more you laughed, the better he liked it.

All I know is that Bill was every bit as good as he claimed to be about the things I personally saw him do, such as carpentering, plain and fancy cooking, and projecting animated shadow pictures on the wall by candlelight.

Now I was satisfied that Bill and I could hammer and saw our way out of any fiscal embarrassment, and in short order, but soon after we had proceeded on our way from Seven Troughs I had to reach a decision on a matter involving a very difficult choice. It was altogether obvious that our two outfits simply did not jibe and, in fact, were in one another's way. Either one or the other was definitely superfluous. Bill appealed to me to give up Dan, Rickey, and Old Gal.

"Vat der hell we want dem for anyway?" he asked. "Any time we gotter pack in some blace we use der mules. Better you turn loose der burros."

We were in Paradise Valley at the time, up above Winnemucca, and Bill was all for going to Jarbidge, the new wonder camp in Elko County, which, as usual, was going to surpass them all. It would take us well over a week to get there by wagon.

"You gotter giff up der burros sometime, ain't it?" Bill argued. "When you wanter get odder ones all you gotter do is help yourself. Dere runnin' loose aroundt effry camp in der state an' dey don't belong to nobody."

Bill was dead right. Burro men were beginning to be a vanishing race. Their abandoned animals were to be seen in increasing numbers, like mendicants, hanging around the mines and camps. Yet, it was not a matter of logic, but of heart, for me to decide to give up mine. I didn't sleep well that night and was awake with the first faint hint of dawn. My burros were still feeding, for ever so faintly I caught a faraway tonk of Old Gal's bell.

Bill was breathing the deep breaths of sound sleep as I noiselessly sneaked away into the chilly twilight silence. About a mile away on a little rise where two streams converged I came upon the gentle trio. All there was to do was to take the bell and hobbles off Old Gal. Dan and Rickey had not been hobbled. It wasn't necessary. They'd never leave her.

Adios, borricos!

My little Dutch prospecting partner, Bill, was the beautiful dreamer of song and fable. He had, to a magnificent degree, the prospector's most essential trait—optimism. For Bill, life was always bursting with opportunities to make not thousands but millions of dollars, and, there, who is to say that he wasn't right again?

So, for three years we seesawed and seehammered between chasing mirages. The houses we built as we moved from place to place fell into three main categories, namely, bunk, boarding, and back. Toward the last I had progressed to the degree of proficiency where the erection of the third-named was entrusted entirely to me, and so, in my humble way, I was enabled to contribute somewhat to the comfort of scores of miners in remote camps.

Lots of times Bill would come up with some wonderful new scheme. It was always "a hell of a big ding." Usually he had been sworn to secrecy by someone whose confidence he had gained, say, some worldly-wise bartender in a saloon who enjoyed mysterious connections with notorious characters.

"Neffer mind who told me," he'd say. "He's a square-shooter. Dot's all I can say."

One of Bill's square-shooter friends had disclosed to him the exact location of a cache of stolen gold bullion somewhere on the coast of British Columbia along the inside passage to Alaska.

"Why hasn't he been up there after it?" I asked.

"He couldn't get away mit it," was Bill's reply. "Der Nordwest Mounties is got deir eyes open all der time. Dey know it's some blace aroundt dere and dey layin' for somebody to show up an' try to get away mit it."

"Well then," I persisted, "why doesn't your friend report it to them?"

"Chust because he kinder likes der idea of stayin' alive a

little longer yet," Bill replied. "Der fellers dot pulled the chob is still in der country, layin' low."

"Oh, that's it!" I began to comprehend. "They'd probably kill him if he squealed."

"You're damn right dey would," Bill agreed.

One thing we did run down was a hot tip Bill had picked up concerning some auriferous black sand up along the Snake River in Idaho. We were at Jarbidge at the time wondering what in the world had ever induced us to go there in the first place. Those black sands, according to Bill's informant, were being secretly sampled by the Guggenheims.

"Better we go up dere," Bill said, "so long we're so near dere anyway. Maybe we get in on der groundt floor. It sounds like a hell of a big ding to me."

It was a case of a month's time delightfully wasted. The black sands were there all right, in greater abundance even than Bill had been led to believe. But we didn't meet any of the Guggenheims anywhere along the Snake, and the only sampling we observed going on was being done by anglers sampling the riffles with their fly hooks.

On our way out we stopped to visit for a while with a man who had hewn out a little heaven of his own up there in the backwoods. Oh yes, the black sands were auriferous, he told us, but only slightly more so than ocean water, just a trace to a cubic yard. Every year, he said, brings its quota of misguided gold-seekers in there to investigate them. The whole thing was simply just one of those rumors that refuses to die.

"You sure got a nice blace here," Bill observed. The man seemed pleased.

"How about staying for supper?" he asked. "I'll cook you some moose steaks." He invited us to see his private snowdrift which reached up to the eaves of his log cabin. We stood by and watched as he burrowed into it with a shovel and brought forth a rack of venison. The meat was expertly broiled directly on the lids of his cookstove. It was as tender as a good porterhouse beefsteak and of excellent flavor. Our host expressed himself as delighted to have us as guests inasmuch as sometimes for weeks on end he saw only bear, elk, moose, buffalo, mountain lion, and other such inarticulate Mammalia as prowled thereabouts, most of them AWOL from their refuge in Yellowstone Park above.

"Better we get der hell outer dis country," Bill said, addressing me. "First ding you know it gets in der blood."

It must have been that we were in the sand era of our joint venture. No sooner had we put the black sands of the Snake River behind us than we were setting our course for yet other sands albeit they were a good thousand miles away on the Amargosa Desert south of Rhyolite, Nevada.

According to another square-shooter friend of Bill's, there was a tidy sum buried in those sands represented by twenty barrels of fine old Kentucky whisky, which at that time would have attained the venerable age of around twenty-five years in the wood. The beverage, along with other merchandise less urgently required, was en route from Ludlow on the Santa Fe to the then booming camp of Rhyolite, via twenty-animal-freight-team. At a point where the wagon road skirted around the great pyramids of shifting sand that rise from the desert's floor some miles below Rhyolite a ripsnorter of a sandstorm suddenly broke loose. The first thing they knew, the teamster and his swamper found their wagons hub-deep in sand. All they could do, and that in a hurry, was to unhitch the big team and get out of there before it too was swallowed up, as the wagons rapidly were being, by the shifting sand monster. The wagons had never since been found.

Along the way we stopped to investigate the activity occurring in a canyon bordering one of the great valleys of central

Nevada. We were just in time to grab off a fair-sized contract to build the usual structures for a newly hatched venture. A very prosperous cattleman had a ranch nearby, where we turned the mules out to pasture. He had a daughter, a spinster, who, next to himself was the brains of the outfit. While she was not strikingly comely, it did not necessarily follow that she had never had proffers of marriage. It was reasonable to assume that hers was a voluntary spinsterhood. Some day she would fall heir to a goodly share of her dad's big estate.

Our job in the canyon was finished in a month, and we moved down on the ranch where Bill was going to make some cupboards and shelves for the lady. I assumed he was to be paid for the work till he told me he was doing it for nothing.

"Dey wouldn't let us pay for der mules," he said.

"Oh, that's different," I replied.

"And besides, I'm going to marry her," he added, meaning the daughter.

"Bill, you're only fooling," I said.

"Like hell I am," he replied. "You can put in a good word for me any dime you get a chance. You help me win dot; you always got a home."

Then he held forth at length about the great ranch with its thousands of acres, thousands of cattle, and thousands of dollars that, no doubt, were reposing in the bank. I told him he shouldn't think of such a serious step as marriage in terms merely of those material advantages. He should be very sure he loved the lady on her own account, aside from them.

"On der dead square," he vowed, "I'm chust nuts about her, belief me!"

Just for ducks, I thought I'd try to find out how she felt about Bill.

"Oh," she said, "I think he's so amusing, and such a darling putting up all those shelves for me."

I reported back to Bill. He merely nodded his head. It was just as he had expected. A couple of days later his work was finished. The first time he could catch her alone he was going to propose.

I was over by the blacksmith shop watching the boys shrink a hot rim on a wheel. Bill, looking more glum than I had ever seen him before, came out of the house toward me.

"Better we pack up an' get outer here," he said.

We drove away in silence. After a reasonable length of time I said "Did you propose to her, Bill?"

"Nah," he replied. "I changed my mind about der whole dam ding."

Then, after another longish pause he added, "I don't know wot I effer saw in dot old maid anyway."

Thus went what was to have been my home, "always."

24

THOSE TWENTY BARRELS OF WHISKY buried in the sands of the Amargosa Desert are close to half a century old by now and are still aging in the wood. Bill and I never got down there to try our hand at finding them. Maybe some day a favoring wind will reshift the sands back where they used to be and leave the wagons with their priceless cargo high and dry on solid ground. Lucky the man that happens by just then. He can stake a claim with something decidedly unique in the way of a surface showing.

The variegated interlude with my engaging, energetic partner, Bill Pfeifer, inevitably had to come to its finale some day.

That day found us at Goldfield. We had been meaning

to take a run over to Cactus Peak about twenty miles to the east where that commanding landmark stands a solitary sentinel over a vast stretch of shadeless wasteland. Bill had conceived a liking for Cactus Peak several years earlier when he first viewed it from a distance.

"I've got a hunch dere's someding bigger dan Goldfield underneat' dot hill," was the way he had put it to me.

But that day in Goldfield was a day of double coincidence. It was a coincidence for Bill that a certain mine operator from Round Mountain up north of Manhattan also happened to be in town and was very happy to see Bill. They had met in the past. He knew all about Bill's skill as a carpenter and wanted him at Round Mountain forthwith to take charge of some construction work there.

For me, it was a coincidence that George Badgett and Andy McCormick were both in Goldfield that same day. They were on their way to Ubehebe, traveling in a sturdy Dodge open touring car. They, in turn, wanted me to go down there with them. There was loads of room for me and my belongings in the tonneau of their car.

That did it as far as Bill and I were concerned. We split up right there. It seemed altogether logical that we should. I explained, and Bill understood that it wasn't right for me to let George and Andy keep carrying me for my interest in the copper claims. They could use me to help with the development. They had come back from Montana with a little stake. I had a couple of hundred dollars of my own, winter was at hand, and, on the whole, Ubehebe was my natural destination. Besides, Bill had made it clear that he was keen to take on the construction job. He would have no trouble replacing me as his helper. Of course I'd miss Bill. No one ever had a more agreeable partner—nor more amusing—than I had in Bill Pfeifer.

Andy was at the wheel and we were on our way in the morning. Our route lay by way of Bonnie Claire and down Grapevine Canyon to the old Steniger ranch where Death Valley Scotty was starting to build a million-dollar edifice of some sort. No one but he and his money-rich pal from Chicago—fellow named Johnson—had the least idea what it was supposed to be. Even at this date no one has yet come up with a plausible explanation of the why and wherefore of the gaudy monstrosity known simply as Scotty's Castle.

Scotty was expecting George and Andy for noon dinner. They had accepted his pressing invitation on their way up from Ubehebe a few days before, and George said it behooved us to be on hand at the appointed hour. Not that George was afraid of Mr. Walter D. V. Scott, or of anyone else, for that matter. The old boy wasn't built along those lines. He was a mild-mannered, blue-eyed Tennessean. In his younger days, as I had learned from one of his cronies, George had survived one of those games they played in the mountains back there, where two men, bent on exterminating each other, clasp left hands while armed with bowie knives in their right hands with which to slash and hack their way to a settlement of their grievances. No indeed, fear played no part in George's punctiliosity. It was just that he didn't "admire" to fall down on his engagements, and the same went for Andy too. Furthermore, a dinner cooked by Scotty was well worth breaking one's neck to get to on time. That fabled character, while on tour with Buffalo Bill's Wild West Show, had made it a practice to cultivate the acquaintance of the most celebrated chefs of the capitals of Europe and to wheedle them out of their most closely guarded culinary secrets.

We arrived there practically on the dot. Scotty emerged from a wing of his partly finished building all togged out in his snow-white chef's uniform, even to the high-domed cap.

"Meet anybody up the road?" he shouted, not bothering with any formalities of greeting.

George said no, we hadn't seen hide nor hair of ary soul since leaving Bonnie Claire. Was Scotty expectin' somebody else, he asked?

"No," Scotty bellowed. "I just gave a man time to get out of here—stepped him up around the heels with my gat. I'll raise my sights on him if he ever shows up around here again."

"Must a-hid out when he heard us comin'," Andy opined. "What was his game?"

"Wobbly—troublemaker," Scotty replied. "Come down from Goldfield to raise a stink. Tried to cook up a strike with my boys."

"Wouldn't surprise me none," George injected, "but what the miners would go on strike pretty soon in Goldfield and Tonopah both."

"Been expectin' that right along," Scotty agreed. "Mines are lookin' too good. Makes the boys want to get in on the gravy. Well, there's no gravy like that down here. It's all goin' out and nothin' comin' in. It's the mine operators' funeral, not mine. Come on in. Dinner's about ready."

"We brought along one extry," George reminded him, indicating me with a toss of his head. "Hope it don't inconvenience you none."

"Hell, no," Scotty said. "I don't calculate that close. He led the way to the kitchen of the castle. After dinner we could look around all we liked, he told us.

The dinner would have been classed as de luxe anywhere on earth. The fried chicken, southern style, George pronounced as good as any he had ever eaten in Tennessee. There was plenty of everything—mashed potatoes with gravy, sweet corn right out of Scotty's garden, hot biscuits by the panfuls, honey and spiced figs, coffee which, to keep George company, I swore was as good as any I had ever drank arywheres, and a multilayered cake which, like Joseph's coat, was of many colors, not to say flavors, and was the creation of our versatile host himself.

"Didn't I tell you," George Badgett said afterwards, "that Scotty's the best cook you ever eat after?"

He certainly was that and then some.

Scotty volunteered the information that the big structure was to be a "bug house," and he invited us to file our applications for admittance then and there as the books were open and he looked for a long waiting list, naming several prominent mining engineers, politicians, and promoters as likely candidates.

He conducted us through the big rooms on the rambling ground floor, none of which seemed to make any sense. In a far corner of one huge, freshly plastered room there was a pile of books in rank confusion, looking as if they had been dumped there out of a wheelbarrow. They were new books, some two hundred of them, I estimated, and they all appeared to be alike. Textbooks, I said to myself, and for a moment I thought here was a real clue—this was going to be a school of some sort. Soon, however, I found out differently. On closer inspection the books turned out to be works of fiction by Dane Coolidge, two of his latest entitled *Lost Wagons*, and *Wunpost*, about a hundred copies of each. They were first-rate lusty action stories, the locale of which was right there in that part of the country, Scotty being the central character in each. I told Scotty I'd like to read both books.

"Help yourself," he said. "Take as many as you want. Take them all. I don't want any of them."

"Have you read them?" I asked.

"Hell, no," he said with disgust. "They're nothing but trash. I wish that feller'd quit sending me his books."

"You know Coolidge, do you?" I asked.

"Guess I ought to," Scotty replied. "He spent a month around here last year, he and his wife. She's okay—got plenty brains. That's more than I can say for him." (That last remark when later it was relayed to Coolidge drew a hearty laugh from him as well as his unqualified endorsement that Scotty had it about right.)

We all had our beds with us and could well have stayed over till the following day as Scotty had asked us to do, but George and Andy wanted to get back on the job at Ubehebe. So, early in the afternoon, we piled aboard the Dodge and with muffler wide open we went roaring down the canyon, the toughest part of our trip still ahead of us—Cinder Hill, the Tin Mountain wash, and the craters on the opposite side of Death Valley.

Ubehebe is a region of deep, barren canyons between rugged walls of varicolored rocks which store the heat of the sun's merciless rays pouring down on them all day long so that at midnight during the summer months the effect on one is the same as being inside a brick oven with the heat up. As places go, Ubehebe is neither beautiful nor magnificent. The effect it has on the spirit is one of awe rather than exaltation. It is one vast frown as far as one sees, silent, locked in the sleep of death, purpling and shimmering in the distance which seems unending.

Our camp was a single-tenter located well out of reach of any cloudbursts that might come tearing down the gulch at any hour of the day or night. We three slept in the open where we had an unobstructed view of the shooting stars and meteors especially prevalent in those skies, each a wicked angel cast out of heaven and en route to Hades, one might well imagine.

We were working in ore, chalcopyrite, which with a minimum of sorting ran forty dollars a ton in copper and gold at prices then prevailing. There were a hundred tons of it, more or less, in our ore pile ready for shipment, all taken out of open cuts and shallow winzes on the surface, but the trouble was the pile just kept growing, along with our investment in it, and we couldn't cash it in for money. No one would come and haul it away for us. The roads were murder. Even the four-wheel-drive trucks wouldn't tackle them. There we were, stuck with the fruits of our own labor, but we wouldn't admit we were licked. That ore would find its way to the smelter one fine day.

Before coming to Nevada, George Badgett had been mining in Montana in association with Charles E. Knox, Philadelphia capitalist. Knox was early on the ground at Tonopah where he acquired a group of close-in claims with which he organized the Montana Tonopah Mining Company. George Badgett followed him to Tonopah and ran the company in its early stages. The property rapidly developed into one of the richest mines in the district, and operations went on a big scale with a forty-stamp mill and cyanide plant running three shifts continuously, the big ore bodies being followed to depth. The company paid dividends for years out of its total production of twelve million dollars. In the meantime, George continued as a scout for Knox, the two men holding each other in the highest mutual esteem.

George had prevailed on Knox to look into a little gold prospect about twenty miles from our camp. It belonged to Andy and was known as the Lost Burros. Knox liked it, and a deal was made with Andy whereby the Montana Tonopah would finance its development on a lease-and-bond basis. There again, transportation was the big snag. However, word got around that Knox was dickering for an old caterpillar tractor that belonged to the Waterson brothers, operators of a chain of banks—very, very shaky banks they were—over in Inyo County, California.

We decided it would be a good idea to have Andy drive up to Tonopah to see how the "cat" deal was coming along.

The day Andy left, George took me over to our group of lead claims which I hadn't yet seen. We had to cross two canyons and two high ridges to get to them. They were about the last word for inaccessibility as far as hauling was concerned, but the showings of lead ore were something to behold. There was stuff that George said was cerusite, carbonate of lead. It looked like granulated sugar, ready to be spooned up and sprinkled over one's grapenuts for breakfast. Every grain was a clear, perfect little crystal with a faint amber tinge. It was hard to believe that someone hadn't planted it there in its crevice instead of its having been deposited there by the forces of nature thousands, yes, millions of years ago.

So, there our lead ore was, and there it would stay indefinitely, for at the prevailing price of lead there was nothing but red ink in it for us.

George was itching to get a shot at a mountain sheep. There were lots of them in the rocks back of our camp. I wished him the best of luck, and he wished me the same, for I was off on a little jaunt of my own. I was going to see what those "badlands," as George called them, were really like. He had pointed them out to me from our lead claims, off to the north and west.

"That's about the kind of a country Scotty's mine would be in," he had remarked, "that is, if he's really got one."

That got me thinking that maybe if I strolled over there I'd be the first one to stumble across Scotty's "if" mine. White men and Indians had tried to trail him to it, but he had always succeeded in eluding them. I had even heard it claimed that Scotty kept a hired killer at his mine so that should anyone succeed in finding it his lips would be forever sealed. Of course, one could suit oneself about believing half the things one heard about Death Valley Scotty.

At any rate, the badlands lived up to their name that day for me at least. The morning had passed almost before I had realized it. I figured I had come about five miles from camp, pretty rough going all the way, and my objective on ahead looked to be about as far again away. I had loafed along with little regard to time, stopping to study rock formations on the way, breaking off specimens and studying them under my glass. The day had become downright hot. Something told me the smart thing would be to turn back to camp, call the thing off, perhaps for some other day. Ah, what the heck! I thought. I had come that far and I might as well see it through. If I'd keep moving, I figured, I could get over there in a couple of hours at the most and then make it back to camp in time for George's venison feast, if he got a bighorn.

I had started out with a quart canteen of water. Half of it was gone. I wondered why I had drunk any of it at all. I hadn't really needed it. I could get along without water much longer than the average person, as I have stated before. It was a fixed notion with me that I could go for at least twenty-four hours under any condition without a drop.

I was shortly to learn that doing without a thing voluntarily is quite different from being inexorably deprived of it. Of course this whole thing was voluntary. I could turn back at the very next step, back to the water cans at camp. That's what I told myself, only it wasn't so. I was committed to going through with it, and I was only lying when I told myself otherwise.

Before long I found myself getting water conscious. Very well, here was my chance to demonstrate that I was constituted somewhat along the lines of a camel. I'd proceed straight on through to the heart of the badlands, see what there was to see, and then go the whole way back to camp without tasting another drop out of my canteen.

Eventually I reached what I believed must be the badlands. I kept on up a short steep canyon which brought me out on a spur from which there was a view of the encircling Hades that would have served Doré as a model in his gruesome art. Before me was spread a vista of dull gray rock, buckled and shattered, that could have been the waste dump of hell itself, an area rutted with deep-cut gullies and jagged ridges running every which way. Here and there up along the higher crests I thought I could discern some dikes that might be in place. The rest, as far as I could see, looked as if it had been run through some Brobdignagian milling process.

I had seen enough. After all, Scotty had the only real system. No doubt he had been all over that region on muleback with another mule or two packing his bed, grub, and—what I tried to forget—gallons of water.

Now I was free to start back. I had carried out what I had committed myself to accomplish. I'd reach camp by six o'clock at the latest. Even George would open his eyes wide when I showed him there was still some water in my canteen and I told him where I had been.

Yes, George was going to be surprised all right but about something entirely different. So would Andy be, who surely would have gotten back from Tonopah in time to sit down to the venison supper George, no doubt, had ready.

Gradually the thought came over me that I might not be heading in quite the right direction. Step by step the conviction grew that I had somehow lost my bearings. At first it had seemed too stupid to be taken seriously. When I stopped to take stock of where I was, I knew I hadn't come down any such wash as the one I was then ascending. Miles back I must have mistaken a certain break in the hills for the gap out of which I had emerged on my way over. It must have been that the sun swinging around to the southwest had misled me. Surely the gap I wanted was back that other way. I certainly was confused. I must have gone 'way past where I thought the right gap was, and still I found no opening in the rimrock that looked at all like it. Then I wondered if after all I hadn't been on the right course in the first place and merely hadn't stayed with it long enough. I was beautifully lost. Now how had I ever gotten myself into such a silly mess? Of course, I should have made notes of landmarks on my way by which to guide myself on the way back. This was a fine time to be thinking of that!

The main thing now was to take it easy. My thirst, with the realization that I might be in a bad fix, began to taunt me, taking what seemed to me to be an unfair advantage of me. The sun's rays, though not broiling, still had plenty of heat in them for a January afternoon. In another hour it would be setting. Then there'd be twilight for an hour or so, and then night, a moonless night.

By sunset I was back in the wash again. This time it looked sort of familiar and friendly, but it still wasn't the one I was looking for. Surely, I thought, the right one must be on beyond only a short way.

Not so, however, and after I had used up about half of the available twilight looking for it, I gave up and decided I'd try that wash anyway. It was the only opening of consequence I had come across in either direction that might lead me over the tall, stubborn ridge which seemed determined to head me off from any other approach.

It cooled off rapidly as night fell. Nevertheless, my thirst continued to crowd all other considerations out of my head as I trudged on in the deepening darkness of the wash. The farther I went, the steeper and narrower it grew, till finally it came to an end at the base of a sheer wall, and I knew that was where I'd have to spend the night, like it or not. I struck a match and saw that it was only nine o'clock. Now, I asked myself, what was I going to do there for the next eight or nine hours?

The first thing on my program was a mouthful out of the canteen, a good big one, yes, but nevertheless just one. That much at least was coming to me, I figured. This business of getting lost hadn't entered into my bargain. Very well, then, just one mouthful it would be.

It didn't work out that way though. Once my lips became attached to the mouth of the canteen I could no more stop at a single gulp than I could have hoped to fly over the cliff before me.

"That settles that," I said aloud, with a degree of satisfaction. "No use packing this thing around any longer," and I slung the empty canteen away and heard it crash in the rocks below. Then I was sorry. I had been a weakling, emptying it completely. Why hadn't I hung on to a bit of the water, just enough so that I could hear it swish around in the canteen under my arm. Just knowing it was there would have afforded me a measure of moral support, slim as it might be. All those eager gulps had accomplished was to put my thirsty craving into high gear. A pageant of wet things and wet places paraded past my imagination, such as a dripping water tank like the one on the Southern Pacific where I had met Bill Pfeifer, and big schooners of cold beer being shoved across the bar by Walter Drysdale in his Bank Saloon in Tonopah, and the Cave of the Winds filled with mist back of Niagara Falls, and the icy riffles in the headwaters of Reese River—all being a sweetly tantalizing pastime I was sure the devil had gleefully arranged for the benefit of my desiccated system.

I backed down the ravine to the first level spot big enough to lie down on, and I had no sooner disposed myself as comfortably as I could, stretched out on my back, than I fell sound asleep.

At midnight I woke up thoroughly wretched with chills and fever. I alternated between standing up, swinging my arms to get warm, and sitting hunched over with my arms wrapped around my knees, longing for my jacket, for something to relieve my burning throat, for daylight so I might see where I was—anything, just anything, no matter what!

The long night was divided into snatches of sleep, sitting or lying, each ending in rude, shivering awakening. Long before dawn I had struck my last match to see what time it was. Between times I thought of George. Of course, I had taken all the joy out of his day's sport, and I hated myself for that. Of course, he was worrying. There wasn't the least doubt he had bagged his bighorn and proudly lugged it to camp, and then—no one there to show it off to—no one to congratulate him. Strangely enough, George loved adulation though he was always pretending to deprecate it. I could see him going ahead anyway and cooking a big venison dinner and then waiting by the hour for me to come and sit down to partake of it.

My final nap carried me well past dawn. I woke with a

start in a world filled with the chill and silence of death, to the sickening truth that it hadn't all been a nightmare after all. Well—already precious minutes had been lost.

There seemed to be but one direction to take if ever I was going to make it to camp. Right or wrong it was now my one and only chance and I had to take it. It called for getting over that ridge somehow and the disheartening part of it was that I had to drop back and down in a wide detour, after which a long, hard scramble over a steep rock slide faced me.

Now I knew, all too well, that everything depended on my keeping calm, going slow, and not trying to force the issue. As for my thirst, I would regard it as my assurance that I'd be all right as long as it held out, that is, kept torturing me, strange as that may sound. When it got beyond that point, then I'd really be in a bad way. The pebble under my tongue did wonders to buck me up.

I made the top of the ridge at last. So what? For all I knew about where I was I might as well have been among the craters of the moon. The sun was about a dozen diameters above the horizon and of an ominous, blazing red. To its left, twenty to forty degrees, was about where camp should be, and that's the way I struck out.

Ridge after ridge I had climbed, crossing in and out of deep, hot gulches. By noon my feet were acting up badly, and for the first time in my life, I learned what was meant by the term headache.

I absolutely had to rest for a while. I simply couldn't go another step. There was no such thing as shade, but a gentle breeze just then got under way. I sat down, propped against a rock, my hat pulled down over my eyes. I began to relax all over, and I dropped off to sleep.

It was in that position that Andy spotted me from some

two miles off. I well could, and I did, thank God for that sleep.

Had I kept on going in the direction I was taking, instead of pausing up there on that ridge, there was every chance that my bleached bones amid the rocks of those deceptive ridges and canyons would have marked the finale to my rudderless peregrinations.

Little sips of water at intervals brought me around in fairly good shape after an hour or so, and by taking it easy, Andy, now joined by George, got me back to camp under my own power. They both expressed the opinion that I had proved myself something of a human camel by having come through as well as I did.

25

THERE WAS PLENTY of cause for rejoicing. Andy had brought back the word that Charlie Knox had closed the deal for the caterpillar. It was already on its way by rail from Bishop to Bonnie Claire. Soon now we'd show those sandy washes who was boss! They might stop the trucks in their tracks, but the caterpillar would eat them up. We were to have the use of it to haul our ore out to Bonnie Claire, paying the Montana Tonopah Company so much a ton as rental. As soon as the broken ore was all shipped, we were to move over to Andy's Lost Burros mine, set up camp there, and get things ready for work to start as soon as a crew of miners could be sent down from Tonopah. Andy would then remain in charge of the development work. George and I were welcome to stay on and work with him if we wanted to.

Well, we decided we'd see when the time came. All depended on how our ore would run when it reached the smelter. A hundred tons or more at, say, forty dollars a ton gross, less haulage, freight, moisture, insolubles, refractories, sundry other smelter excuses, should net us about two thousand dollars and put us in shape really to go after those ore bodies and bring in a big producing copper–gold mine.

All of which was great on paper, but that's as far as it went. Even to the most casual eye, the caterpillar, as soon as it had been unloaded off the flat car at Bonnie Claire, gave disquieting symptoms of being just about as shaky as the bank in Bishop from which Charlie Knox had bought it sight unseen. It behaved like a chicken taking a dust bath; literally shaking itself to pieces, rattly old junk heap that it was, it died in the road half way down to Scotty's.

"Stung" was the word for it. The Montana Tonopah Company had given its promissory note for forty-five hundred dollars for it and quite understandably refused to pay it on presentment. The slick bankers had seen to it that they got a negotiable note from honest, unsuspecting Charlie Knox. It was just about at that time that their all-round crookedness caught up with them, and the gates of San Quentin prison swung wide to receive them. Meanwhile, the California State Superintendent of Banks seized the bank and, strictly in line with his sworn duty, sued on the note in behalf of its victimized depositors. Thus, the Montana Tonopah Company, which was forced to pay the note plus interest, plus costs, became an involuntary contributor toward the meager funds that were distributable to the hapless depositors of the wrecked bank.

Under the circumstances, there was no immediate incentive for us to mine any more ore on our ground in Ubehebe. Hence, we all moved camp to the Lost Burros. Charlie Knox sent down load after load of materials and supplies, and before we knew it, we had a nice little settlement of tents with board floors and walls all set up and furnished ready for occupancy.

Of one thing I was sure—I would not stay on at the Lost Burros. The next vista in the kaleidoscope of my happy-go-lucky way of life, what would it be like?

We had just knocked off work for the day, taking turns at the wash basin. George was all set to start a mulligan of mountain-sheep jerky, canned tomatoes, red pepper, and onions. He had been saying that if you ate red pepper regularly in your food the coyotes wouldn't eat your carcass in case you died in the hills. In that case, Andy and I agreed that George surely had his body thoroughly immunized against the danger of ever winding up inside the bellies of those prowling carnivores.

Just then Andy said, "Listen!" We all came to attention, Andy still holding the basin which he had been about to empty, George with comb in hand, his toilet not quite completed, and I waiting to take over as soon as Andy got through.

There it was, the distant drone of an automobile making its way in low gear up our canyon.

"Better wait till I see how many there is to cook for," George said, adding the finishing strokes to his wet hairdo.

By the time I was washed, the roar of the motor with its muffler cutout was well-nigh deafening as it reverberated between the canyon walls. We were all agreed it must be Charlie Knox, probably accompanied by an engineer or some of his eastern associates. None of us would have bet a nickel at any odds that there were ladies in that car.

However, that is just exactly what there were.

The first thing that caught my eye was the dazzling new Hawaiian-tan Cadillac touring car, unquestionably the

235

swankest thing on wheels that had ever struck the desert. At the wheel was Charlie Knox himself. I had never met him, though I had seen him a few times around Tonopah. With him in the front seat was a girl whom I took to be his daughter. Behind them sat a cherubic little lady with an alert, impish look on her face. George and Andy hurried to open the car doors and help the ladies get out. There followed handshaking all around and a general powwow during which George motioned me over to be introduced.

I had heard the boys speak of a Miss Someone-or-Other, who was secretary and treasurer of the Montana Tonopah Mining Company. I understood that she had been written up in the American Magazine. Well, here she was! Impossible! I had pictured her as a sharp-featured spinster with horn-rimmed spectacles and her hair done up in a tight knot behind, but here was a mere girl, definitely younger than I. Maybe I hadn't gotten it straight. Probably the other lady, the short, little, dumpy one, was the high official in question. That, however, didn't seem to make sense either. She was such a funny little dickens and looked as though nothing had ever worried her in her whole life. Incredible as it seemed, she was the mother of the girl with the responsible company executive job.

The girl held out her hand which I took for an instant during my introduction. Such amazing eyes she had! They could have played havoc with one looking into them had she elected to put them to such use. Indeed, that's exactly what they did to me anyway, without any artifice whatever on her part.

Charlie Knox was the personification of manly polish, about in the prime of his days, just a shade over forty. I esteemed it a privilege to make his acquaintance. He had the easy bearing of a real gentleman, was educated, had traveled extensively, and had been highly successful in promoting big enterprises. A man of fine presence, he would stand out in any company.

Nevertheless, it was the little chubby one that stole the whole show.

"This is a hell of a place to bring a fellow to!" was her first observation as she set foot on solid ground. Naturally, we all burst out laughing, all, that is, but her daughter whose face betrayed a kind of hopeless despair, as if she had long since given up hope of ever bringing up her mother properly.

Poor George was sorely disappointed. There would be no mountain-sheep mulligan after all. Our visitors had brought along beefsteaks, green vegetables, fruit, a homemade cake, and heaven knows what all in cans, bottles, and jars. Obviously the perishable viands had the right of way over George's thoroughly mummified jerky which would keep till it became petrified.

Charlie Knox, the man who always did the right thing, it seemed, came out of his tent with a Thermos bottle of ice-cold cocktails, extra special, made up for him at the famed Waldorf Bar in San Francisco. We all had one, then an encore. We toasted the ladies and wished the Lost Burros Mine success. Morsels of cheese and other tidbits were passed around on our best tin plate, till finally, Mumpsie, the little mother, said it was a waste of time fooling around with those odds and ends.

"Let's get at those beefsteaks," she urged. "I'm as hungry as a bear!"

Well, the breakup was at hand. Charlie Knox had come down there to try to inveigle George into taking on the job of reopening the old Klondyke Mine which the Montana Tonopah Company had taken over. It was going to be a good-sized operation, and George was just the man to make a go of it. Miners would be coming down to the Lost Burros within the week, and Andy would run the show there. I commenced to wonder where that would leave me.

After breakfast the next morning, while chatting with Charlie Knox, I mentioned that there seemed to be no sense in my staying around there any longer, not for the present, at least. With Andy's work cut out for him and George gone, plus our copper ore tied up for lack of transportation, I was thinking of doing a bit of looking around for a while. Yes, I could have a job right there in the mine, but I explained that I drew the line at working underground.

Well then, Charlie Knox suggested, how would I like to work with George up at Klondyke, driving a truck between there and Tonopah, helping around the blacksmith shop, and what not, just by way of filling in the time until I decided what I wanted to do next?

How would I like it! I'd be delighted! I had visions of trips to the Montana Tonopah Mine where I'd probably have to report to Miss Secretary-Treasurer. A lot of good that would do me, wouldn't it? Of course she had been gracious toward me. That was just her nature, and certainly nothing to jump to foolish conclusions over.

George and I drove back in the car that brought down Andy's first contingent of miners. The Klondyke camp was all set up and provisioned by Mrs. Beecraft, who was going to stay on as cook while her husband worked in the mine. George insisted that I put my bed in his private cabin, although there was a spacious, comfortable bunkhouse which would have done well enough for me.

Was it fate that at Klondyke I was practically back again at my old Gold Reef diggings? Up there on the Reef, not five miles away, some of the boys were still pounding away on their drills, so Beecraft told us, and the talk was that Cal Brougher was going to sink a deep shaft on his group of claims in Gold Mountain where the showings were exceptionally promising.

There was a world of tonnage in the old Klondyke that just about would measure up to shipping. It was like a routine manufacturing proposition, but the accommodations were excellent, and there were those trips to town with the company truck!

As for the girl, I was laying siege to her heart in a roundabout way. I was trying to ingratiate myself with Mumpsie, who never missed a chance to tell me I wasn't worth the powder to blow me plumb to. Yet, bless her, she never failed to come across with a cut of pie or cake, and, best of all, a bit of reminiscing when she was in the spirit.

Mumpsie was born and "drug up" in the Mother Lode country of California where the Yuba River cuts through it. Her father had owned a big ranch up that way and ran it like a squire, always garbed in the height of style, boiled shirt, hard hat, and polished boots. Mumpsie recalled that he was quite a ladies' man and pretty handy with his dukes.

The ranch was a bustling stop-over station for big freight teams which kept an endless flow of merchandise pouring into Virginia City on Nevada's great Comstock Lode, where a good California watermelon would fetch ten dollars any old time.

There wasn't a word in the mule skinner's vocabulary that Mumpsie couldn't spell. At Marysville, where she went to school, she came to know some of the survivors of the tragic Donner party. At school, alas, she apparently was in hot water most of the time. One of her exploits was to scale the Marysville buttes. A party of boys and girls drove out to them in wagons one especially hot day with the intention of making the difficult climb. All except Mumpsie and one other girl gave up the battle soon after the start. Those two somehow made it to the top of the highest butte but not without getting covered with bruises and their clothes all but torn off.

Another of her experiences was engineered by a boy in her class at school whose father was an undertaker. One day he asked her how would she like to see a couple of dead Chinamen? Mumpsie gave him to understand that that had always been the height of her ambition, and so the boy took her into his dad's morgue where two "Celestials" were laid out on a marble slab. The boy explained that he was going to have to wash the corpses and asked Mumpsie if she would like to turn the hose on them? Sure she would, she told him—anything to oblige. So there she stood holding the hose and directing its lively stream all over the blissfully unaware bodies.

"I don't suppose you relished the job very much," I observed, though I had my doubts.

"Oh well," she replied, "it was something different."

I saw quite a lot of Mumpsie but precious little of her daughter who was too busy in her office to be bothered with me and my trucking work. She had directors' meetings to attend, stock certificates to transfer, dividend checks to make out and mail—always something, always busy. What I was dying to find out was who, if anyone, had the inside track with her. Mumpsie was no help at all on that score. She hardly ever mentioned her daughter, and I couldn't come right out and ask. They were so utterly different that it was hard to believe they were mother and daughter.

There was a considerable social activity at Tonopah which

climaxed each Christmas season in the Elks Charity Ball preceded by a banquet. The food, drink, gaiety, and beautiful women elegantly gowned couldn't be excelled anywhere. Now, if ever there was a good Elk it was I, and I defied the Grand Exhausted Rooster to name me one good reason why I should absent myself from that lavish affair. Indeed, if I had been able to reach that dignitary's ear I could have whispered into it a valid reason why I must be there, namely, that the girl from the Montana Tonopah Mine was going to be there. Actually I didn't know for sure, but I would have bet that she couldn't resist the lure of that brilliant night with all its attendant glamor, its fine dance orchestra imported for the occasion from San Francisco, the elaborate banquet, the throng of importunately aspiring escorts—in short, the once-a-year lustre and excitement of the Elks Charity Ball.

I went to the party and had a very attractive miss, whom I had asked several weeks in advance, as my partner. The feasting was already under way when we arrived on the festive scene.

Immediately, I spotted Miss Montana Tonopah. At her right sat a husky blond chap, who no doubt traced his lineage clear back to Leif Ericson, and at his right sat Mumpsie. Everyone around there was having a great laugh over something or other, everyone, that is, except Mumpsie and her daughter. It must have been a good one, whatever it was, that Mumpsie had sprung. I could almost read her mind. She was probably saying to herself, "I wonder what strikes these damn fools so funny?"

I knew who the big fellow was and, worse luck, I couldn't find any fault with the young lady's choice of escorts. He was a rising young engineer, a metallurgist, connected with one of the big Tonopah companies. So, he was the one! This handsome viking was an officer in the Elks Lodge to boot!

After the banquet, who should be leading the Grand March around the ballroom, with whose arm resting on his, but— well, what the devil! If it hadn't been for my partner, on whom I couldn't very well run out, I would have hunted the nearest exit without further delay.

Once around the hall and the sedate march broke into a spirited one-step. The band cut loose for fair. Trumpets and sliphorns blared brazenly. Fiddles squeaked and squealed like frenzied mice. The trap drummer went on a murderous rampage evidently designed to annihilate the very implements of his livelihood. Come on, boy, this is no place for a kill-joy! Okay, I'd make a night of it. After all, I did have a swell partner!

The music, if such it could be called, abruptly stopped. In a matter of seconds my partner was besieged by applicants for a spot on her program. I made a beeline for the group clustered around the girl from the Montana Hill. I gave myself big odds I'd never get a dance with her.

I worked my way right up face to face with her and was rewarded with a cold stare. It lasted only an instant and was followed by a sudden, spontaneous smile.

"Oh," she said, "for a second I didn't recognize you." No wonder, for she had never seen me before in anything but my work clothes. I asked and received the promise of a dance with her.

When my number came around, and when I had had that dance, so tantalizingly brief, a sudden recklessness came over me. I had to be quick, because Leif Ericson was steering a course toward us. I asked her if I might drop in on her and her mother some evening—soon?

"Why, of course," she said. "We'd be delighted." She smiled as I thanked her.

But, rats, what else could she have said? That's what I asked myself as I walked away.

26

CAL BROUGHER was one of that select company of old-timers who got in on the ground floor when Jim Butler discovered Tonopah. A true son of the desert was Cal and, unless perchance it be in a poker game, men of his caliber are not given to bluffing. So, when Cal announced that he was going to put down a deep shaft on Gold Mountain, it was as good as sunk, timbered, equipped with hoist, and all set to go.

Gold Mountain rises boldly out there on the desert just eight miles southerly from Tonopah. Cal had a group of claims on the mountainside which he had held on to since the early days, and now he incorporated the Tonopah Divide Mining Company with the object of developing them.

Prince of a man that he was, he reserved for me, out of pure kindness of heart, a few thousand shares of the stock at less than ten cents a share. What was I to do? It meant nothing to him whether I took up the stock or not. He didn't need any part of my insignificant bankroll. I am sure he would have given me the stock for nothing if I had asked him to. Above all, I wanted him to know that I did appreciate his thinking of me, and so I thanked him sincerely, snapped up the shares, and inwardly kissed my money good-by.

In what seemed like no time at all, Tonopah Divide was selling on the New York Curb Exchange at fourteen dollars a share. It went up so fast that I couldn't have gotten out without a profit, even if I had wanted to. No, I didn't get the very top price for my stock, but then, as I once heard a race track tout remark, "I done all right."

Cal Brougher had indeed made a magnificent strike of

unbelievably rich silver ore in his shaft, and then George Wingfield stepped into the picture, and it was as much the lending of his magic name to the big goings-on as it was the glowing reports sent out by high-priced geologists that got the so-called Divide Boom into high gear.

Now for once I happened to be in the right place at the right time.

After operating the old Klondyke for the best part of a year, Charlie Knox decided she wasn't worth bothering with any longer. Month after month it had just been a case of breaking even, or a little better, or a little worse. So, he shut her down. Immediately George Badgett hurried back to the State of Montana where he had a deal on for the old Monarch Mine. Automatically, I became mayor of Klondyke and its entire population, and in that capacity I continued to occupy the comfortable cabin with all its refinements at my disposal while an excitement of major proportions was breaking out right in front of my door.

Wildcat companies were being incorporated right and left. The secretary of state of the State of Nevada sat up nights signing charters. Grumpy printers ground out stock certificates on groaning, smoking presses. Brokers' offices in Tonopah and Goldfield were jammed with clients and swamped with orders to buy this, that, and the other stock—anything that had the word Divide in its title, such as Brougher Divide, High Divide, Silver Divide, Gold Divide, Pay Divide, Let's Divide, and a raft of others, each one purporting to possess the only true extension, projection, and apex of the vein intersected in Cal Brougher's shaft. No sooner was a company organized than its entire treasury stock was oversubscribed, far in advance of its listing on the San Francisco mining exchange.

Charlie Knox arrived somewhat late on the scene having

missed most of the first act. He had been kept on the jump directing the operations of his far-flung properties. By the time he got around to the Divide district, prices for close-in ground had skyrocketed, and everything was tied up in options to promoters.

I was at the big Tonopah Divide Mine watching car after car of the beautiful white talcy high grade being hoisted out of the shaft the day Charlie Knox drove out there to have a look at the strike that had the mining world agog. Miss Montana Tonopah and Mumpsie were with him in the big Cadillac, as was George Garrey, a hundred-dollars-a-day engineer and geologist and a good egg for all o'that. All but Mumpsie were going underground. I was invited to join the party, but in an off moment of mental aberration—I guess that's the word—I declined with thanks, explaining that I had already seen the big strike. I kicked myself black and blue, figuratively, as I watched the cage drop below the collar of the shaft, girl and all. I had talked myself out of a ready-made opportunity to spend an hour or so in adding to my paltry knowledge of geology under peculiarly agreeable circumstances.

Little Mumpsie, though, had the world beat for good company. I had discovered before then that there was a deep well of understanding and affection beneath her devil-may-care exterior she presented to the world at large.

The time passed quickly enough till the party returned from down below. As I got out of the car, Mumpsie blandly asked how things had looked down there.

"There's some good-looking ore down there," the ever-conservative George Garrey admitted.

"Is that the best you can say for it?" Mumpsie asked scornfully. "I'll bet you don't know a bit more now than you knew before you went underground." It was the sort of thing that no one but Mumpsie could get away with, and right there

George Garrey showed his breadth of mind by laughing delightedly at Mumpsie's frank little dig.

Charlie Knox expressed his regret for not having some close-in ground tied up there. He was leaving the following day for New York where his associates would leap at a chance to get aboard the Divide Boom if he had something to present to them. I promised him I'd rustle around and see what I could do about it.

"Wire me right away if you succeed," he replied.

Day after day a young Jewish fiddler, Julius Goldsmith, who played in the orchestra at the Big Casino dance hall in Tonopah came out to the cabin at Klondyke, and together we did our location work on some claims we had staked out close to the extreme southern end of Gold Reef, which was now all embraced in what was called the Divide District. Julius was a companionable little chap, tough and scrappy but generous to a fault. I couldn't see how he stood it, playing all night in the dance hall and working a shift out there in the daytime. Julius had made a stake some years before mining at Randsburg down on the Mojave Desert—in spite of which he had left there broke. Early in the game he had located a fine group of claims which almost adjoined the big Tonopah Divide mine. It would have made an ideal promotion for Charlie Knox, but a deal had already been closed, and the ground now belonged to the Tonopah Dividend Mining Company whose stock was selling in volume on the exchange. Julius had made me a present of a block of the stock with absolutely no strings attached, and I was to use my own judgment about when to sell it. That I did shortly afterwards, luckily timing it just right. I, in turn, made Julius a present of my half interest in our joint holdings up back of Klondyke. Blest if he didn't put over a deal on them, cashing in handsomely once more. Julius was now a rich man. With his wife and family, he moved to San Francisco and invested in real estate, which was his undoing. He died broke.

I had made the rounds looking for something suitable for Charlie Knox, but no use talking, the good ground was all taken. Then one day I casually asked a young Slavonian, Novak Achimovich, when he expected operations to start on the ground on which he had given an option. It was a very choicely situated parcel of claims. Novak said work would have to start and a down payment be made within a week or Frank Dunn would forfeit the five hundred dollars he had put up for his option.

Frank Dunn! Why, Frank was a good friend of mine, the district attorney of Nye County. I dashed right up to his office. Why, yes, he told me to go ahead and see what I could do. He had just learned that his people had fallen down on the deal, and he was getting ready to put it up to others.

I sent a long, hot wire to Charlie Knox in New York. Next morning I got a reply from him saying that his people were all set to shoot, but they wanted an engineer's report on the property first. I sent back a long answer telling him it would be impossible to get a report in time, that these were boom conditions, that the owner, Novak Achimovich, had already given another option—which was gospel truth—to become effective in case of default by Dunn, and to tell his people to stop fiddling a la Nero.

Two days before the option was to expire I found two interesting bits of intelligence awaiting me on my arrival downtown. First, the Tonopah Banking Corporation had a large telegraphic transfer of funds for me from Charlie Knox. I knew what that was all about. His people had seen the light. This was the initial payment on the option. Things were coming my way. I was in on the deal in a very substantial way. Pay dirt at last!

My jubilation, however, was short-lived. I ran into Johnnie Weaver on the street. He was just in from Divide and told me that a fellow named Degenhart had jumped Novak Achimovich's claims. Good Lord! The deal was off! Jumped the ground! That would mean litigation, and litigation would mean time, of which there wasn't a minute to spare. I slunk into Western Union and wired the sickening news to Charlie Knox. Naturally, I didn't disburse the funds he had wired me. Along about noon I got an answer. I was to see what I could do about buying off Degenhart and getting a quitclaim deed to his alleged interest in the ground.

Late that afternoon I rounded up the man. He was defiant—claimed there hadn't been anywhere near the legally required amount of location work done on the ground, that he was now in lawful possession, and he meant to secure his rights by performing the required amount within the next ninety days.

It made no difference that his contentions were utterly preposterous. Title to the ground was now clouded. No one in his right senses would touch it with a ten-foot pole. I asked him what he would take for a quitclaim deed.

He said he would take ten thousand dollars—not a damned cent less! I told him I'd give him five hundred, and was told I could go to hell. Instead, I went to the Belmont Grill and pecked at an order of ham and eggs. Later I encountered Degenhart in the Tonopah Club. We went to a back room and sat at a card table while I did my best to get it through his head that neither of us could hope to interest anyone in the ground as long as his monuments were up. Both titles were clouded. The thing was deadlocked, and he held the key. I reminded him that Achimovich had put his case in the hands of an attorney, Jack Thompson, who had readily taken it on a contingent basis for an interest in lieu of a cash retainer. Didn't that indicate that he, Degenhart, couldn't have much of a case? I told him to consider the Litigation Hill deal. That mess had demonstrated beyond the shadow of a doubt how claim jumpers stood with either a judge or a jury. All the litigants were left holding the sack. The boom had come and gone while they were wrangling. I made it clear that my interest in the squabble was strictly one of immediacy. Unless I could clear the deck forthwith, I wouldn't give a hoot about the outcome of his battle with Achimovich. At the moment there was some cash for me and for him too, if he was smart enough to see it, but if he preferred a long lawsuit of extremely dubious outcome, even after doing all of his required location work, to five hundred dollars spot cash—well, good luck to him. I'd hunt up something else for my principals. With that, I ordered two more bottles of beer. We stayed at it till well into the small hours.

"It's three o'clock," I said. "I'm going to bed as soon as I finish this." I was itching to tell him what I thought of him and his kind—remind him how they used to settle such cases in bygone days, but all through these hours I was convinced that he would finally give in; otherwise, he would have named his terms, demanded immediate acceptance or vice versa, and the session would have ended right there.

At 3:00 A.M. he just set down his glass and solemnly announced that just for the sake of seeing me put over my deal he was cutting his price in half, to five thousand dollars.

"That's your final rock-bottom figure?" I asked.

Drawing on his extensive stock of profanity, he assured me it was, but his very vehemence seemed to tell me it wasn't.

"Then I'll tell you what mine is," I countered.

"Let's have it," he said, defiantly.

Enunciating slowly and deliberately, I replied, "One thousand dollars!"

"I'd see you in hell first," he declared.

Now for my last card, I said "I guess that ends it." I pushed my chair back and getting up I started for the door.

"Here, wait a minute," he called after me. "No use getting sore."

It was working. I made as though I hadn't heard him and just kept going. He followed me outside.

"Now listen," he said. "I've got just as much right to get sore as you have. Let's cut out the stalling. Tell you what I'll do. Make it fifteen hundred, and I'll sign up."

It was a deal. We shook hands. We met at Frank Dunn's office before noon that same day. I had a certified check with me for fifteen hundred dollars. Frank drew up the necessary papers stripping Degenhart of any past, present, or future interest in the property. Degenhart's signature was witnessed, and Frank affixed his notarial seal while I handed over the check.

That was the way the Knox Divide Mining Company was born. For my obstetrical efforts, I was paid a commission and stock in the company. As had been foreseen, the stock leaped promptly into popularity with the speculative hungry public from coast to coast.

I was now associated with the Knox interests and accepted an invitation to take up residence at the Montana Club up at the mine on the slope of Mount Oddie, where Charlie Knox himself stayed when in camp. The commodious establishment was presided over by two highly proper German old maids, the Misses Jacobs and Vietsen, the former an accomplished cook and the latter the most fastidious housekeeper in all Christendom. Not fifty yards on up the hill stood the cottage where little Mumpsie (and someone else) lived. All of the boys at the club, about fourteen of them, were engineers, mine- or mill-supers, assayers, surveyors, some newly out of college and working regular shifts, like interns doing post-graduate work, polishing up to become big-name geologists, as in the case of Henry C. Carlisle, who was one of the club boys.

There now followed for me a kind of dream period, a sequence of golden days in a great silver camp. Seated on the club's porch of a balmy summer's evening, the whole of Tonopah spread out down below, while off to the west, across thirty miles of desert silence, loomed Lone Mountain, darkly silhouetted in the fading sunset, I felt myself apostate to the true calling of my heart. Lone Mountain, as mysterious as the Great Pyramid, was pulling, pulling me mightily. It wanted me, and all the hills and desert beyond and round about did too. I wanted to spread my bed down there on the clean floor of that parched expanse, where I could see the stars unobstructed and again experience that exquisite sense of lonesomeness that the desert and its denizens had taught me to revel in.

Maud (Miss Montana Tonopah) and I had played some tennis on the club court. One evening she went with me to the early picture show at the Butler theater and we walked both ways. On the way home, coming up the trail from town, she took my arm. To be sure, we were at an altitude of sixty-five hundred feet, but I could hardly attribute the quickening of my heartbeat to that factor. The heavens seemed unusually crowded with glittering stars. We stood a moment to gaze and absorb. I was a goner.

I pulled myself together to ask her something I had been doing my best to find out ever since the Elks Ball.

Was there anything serious between her and the big Norseman who had escorted her there?

Not at all, she told me. He was engaged to some mighty lucky girl back East somewhere.

When I heard that, I told her she must marry me. She didn't act at all surprised and merely replied that she wasn't ready to consider such a momentous step. Nor did she intimate that she might some day. Her attitude was negative, noncommittal, disappointing.

I carried my case to Mumpsie.

"What, marry you?" Mumpsie practically gasped. "What on? You're in no shape to get married!"

So that was it! And I thought I had been doing fine. I had a nice comfortable stake, nothing fabulous but definitely more than ample, I thought, to get married on. Nevertheless, Mumpsie didn't think too highly of my hit-and-miss style of life. She even brought up the unpleasant possibility of my losing my stake at a single stroke. Then where would I be?

"I suppose if I were a doctor," I said, "or a lawyer, or a banker, I might have a chance."

"A banker!" she repeated with spirit, her eyes all a-sparkle. "My baby married to a banker! Now that would be something like!"

Banker! I thought, disgustedly. It flashed through my mind what Snowshoe Charlie once said on the subject. "You don't have to know anything to be a banker," quoth he, "just so's you can sign your name so nobody can make it out—hide behind your signature." If that was all it took, then the presidency of the Chase National Bank was within my grasp!

There were matters of pressing urgency pending right about that time, but I must admit the banking idea struck me as not being entirely without its points. I would file it away in the back of my head. It might be worth looking into some day.

We had a new one going then—Tolicha! I had taken an option on a group of claims down there, fifty miles southeast of Goldfield. They were known as *the Landmarks* because they stood out boldly above the surrounding desert flat. The owners were two knights of the green cloth, Nick Abelman and Jimmie McKay, plus two prospectors, Jack Jordan and Jumbo Yeiser. Time was of the bitter essence of my contract, especially as regarded the grasping, cold-blooded McKay. Nick Ableman was just the opposite—fine to do business with. The total price was one hundred and fifty thousand dollars, and I had just thirty days to find a backer and make an initial payment of fifteen thousand. It would have to be an individual or a syndicate able to underwrite both the property payments as they fell due and the development program which could conceivably run into fancy figures for equipment and labor before any substantial production would start. There was a showing of spectacularly rich gold ore in a raise from the level of a short tunnel.

Charlie Knox was in New York. I painted him a vivid picture by wire. He rounded up a man game enough to take a gamble on what might turn out to be another Goldfield. He was James W. Gerard, the former United States Ambassador to Germany.

In due time, along came a draft for the fifteen thousand. Now I sure had a real he-man job on my hands. Three engineers in succession came to Tolicha to examine and report on the property, namely Van Wagenen, Holland, and Crawford, each important enough to have his every move reported in T. A. Rickard's Engineering and Mining Journal. I don't know what their findings were, but they didn't occasion any letup in the heavy flow of funds from New York to meet the huge expenses.

Tolicha was on the order of Ubehebe when it came to terrible roads, or no roads at all. The only water supply was a feeble spring seven miles down a narrow, sandy canyon. We were committed to have a fully equipped plant with hoist, compressor, gallows frame, shops, boarding house, sleeping quarters, and change room. It was all up to me, and I had no time to lose.

Fortunately, I got hold of Johnnie Weaver. There never was a man like him for setting up machinery in out-of-the-way places and in a big rush. Johnnie was nervy and fast. He lined up everything by eye, not wasting any time with transits and levels.

Johnnie and I scouted the countryside till we found a big hoist and compressor in the hills back of Walker Lake. I bought them from the owner, Johnnie Miller, state senator from Mineral County and one-time unsuccessful candidate for governor of Nevada. Herb Pickle hauled them separately the hundred-and-fifty miles to Tolicha, and but for the ingenuity of Weaver, Herb never would have gotten his big truck up the roadless hill where the stuff was to be unloaded for setting-up.

Jack Aylward was the big secondhand machinery man of the desert. In me he had something of an angel for a while. Jack's yard in Goldfield was a Sargasso Sea of mine wreckage representing millions of dollars that had gone the way of fond hope and fruitless search. Jack was a handsome, picturesque fellow with a marvelous baritone voice. No one, not even the great David Bispham, could have topped him in his singing of "Nights of Gladness." All the prospectors liked him, and he never turned one of them down.

We kept Herb Pickle busy with his truck even after the heavy hauling was out of the way. From on up the hill we could see him coming fifteen miles away. One day the boys wondered what in the world made his load appear so lofty. I knew what it was. I had told him to load on a backhouse in Goldfield. We needed one for our cook, Mrs. Beecraft, who had proved her worth at Klondyke and was now the only feminine member of our budding community. Herb Pickle brought his truck with the old weatherbeaten relic right up in front of the cookhouse. There it stood in all its majesty while all hands went in to dinner. Later our handyman, Dutch Badewitz, took command, selected the site it was to grace, and assisted in its careful unloading. Whatever his faults might have been, Dutch was a realist, and to Mrs. Beecraft's credit let it be said that she took it in good part when Dutch, at what practically amounted to a grand unveiling ceremony publicly dedicated the edifice to her exclusive comfort and enjoyment.

Of course the townsite boys got busy. A street was even named for me, but the Broadway of Tolicha was named Gerard Boulevard and the main cross street, Knox Avenue. As was to be expected, the press played it up big, stressing the fact that we were lined up with the Marcus Daly millions through Gerard who had married into that family of fabulous copper wealth.

All sorts and conditions of outfits streamed into camp— wagon, burro, automobile. No one went away without locating a claim or two up to and beyond five miles away from the Landmarks. Even the Tonopah and Tidewater Railroad banked on Tolicha to the extent of putting in a siding at Ancram, its point of nearest approach, where there was nothing but a water tank.

While our shaft was sinking, we gouged out all the ore in sight from the tunnel level up, scraping together a hundred and fifty tons which went out in four railroad carloads. Though we made record time putting our shaft down with air hammers and reached a depth of two hundred feet and then crosscut another hundred feet each way from the bottom, we never got through the reddish rhyolite we encountered the minute we dropped below the tunnel level.

At that stage of the game another payment of thirty thousand dollars was due on the property. I requested a thirty-day extension. All the owners but the notorious McKay were agreeable, but that callous schemer insisted on his pound of flesh. My wire to Charlie Knox brought a prompt reply. Gerard was prepared to make the payment, if I so recommended. I advised against it.

Under our agreement we had to leave all the machinery on the ground when we left, and an exceptionally good plant it was. Several attempts have been made by others from time to time to pick up the downward extension of the sweet little ore body which cropped on the surface up above the tunnel. To date, all that has come of them has been to advance our openings farther and deeper into the sterile red rhyolite.

Time may yet show that we were too hasty about throwing up our option on the Landmarks, though I, for one, am of the school that holds we had merely been toying with a little slice off the top of a wonderfully rich, true fissure vein which lies asleep somewhere thereabouts, probably in the chain of hills some miles south of Tolicha. That entire area, for the entire foreseeable future has since been taken over by Uncle Sam as a bomb-testing site, and hence is closed to prospectors. *Requiescat* aurum! Selah!

27

I CANNOT RECALL what it was that Charlie Knox wired me from New York to see George Wingfield about. Anyhow, I called at the Tonopah Banking Corporation, control of which Wingfield had only recently acquired from Cal Brougher thereby adding to his chain of banks which held the bulk of the banking resources of the State of Nevada.

I had but a few minutes to wait before I was shown into the

directors' room where Wingfield had been dictating a letter to a stenographer who got up and withdrew as I entered. He asked me to take a seat, and I got right to the point of my mission, whatever it concerned. All I can recall about it is that his response was favorable and cooperative.

As I got up to leave he asked me what I was doing those days. I had never actually met him before, though he was a familiar figure around Tonopah and Goldfield.

"How would you like to come into the bank here as an officer?" he asked.

I looked to see if he wasn't just fooling, but he was a man who did not go in for much of that sort of thing. I replied that I didn't know the first thing about the banking business. He brushed that aside as being of no consequence, mentioned the salary, which was a bit disillusioning, and went on to say a few things about the bank, to which I wasn't paying too much attention. My thoughts had become all jumbled up as a result of that totally unexpected development. What would Mumpsie say to that? Surely this ought to boost my stock with Maud! What about Charlie Knox? They all seemed like one closely knit family. He called Maud "Daughter," and she did look up to him virtually as a father, her own having died when she was a child. Suppose she married me—where would that leave Charlie Knox? He would be lost without her. She was closely tied in with all his plans and operations.

I even thought of Daniel Webster Morgan. How disgusted he'd be to hear of my defection if I went to work in a bank! I thought of Snowshoe Charlie's estimate of bankers as a class. And to think of becoming an officer in the very bank that had once found occasion to have a check of mine protested for dishonor!

In short, I accepted Wingfield's offer.

My immediate concern was to get up on Montana Hill as fast as I could with my epochal news. I would try it out first on little Mumpsie. Hadn't she practically asked for it?

Alas, she didn't respond to my enthusiasm. She said—and how right she was—that I'd never get used to being cooped up in a bank. No, I had no illusions then that Mumpsie had any immediate intentions to start campaigning for my cause.

With what was left of my enthusiasm, I wandered across to the company office, hoping to find Maud alone there in her inner sanctum.

She was. I told her the big news and what I hoped it might mean for us both.

"Don't you think you should wait and see how things work out?" she asked.

"But what if I make good?" I persisted.

"Then we'll see," was all she replied.

I had no right to expect more nor, for that matter, as much. Nevertheless, I was hurt. I told her there was nothing left but for me to go back to the hills. I meant it, every word of it. She made no reply—just sat there at her big polished desk, gazing out of the open window toward somber old Lone Mountain and the pastel-tinted Monte Cristo Range. I said good-by, and our eyes met.

"Good-by," she said, hardly above a whisper. All I saw in her look at the time was compassion. Not for a moment did it occur to me then that there might be something more than that, but I did know that I could never forget that look. I knew right then that I would always love her.

I went back down the hill and made straight for the bank. Wingfield was gone. He had just left a few minutes before I got there and was on his way to a directors' meeting at his bank in Goldfield, The John S. Cook Bank, from which he would return to his headquarters in Reno.

Ah, well, I'd simply write him a letter. No need to go into details. I'd just say that after thinking it over I had decided not to go into the bank but thanks all the same.

However, I changed my mind back again bright and early the next morning after having slept on the situation. I saw myself as the fool of yesterday. I hadn't actually been rebuffed at all. Both Mumpsie and Maud had been as encouraging as I could possibly have expected. I must have been blind not to see that.

One week later I was at my desk in the bank. For days all I had to do was to countersign stock certificates of dozens of mining companies for which the bank acted as registrar—that and jump up every few minutes to acknowledge congratulations.

All the heavy-duty brain work was taken care of by a man named Doyle, a keen, rapid-fire individual whom I greatly admired. Not only did he know what it was all about, but he was willing to help a greenie over the rough spots. Moreover, he was nobody's yes-man—least of all Wingfield's. He had all seven of the Wingfield banks to look after. I was sorry when he left the organization after some kind of clash with Wingfield. None of his successors in the big job came anywhere near to measuring up to Doyle's stature.

It was with quaking knees that I went to Charlie Knox to gain his consent to my marrying "Daughter." He gave it on condition that we would leave his organization intact. That seemed to Maud and me more like a reward than a condition.

Omar Khayyam must have been a prospector. Listen to what he said:

> *Into this universe, and why not knowing*
> *Nor whence, like water willy-nilly flowing:*
> *And out of it, as wind along the waste,*
> *I know not whither, willy-nilly blowing.*

From the Unknown, so it seems, we swing into this terrestrial existence in orbits which for a time we share with those we love. For ten years we four, Maud, Mumpsie, Charlie Knox, and I, were in the happiest of associations, till Charlie Knox swung out of our common orbit, back into the Unknown, his place forever impossible to fill as we three continued on our way grateful, at least, for a world of happy memories. Wherever he went, he was joined fifteen years later by that brightest, most adorable little pal a fellow ever had—Mumpsie. As she was nearing the end of her days she looked up at me from her pillow and said, "Life is a waste of time, but I wish I had mine to waste all over again."